OUR PARTNERS

Principal Partner

Major Cultural Partners

Partners

BOMBAY SAPPHIRE

Published in 2007
by Alphabet Press
alphabet.com.au

Text © The Melbourne Design
Guide Company
editor@sydneydesignguide.com

Design © Round

Photography supplied courtesy
of the featured designers and
venues. Copyright rests with
the photographers.

All rights reserved. No part
of this book may be reproduced,
stored in a retrieval system,
or transmitted, in any form
or by any other means,
electronic, electrostatic,
magnetic tape, mechanical,
photocopying, recording or
otherwise, without the prior
permission in writing of the
respective copyright holders.

Editors
Viviane Stappmanns
Ewan McEoin

Founder
Paul Charlwood

Design & Art Direction
Round
round.com.au

Printed in Victoria by
Finsbury Green
finsbury.com.au
Fonts: Janson and Leger
Stock: Precision

Although the authors,
editors and publisher have
endeavoured to make all
information as accurate as
possible, they accept no
responsibility for any loss,
injury, or inconvenience
sustained to any person
using this book.

ISBN 978-0-9804425-0-2

The Sydney Design Guide

Edited by
Viviane Stappmanns
Ewan McEoin

<u>The Sydney Design
Guide Editorial Team</u>

<u>Editorial Assistant</u>
Caroline Clements

<u>Sub-Editor /
Production Editor</u>
Josephene Duffy

<u>Section Contributors
& Advisors</u>
Architecture
Eoghan Lewis
Vincent Lam
David McCrae
Stella de Vulder

Products & Objects
Grace Cochrane
Brian Parkes
Peter Salhani
Anne Watson

Industrial Design
Angelique Hutchison

Fashion
Clare Buckley
Kym Ellery
Edwina McCann

Art
Katrina Schwarz
Dominique Angeloro

Visual Culture
Anne Marie Van De Ven
Zoe Sadokierski

Eat / Drink / Sleep
Lisa Dabscheck
Joel Meares

Contents

17 Introduction & Maps

36 Architecture & Built Environment

82 Products & Objects

150 Industrial Design

160 Fashion

226 Art

250 Visual Culture

292 Eat / Drink / Sleep

330 Out of Town

338 Design Resources, Events & Team

above
Customs House

photography
Peter Murphy

A Message from the Lord Mayor

Design: To create or execute in an artistic or highly skilled manner.

Sydney is a vibrant, diverse and sophisticated city. Contributing to the city's rich texture are innovative design and contemporary design practitioners who shape our daily lives, from the clothes we wear, the interiors and exteriors of our houses, to the sense of excitement we feel walking through the city and our urban villages.

Good design can revolutionise the way we occupy our environment, and the cities we live in. If good design is doing its job, it quickly becomes such a part of our lives it almost becomes invisible – we only notice when it is lacking. The City of Sydney is committed to fostering, inspiring and supporting creative thinking and practice, to ensuring that we are not lacking in innovative design solutions and experiences. As the Lord Mayor I recognise the value of the design industry and its economic impact on our City. I am pleased to support a truly unique guide, reflecting Sydney's truly unique design industry.
Clover Moore MP

$$E=TT^2$$

The new Audi TT Roadster.

The Audi TT Coupe changed the formula for energy in a luxury sports car. Now the TT Roadster builds on the same principles, while bringing you the kind of visceral driving experience that is only possible with an open top Roadster. Select from the powerful turbo-charged 2.0 TFSI or the blistering 3.2 V6 quattro and discover how energy plus oxygen equates to a new formula for excitement. Visit your nearest Audi Dealer, call **1800 50 AUDI (2834)** or SMS: **Roadster** to **1999 AUDI (2834)** or **0427 262 265** for a brochure.

* Audi Q7 7-adult seat option RRP $1,700. Each SMS you send will cost you 55c (incl. GST). Terms and conditions available at audi.com.au

Pinnacle of the design profession: what it takes to create a design icon

Automotive design is known as the pinnacle of industrial design. A car designer won't hesitate to tell you why that is so: the mammoth journey from concept design to serial production is no mean feat. There are the endless refinements, myriad restrictions, precision engineering, production hurdles and marketing requirements an automotive designer faces in tackling the challenge of creating cars that exist not just on paper, but that enjoy popularity on the road.

When the Audi TT was launched as a concept study at Frankfurt's International Automobile Exhibition in 1995, it caused an instant furore. Its unique, symmetrically shaped exterior was described as both organic and minimalist, its low-slung chassis and sporty dynamic immediately recognised as a sports car design of the highest order.

However, while thousands of petrol heads excitedly paced around the showpiece, they knew there was a glitch. Rarely does a concept design make it onto the road, and if it does, significant modifications to its look are the norm, not the exception. Three years later, fans were once again stunned. The Audi TT (named after the Tourist Trophy motorsports event held on the Isle of Man, not – as many believe – to suggest 'twin turbo') had made it off the production line

above
An instant icon down to the finest detail: design sketch for the new Audi TT (2006).

looking astonishingly similar to its earlier concept cousin. Known for its attention to design and detail, which had been cemented many years earlier with the sleek Audi 100, the German car manufacturer's management and design team knew they were onto a winner when they exhibited the concept TT. They had decided to refine every detail, perfecting all nuts and bolts to seamlessly integrate form and function, instead of sacrificing one for the other. Thanks to its ingenious design and the uncompromising production process, the TT became an instant icon, with immediate customer waiting lists of over two years. Fans loved its blistering power equally as much as they did the retro-minimalist styling of its interior, in which all fixtures communicated Audi's respect for great design. In fact, this interior is now regarded as a watershed in automotive design history, with many car manufacturers subsequently emulating its sporty, sleek feel.

And while new TT owners and admirers still marvelled at its astonishing on-road performance and ability to stand out from the crowd, the design team had already retreated back to the drawing board to deliver the next sensation: the TT roadster. Like its older sibling, it entered the market with much gusto two years later, another breath of fresh air in the world of car design.

Finsbury Green Printing

One of the objectives of producing this book was to collaborate with innovative companies who deliver creative results while maintaining social responsibility. Printing with Finsbury Green means printing with one of the most environmentally sustainable printers in the world.

Finsbury has a clear commitment to minimising the environmental impact of printing while producing a high-quality, design-literate product. Australia's only carbon-neutral printers, they have made a conscientious effort to achieve global best practice, reaching ISO14001 Environmental Management and ISO9001 Quality Management Systems certification. They are Forest Stewardship Council and Chain of Custody certified. All of their printing plates are digital; 99% of their inks are vegetable-based; 97% of their printing is alcohol-free, and they produce an annual sustainability report that is independently audited. For us, working with Finsbury has meant that we have done all we could do to make the production of this book as environmentally ethical as possible.

We encourage you to do the same next time you are printing – it all helps.
finsbury.com.au

SYDNEY DESIGN GUIDE_FOREWORD

Introduction to the Guide

Hello!

Here we are; the months of research, writing, talking, interviewing and piecing together the puzzle have resulted in this wonderful stack of ink and wood pulp that is the Sydney Design Guide. We aim to show you a side of Sydney often disregarded by conventional travel guides: the city's creative heart and the people who keep it pumping. We set out to establish connections, point toward creative hotspots and unearth the talent beneath them. Of course, we didn't do all of this by ourselves. All our partners share our passion for design. Also, we want to thank all our creative collaborators – and there were many – who happily shared with us what they know, love and loathe around this city. They have ensured that this is a book made by a city, not just about it.

How to use this book

There's more than 50,000 words in this guide, so digging your way through all that information is no mean feat. But we've done everything we could to help. Each of the nine sections of this guide has its own distinct colour scheme, so you don't get lost in jewellery if you're really after independent art galleries. Each section features walks, stories, as well as profiles of designers and makers. Then of course there are the key stores where you can buy their frocks, products, homewares and so forth. To find them, look out for the orange tag that sits on all the pages that feature stores and boutiques. Also, there are websites or phone numbers provided with the designer's entries, so you can get in touch and tell them you love them. Have fun!

City

TRAIN
MONORAIL
FERRY

Architecture
1. 363 George Street
2. AMP Building
3. Andrew 'Boy' Charlton Pool
4. Aurora Place
5. Australia Square
6. Castlereagh Centre / Capita Insurance Company
7. City Mutual Life Assurance Building
8. Cook and Phillip Park Aquatic and Recreation Centre
9. Customs House
10. Deutsche Bank Place
11. Governor Phillip Tower and Governor Macquarie Tower
12. Hyde Park Barracks
13. Ian Thorpe Aquatic Centre
14. MLC Centre
15. Museum of Sydney
16. Qantas House
17. Sydney Conservatorium of Music
18. Sydney GPO
19. Sydney Opera House

Object
20. Museum of Contemporary Art Store
21. The Strand Arcade
    Dinosaur Designs / Venerari

Fashion
22. Belinda
23. Carla Zampatti
24. Incu
25. Vintage Clothing Shop
26. Von Troska
27. The Strand Arcade
    Alannah Hill / Akira / Alex Perry / Bowie / The Corner Shop / The Graduate Store / Jayson Brunsdon / Leona Edmiston / Lisa Ho / Wayne Cooper / Zimmermann

Art
28. Art Gallery of NSW
29. Museum of Contemporary Art

Visual
30. Ariel Booksellers
31. Borders
32. kikki.K
33. Kinokuniya
34. Museum of Sydney Bookstore

Eat / Drink / Sleep
35. Bambini Trust Restaurant & Wine Room
36. BBQ King
37. Becasse
38. The Blacket Hotel
39. Commercial Travellers Association Club
40. est. at Establishment
41. Golden Century
42. Guillaume at Bennelong
43. Hemmesphere
44. Hilton Hotel
45. Opera Bar
46. Sailor's Thai Canteen
47. Sea Bay
48. sushi-e
49. Summit & Orbit Lounge
50. Tetsuya's
51. Via Abercrombie

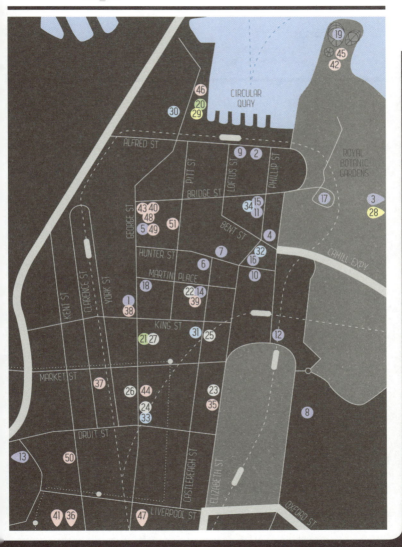

Surry Hills

Object
1. Beautiful on the Inside
2. Chee Soon & Fitzgerald
3. cloth
4. Collect
5. Courtesy of the Artists
6. Davidmetnicole
7. Format Furniture
8. Hub Furniture
9. InDestudio
10. Koskela
11. Living Edge
12. Metalab
13. Object Gallery
14. Orson & Blake
15. Planet Commonwealth
16. Planet Furniture
17. Sabbia Gallery
18. Schamburg + Alvisse
19. Spence & Lyda

Fashion
20. 32 Riley St
21. Capital L
22. Dobry Den
23. Hope Street Market
24. Paris Texas
25. Orson & Blake
26. Somedays
27. Surry Hills Market
28. Zoo Emporium

Art
29. Chalk Horse
30. China Heights
31. Firstdraft
32. Gaffa Gallery

Visual
33. Published Art Bookstore

Eat / Drink / Sleep
34. Bodega
35. Billy Kwong
36. Bourke Street Bakery
37. Gaslight Inn
38. Hollywood Hotel
39. Il Baretto
40. La Sala
41. Longrain
42. The Lounge Cafe
43. Matsuri
44. Mohr Fish
45. Pizza e Birra
46. Pizza Mario
47. Red Lantern
48. Single Origin Roasters
49. Spice I Am
50. Uchi Lounge
51. Vini
52. The Wall Cafe

MAP_SURRY HILLS

Darlinghurst & Potts Point

Architecture
1. Elizabeth Bay House

Object
2. de de ce
3. Euroluce

Fashion
4. Alfie's Friend Rolfe
5. Arida
6. Blood Orange
7. Blue Spinach
8. Our Spot
9. Via Alley

Art
10. Artspace
11. Monster Children Gallery

Visual Culture
12. Architext Bookstore

Eat / Drink / Sleep
13. Baron's
14. Bayswater Brasserie
15. Bill & Toni's
16. bill's
17. The Blue Hotel
18. Fish Face
19. Fratelli Paradiso
20. Judgement Bar
21. Kinselas
22. The Kirketon Hotel
23. Lotus Bar
24. Medusa Hotel
25. Onde
26. Otto Ristorante
27. Phamish Asian Cuisine
28. Regents Court Hotel
29. Cafe Sel et Poivre
30. Tropicana Caffe
31. Una's Coffee Lounge
32. Will & Toby's
33. Yellow Bistro

MAP_DARLINGHURST/POTTS POINT

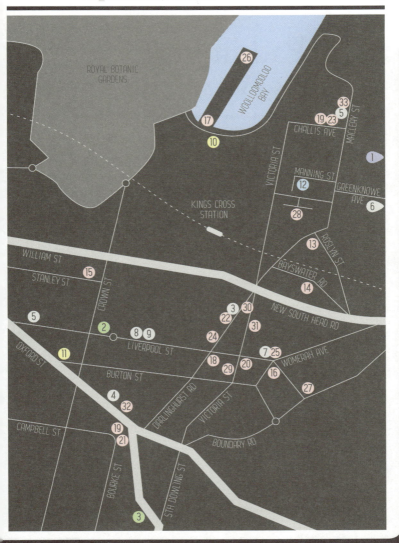

Paddington & Woollahra

Object
1. Dinosaur Designs
2. Orson & Blake
3. Tibet Gallery

Fashion
4. Akira
5. Alannah Hill
6. Belinda
7. Body
8. Collette Dinnigan
9. The Corner Shop
10. Easton Pearson
11. Fleur Wood
12. Gorman
13. Ginger & Smart
14. Incu
15. Kirrily Johnston
16. Ksubi
17. Leona Edmiston
18. Lisa Ho
19. Melvin & Doyle
20. Paddington Market
21. Parlour X
22. Poepke
23. Reads
24. Riada
25. sass & bide
26. Scanlan & Theodore
27. Von Troska
28. World New Zealand
29. Zambesi
30. Zimmermann

Art
31. Australian Centre for Photography
32. Australian Galleries #1
33. Australian Galleries #2
34. Harrison Galleries
35. Ivan Dougherty Gallery
36. Josef Lebovic
37. Kaliman Gallery
38. Roslyn Oxley9
39. Sarah Cottier Gallery
40. Sherman Galleries
41. Stills Gallery
42. Sullivan & Strumpf

Visual
43. Ariel Booksellers
44. Berkelouw Bookstore
45. Egan
46. Paper Couture

Eat / Drink / Sleep
47. Bistro Moncur
48. Buon Ricordo
49. Buzo
50. Love Supreme
51. Paddington Alimentari
52. Paddington RSL

MAP_PADDINGTON/WOOLLAHRA

Bondi

Architecture
1. Bondi Icebergs Pool

Fashion
2. Bondi Market
3. From St Xavier
4. Ksubi
5. Mambo
6. Tuchuzy

Eat / Drink / Sleep
7. Icebergs Dining Room & Bar
8. Fishmongers
9. Gertrude & Alice Bookshop Cafe
10. Green's Cafe
11. North Bondi RSL
12. North Bondi Italian Food
13. Pompei's
14. Sean's Panaroma
15. Three Eggs Cafe

MAP_BONDI

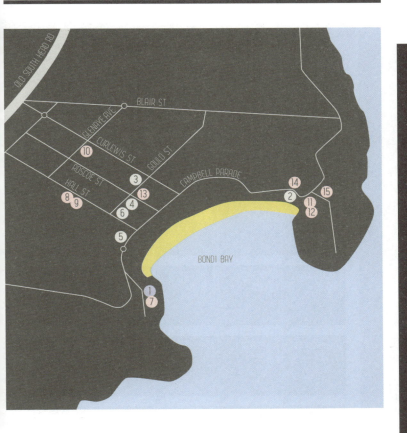

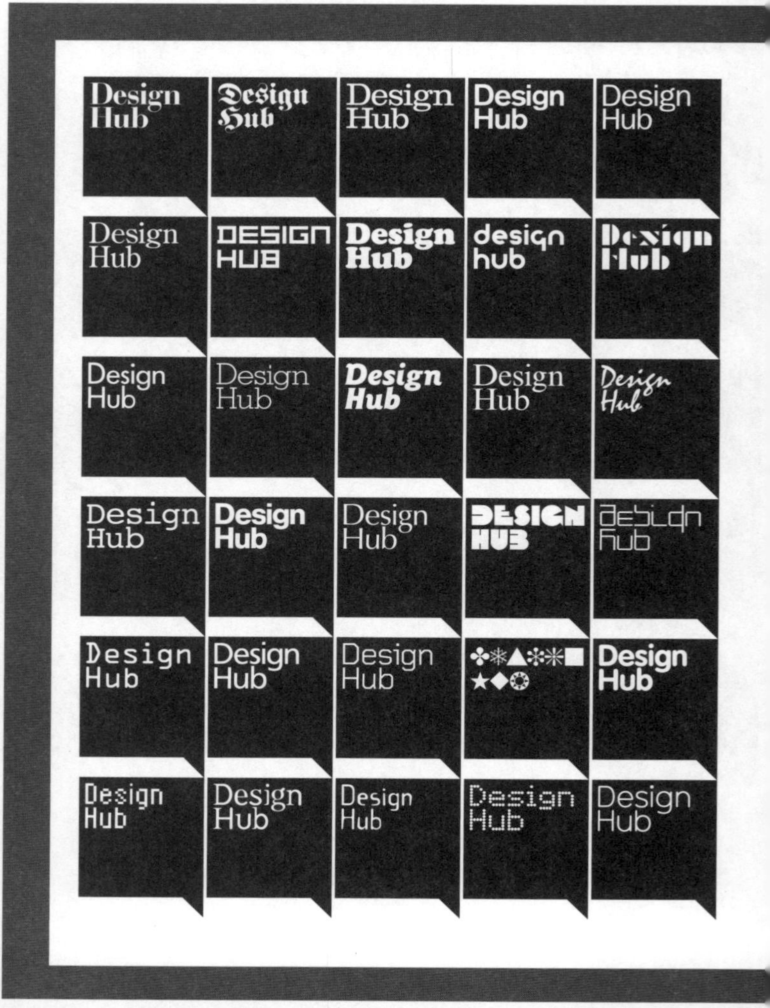
Design Hub
Design Hub
Design Hub
Design Hub
Design Hub
Design Hub
DESIGN HUB
Design Hub
design hub
Design Hub
Design Hub
Design Hub
Design Hub
Design Hub
Design Hub
Design Hub
Design Hub
Design Hub
DESIGN HUB
Design Hub
Design Hub
Design Hub
Design Hub
Design Hub
Design Hub
Design Hub
Design Hub
Design Hub
Design Hub

Your online design resource from the Powerhouse Museum

Explore design collections and read the latest news, interviews, opinions and ideas across the breadth of design.

www.dhub.org

Design Hub is a project of the Powerhouse Museum funded by the Australian Research Council with the University of Western Sydney and the University of Technology, Sydney.

MAJOR CULTURAL PARTNER_UNIVERSITY OF TECHNOLOGY SYDNEY

IMAGINE.

INNOVATE.

CREATE.

UTS:Faculty of Design, Architecture and Building has an international reputation for its innovations in design, sustainability and urban environments.

Our graduates are passionate professionals who design and produce the products, places and spaces of contemporary cities.

Start your design career with a degree in Industrial Design, Interior Design, Fashion and Textile Design, Visual Communication or Architecture.

Join the best in your profession with a Masters degree in Design, Animation, Architecture or Digital Architecture.

**Start here:
www.dab.uts.edu.au**

UTS CRICOS PROVIDER CODE 00099F UTS673DAB

MAJOR CULTURAL PARTNER_OBJECT

SHOWCASING THE BEST CONTEMPORARY CRAFT AND DESIGN

MAJOR CULTURAL PARTNER_OBJECT

Hardware solutions for residential, commercial, retail and hospitality projects.

Visit our Häfele Sydney Design Centre, our experienced architectural consultants can assist you with selection and specification of the right product for your building project or furniture design.

Experiencing is believing

HÄFELE
FINDING BETTER WAYS

Sydney Design Centre, 17 - 19 Pyrmont Bridge Road, Pyrmont 2009
t: 8788 2200 f: 9692 0711 e: info@hafele.com.au www.hafele.com

ARCHITECTURE_CONTENTS

Architecture & Built Environment

40   Introduction

43   Accidents & winding roads_history_feature

45   Take a walk_architecture tour

62   Architectural adventures_things to do

65   Olympic efforts_feature

69   Ten things you didn't know_the Opera House

73   Books & Buildings_things to read

77   Making waves_the architecture of swimming

PARTNER_EUROLUCE

FLOS

Toio by Achille & Pier Giacomo Castiglioni

ARCHITECTURE_INTRODUCTION

Introduction

left
The Rose Seidler House, open to the public, made a great impact on the development of Sydney's residential architecture.

Sydney architecture is not just the Opera House, though we know that's what a lot of folk come here for. But there's a lot more to the place to discover too, not all of it, unfortunately, accessible to the public, since a lot of the great building design that Sydney is so famous for around the world is residential only (yes, the lucky buggers who own those amazing beach houses). So, without delving too much into critique-y natter, and not guiding you in droves to the homes of hapless private owners, we present a selection of the most accessible Sydney sites, and attempt to highlight some major structural themes: heritage points, business and cultural developments, swimming spots (of course!), and the over-riding Sydney theme of old-meets-new. There's a walk, which is really the only way to soak up the living, breathing city, and there might just be a thing or two about the Opera House as well.

right
Sydney Harbour from 16,000 feet – 1966.

photography
David Moore (Estate of David Moore, image courtesy Lisa Moore)

ARCHITECTURE_HISTORY_FEATURE

The early days: accidents and winding roads

Serendipity, ancient traditions and confusion were the forces that shaped many of the urban patterns evident in Sydney today. Eoghan Lewis tells us why.

If Captain Cook had had his way, the city would not be here at all. On his reconnaissance voyage to the continent he had elected his first landing spot, Botany Bay, as the site for a potential settlement (fittingly, new Australians still arrive here by plane every day). Cook reported home that he believed the trees would bear fruit in different seasons – they don't – and that the diverse flora might support a thriving animal population – it doesn't.

Seventeen years later, nearly 1500 men and women, two-thirds of them convicts, arrived on a fleet of 11 recycled boats from the British Navy at Botany Bay in the height of summer. Cook's subtropical paradise was a bland expanse of dry grass and barren trees. Governor Phillip knew they were in trouble; within two weeks they found an alternative site just half a day's sail to the north. Nestled behind the massive sandstone sea walls deep in the natural harbour, divided by a freshwater spring they named Tank Stream, the settlement is now known as Circular Quay.

The site conformed to an ancient pattern of Aboriginal campsites. The harbour provided excellent fishing and maximum winter sun, yet its topography protected it from hot, dry westerly winds and bitterly cold southern gales. Meanwhile, the fresh north-easterly breeze flows through the harbour mouth from the same direction as the view and mid-morning sun.

From its earliest days, the campsite marked out a social hierarchy that is still evident today. Convicts were relegated to the rocky western edge of the Tank Stream, The Rocks, now a distinctively working-class suburb. Meanwhile, the officers took possession of the gentler eastern slopes. Four of Australia's ten wealthiest postcodes still lie directly east of the Tank Stream: Darling Point and Point Piper, Rose Bay and Vaucluse, Bellevue Hill and Woollahra.[1]

Unlike other Australian capitals, Sydney was not a carefully planned city. For a long time it remained a camp; permanent structures were rare, town planning unheard of. As the city grew, governors occasionally tried to assert their influence over an unruly sprawl, with little success.

The topography and paths of the area's original inhabitants dictated the town's arrangement. Winding main roads, like Oxford and King Streets, sit on old walking tracks along ridges – the most efficient way to crisscross the land on foot. These snaking ridge roads drop down to points on the peninsulas where the water is deep; a logical spot for ferry wharves. This natural connection between land and sea, turned to advantage from its earliest days, is the essence of Sydney life.

---

1. 'How wealth is delivered to the top 10 post codes', *The Sydney Morning Herald*, June 8 2007.

Take a walk

The Australian Architecture Association has developed several architecture walks. Here, <u>Vincent Lam</u> and <u>David McCrae</u>, who chair the Association's volunteer tour guide group, share the highlights of the most popular tour through the inner city. Learn more about the connections between colonial and corporate design and the new themes emerging in Sydney's built environment.

First, there's the so-called 'adaptive reuse' of buildings that date back to the colonial era. For their architects it is a challenge to remodel and rework the existing fabric to stay true to the original character yet, simultaneously, to breathe new life and new purpose into the shell.

Secondly, there's the continuous development of the corporate high-rise. In the world's third largest financial centre after London and New York, the significance of corporate structures shouldn't be underestimated. Visiting new and historic examples, our tour charts the evolution of Sydney's office towers, their architectural advances, as well as their cultural significance for this city.

Finally, there's the arrival of the international 'starchitects'. Like many other global cities, Sydney now boasts its own Foster and its own Piano. Three of the tour's buildings are by the same architecture practice, Harry Seidler & Associates. Known as Sydney's godfather of modernism, the late Harry Seidler's contribution to the skyline of the city is lauded – as well as critiqued – by many of his peers, and is so prominent that it's impossible to ignore.

ARCHITECTURE_TAKE A WALK

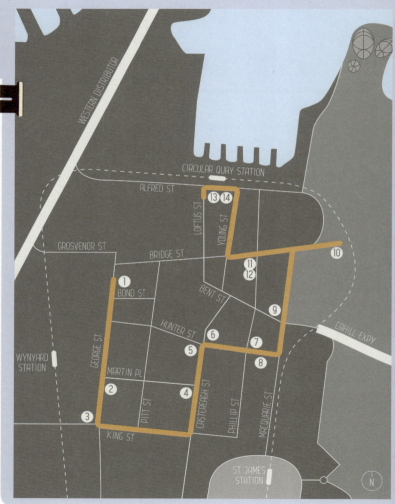

ARCHITECTURE_TAKE A WALK

❶

<u>Australia Square</u>
264 George Street
Harry Seidler & Associates
1967

Our initial stop introduces some central issues and figures in Sydney's architectural landscape. The 58-storey tower was the pioneer high-rise built after height restrictions were lifted in the early 1960s, marking a significant shift in Australia's urban environments. Hard to imagine now, but many Australians remember being awe-struck by what was the country's highest and the world's largest lightweight concrete structure. Their experience was – literally – heightened by visiting the revolving restaurant on the 48th floor, aptly named the Summit and still operating today. Seidler designed Australia Square after his former Harvard classmate, IM Pei (the architect of Paris' Louvre) had suggested another scheme for the site.

Like many on our walk, this building also houses some internationally significant art: the American artist Alexander Calder's black mobile sculpture *Crossed Blades*, and the colourful panelled mural by compatriot Sol LeWitt, which was installed in 2003, replacing the original fading tapestry designed by modernism's granddaddy Le Corbusier and French abstract painter Victor Vasaly.

As you look up, the tower might appear round (Seidler himself said it was built like a tree trunk), but it is actually a 20-sided polygon. Compared with other structural designs, it casts the smallest shadow and offers the least wind resistance. Seidler believed that architecture was best expressed in a freestanding building and opposed the 'walled street'. Thus, he created a substantial public plaza. It was the first of its kind in the city, and many architectural critics and historians view it as one of the most significant developments for civic space in Sydney.

❷

<u>Sydney General Post Office and Martin Place</u>
1 Martin Place
James Barnet / Buchan Group and Howard Tanner
1874 / 2000

The General Post Office is the best-known building of James Barnet, colonial architect of the late 19th century, who is said to have defined the character of Victorian Sydney. It was

ARCHITECTURE_TAKE A WALK

ARCHITECTURE_TAKE A WALK

left
The ribbed floor structures of Australia Square came courtesy of Seidler's collaborator, the Italian engineer Pier Luigi Nervi, who went by the moniker of 'the 20th century god of concrete'.

photography
Max Dupain

built in stages and completed in 1881, then added to in various ways until 1927. Originally visible from remote points, it was the symbol of the city until the Harbour Bridge defined the skyline 40 years later. Indeed, its makers thought of it as Sydney's Eiffel Tower. To reveal the structure in all its Italian Renaissance, palazzo-style splendour, it was decided to widen the unspectacular St Martin's lane running in front. The initial idea of the pedestrian plaza was not realised for another century, until 1970, when Martin Place finally became free of vehicles, now providing a major east-west link through the city. In the late 1990s the building joined many others in a process of adaptive reuse and now houses restaurants, a mall and function centres.

363 George Street
Denton Corker Marshall
1999

A further example of adaptive reuse is this complex, which includes five buildings, two of them heritage-listed, with one housing the Blacket Hotel originally designed by GPO architect James Barnet. The project highlights the architects' respect for heritage works and demonstrates a successful merger of historic buildings with cutting-edge contemporary design. The new tower was designed by Richard Johnson, now a partner in the Sydney firm Johnson Pilton Walker (JPW), but who was at the time with Denton Corker Marshall, a Melbourne-based practice. The new tower's service core also serves the heritage buildings, leaving their structures and floors unencumbered. At the front is a three-sectioned sandstone-clad colonnade that relates in height and detail to the neighbouring buildings. The complex was recognised with the Commercial Architecture Award by the Royal Australian Institute of Architects in 2000.

MLC Centre
Martin Place
Harry Seidler & Associates
1978

Again, we're standing in front of one of the Seidler-designed, Nervi-engineered towers that have become synonymous with inner-city Sydney. It's recognised by architectural aficionados as an outstanding building of its period, demonstrating the vitality and evolution of modern Australian architecture. The tower was positioned towards King Street to avoid building over the underground railway lines diagonally crossing the site, thus allowing space for a north-facing sunlit plaza. Eight massive columns take the weight of the tower. They thicken and turn outwards at the lower levels in response to the increased loads from the building above and the wind from the side. The exterior was constructed using concrete poured on-site and precast concrete elements with white quartz and glass panels. Horizontal pieces under the windows on every floor are structural beams, tapering in from rectangular ends to L-shape sections. This developing pattern of beams expresses the structural strength required, and also gives the building its distinctive character. Again, here's another place to admire some international art. Tapestries by Alexander Calder and German-born American artist Josef Albers are suspended in the tower lobby, and another Albers' wall relief, Wrestling, is on the outside wall overlooking the plaza.

Castlereagh Centre /
Capita Insurance company
9 Castlereagh Street
Harry Seidler & Associates
1990

The last Seidler project on our tour, this building was completed almost half a century after his first, Australia Square. Although Seidler was interested primarily in freestanding towers, space was tight and he proposed a different approach for this site. About a third of the facade is hollowed out on each of the 31 floors, creating a stepped atrium that rises through the full height of the building toward the north, bringing sunlight to the offices inside. In the deep soil on top of these shelves grow figs and palms, transplanted as mature plants after being shaded progressively in the nursery for almost two years so they could adjust to this low-light environment. The effect is certainly beautiful to look at, but there was also a practical consideration – reduced floor space meant the building could be constructed at almost twice the height it would be allowed under other circumstances.

ARCHITECTURE_TAKE A WALK

City Mutual Life
Assurance Building
60–66 Hunter Street
Emil Sodersten
1938

This 12-storey building is considered one of the best examples of the aesthetic principles and construction techniques of the inter-war art deco period. Its architect, Australian-born Emil Sodersten, is responsible for many residential buildings in Sydney and is known as one of the country's major exponents of art deco style, which he cultivated on overseas journeys. Sodersten was a reputed groundbreaker, forming a link between the city's predominantly Victorian conventions and modern architecture. The completion of the City Mutual Life Assurance building also stood testament to a newly found architectural confidence after the 1930s Depression. One of the city's first air-conditioned buildings, the zigzag windows were designed to reduce the heat load on the cooling system. The building still retains remnants of one of the first automated lift systems in Australia, and displays the full range of 1930s modern detail.

Above the entry hovers a bronze sculptural relief by Rayner Hoff, whose art also features prominently on the Anzac Memorial in Hyde Park. The statue represents a Pompeiian family fleeing from the ash and lava of an erupting Mt Vesuvius. The sculptor interprets the figures as heroic Australians and sets them among native flora.

Qantas House
1 Chifley Square
Rudder, Littlemore & Rudder
1957

Qantas House curves with the semi-circular shape of Chifley Square. The building, a corporate icon, was designed by 27-year-old architect Felix Tavener with the firm Rudder, Littlemore & Rudder. Like many buildings we've seen, this one brought a new international trend to Sydney – the curtain-walled office building. An example of moderate 1930s European modernism, it combined quintessentially Australian materials (such as locally quarried granite, sandstone and native timber) with global design and technology standards, an expression of the confidence

above
In front of the MLC tower, the mushroom-shaped Commercial Travellers Club is supported on a single curved, tapered column.

photography
Max Dupain

right
An external steel truss acts as a brace for this stacked building, which houses the head office of the Capita Insurance company.

photography
Max Dupain

and future plans of Qantas. At 46 metres, it reached the maximum height allowed in the 1950s. It was the home of Australia's national airline for 25 years, and was described by architect Peter Rudder as 'reflecting the aesthetics of flight'.

Deutsche Bank Place
126 Phillip Street
Foster and Partners / Hassell
2005

Architect Lord Norman Foster's landmarks include the 'Gherkin' in his London hometown and the German Parliament in Berlin. With the Deutsche Bank building opening in 2005, Sydney finally received what many other cities already had – her very own Foster building. Foster is acclaimed for his exceptional play with form and structure, his reinvention of workplace environments and his sustainable building methods. He was rewarded with the Pritzker Prize, the closest thing to a Nobel of Architecture, in 1999. Foster used many tried-and-tested ideas on this project, as well as throwing in a few new ones. The central concept was to take the core of the building – lifts, air conditioning and other utilities – and transport it from its traditional centre to the building's side. Thus emerged the largest column-free floor plate in the country, while the west-facing core doubles as a heat shield. The mechanical ballet of the sixteen transparent lifts is spectacular both from the inside and out. The stunning, semi-public, four-storey entry concourse (called the Assembly after the Assembly Hotel formerly situated here) manifests the architect's belief that buildings should contribute to the public life of a city. Between office floors and lifts, a full-height atrium measuring 140 metres to the roof allows light to penetrate office floors on all sides. The style of this building – which expresses, rather than conceals, its structure – is a grand example of structural expressionism. The original concept was for the roof element to contain a glazed biosphere with plants to cleanse and recycle air from the building. Unfortunately it was eliminated due to cost and council constraints. As a result, the crown of the building remains empty.

ARCHITECTURE_TAKE A WALK

above
A crown where a thriving biosphere should have been: the striking structure of Norman Fosters' Deutsche Bank Building.

photography
Martin van der Wal

⑨
<u>Aurora Place</u>
Office - 88 Phillip Street
Apartments - 114 Macquarie Street
Renzo Piano Building Workshop / Lend Lease Design / Group GSA / HPA Architects
2000

Consisting of a 44-level office tower and a 17-storey residential apartment block separated by a public plaza, Aurora Place is Australia's most expensive piece of real estate. Revealed just before the 2000 Olympics, it was designed by Italian superstarchitect Renzo Piano (he too was handed a Pritzker Prize, the year before Foster). Piano's design references the Opera House, suggesting that the shape of his building is in direct dialogue with the other's curvaceous forms. Piano's love of working with light is reflected all over this building, with white ceramic paint applied to the glass frontage creating a ghost-like appearance as the fins disappear into the sky. Notice that the tower flares from the bottom to the top. This clever device creates the public piazza at ground level while maximising the floor space on upper levels, where rents are generally higher. In the offices, wintergardens are conceived as social spaces, allowing workers to enjoy some of the most spectacular views of Sydney. The apartment tower boasts glass louvres as natural ventilation spaces and a terracotta tile cladding system similar to a meccano set.

Sydney Conservatorium
of Music
Macquarie Street, opposite
Bridge Street junction
NSW Govt Architect Johnson
/ Daryl Jackson Robin Dyke /
Tanner & Associates 2002

The Sydney Conservatorium of Music, now part of the University of Sydney, is an important reminder of Sydney's colonial days, and was completed in 1821 using convict labour. The original castle-like building was designed by colonial architect Francis Greenway for Governor Macquarie with elaborate, stuccoed brick stables and servants' quarters. It became the Conservatorium almost a century later. The building to the right is a recent addition, completed in 2002. The new additions, opposed by some conservationists, were built within a large excavation and located under two extensive landscaped terraces. Although they are hardly in evidence visually, there are around 600 rooms, including six substantial public performing spaces, all located below street level. Glass and steel frames help the new building sit gently and silently next to the old one.

Museum of Sydney at the site
of the first Government House
Cnr of Bridge and
Phillip Streets
Denton Corker Marshall
1995

The relatively new Museum of Sydney on the site of the first Government House shares an entire block of land with two office buildings: Governor Phillip and Governor Macquarie Towers, the latter of which houses the NSW Government. As the name suggests, the site was first used as the residence of the Governor of NSW. That was in 1788, when European settlers assembled their first permanent building from materials imported on the first fleet. You can see the plan of the first Government House in the granite pavement, in one area showing archaeological

left
Saluting the Opera House: Renzo Piano's Aurora Place.

photography
John Gollings

remains of the building's footings. The pattern extends into the museum's interior. At the end of the forecourt, Janet Laurence and Fiona Foley created the sculpture installation *The Edge of Trees*. Its 29 posts of different materials and heights symbolise the 29 clans of Aboriginal groups in the area as well as the layers of occupation since 1788.

In contrast to the metal and glass tower behind it, the facade of the museum consists of three dark, orange-brown sandstone blade walls, complementing the other 19th century buildings in the district.

The sandstone has five handcrafted textures, from rock-faced stone at the bottom to a smooth finish on top. The architects intended the glass 'viewing cube' and its twin, the 'entry cube', to be the two windows through which the early history of Sydney can be understood. A note for film buffs: some scenes from *The Matrix* were shot here.

Governor Phillip Tower and Governor Macquarie Tower
Cnr of Bridge and
Phillip Streets
Denton Corker Marshall
1993–95

The entry to the two office towers is completely separate from the Museum. Governor Phillip Tower rises to 223 metres with 38 floors, while the smaller Macquarie Tower comprises 25 floors. They share the entry loggia located under the gap between the two towers. Both the loggia and the lobbies are high-ceiling spaces lined with extensive sandstone walls. The office tower displays an international modernism aesthetic with the simple grid of the curtain-wall facade (so-called because it is literally suspended from the frame). At the same time, the tower reflects the classic Greek three-part proportion system: a substantial base, a regularly patterned torso and an elaborate crown. The distinctive crown of intersecting stainless steel blades defines this building in the crowded Sydney skyline. The actual tower commences ten storeys above ground, so offices are high above many

ARCHITECTURE_TAKE A WALK

right & below
Tradition meets modernity in the construction and materials of Governor Phillip and Macquarie Towers and the adjacent Museum of Sydney at the site of the first Government House.

photography
John Gollings

of the surrounding buildings and all enjoy the spectacular views. The monumentality of the towers is reinforced in their somewhat intimidating foyers. This project won almost every architectural award in Australia, including the Urban Design Award from the Institute of Landscape Architects.

Customs House
31 Alfred Street, Circular Quay
James Barnet / Walter Liberty Vernon / Tonkin Zulaikha and Jackson, Teece, Chesterman & Willis / Lacoste + Stevenson, Peddle, Thorp & Walker Architects and Tanner Architects
1887–1997

Adjoining Circular Quay, Customs House stands as a reminder of the importance of the quay as the original maritime and civic centre of the colony. It was the hub of early trading, where imported goods were taxed, stored and cleared for sale. The six-storey, sandstone-faced classical revival building was modelled on the London Customs House and is mainly the work of colonial architect James Barnet, who added to the structure of an earlier building. The story of Customs House is one of continuous transformation. By 1990, the Australian Customs Service Headquarters moved out of the city, and the building was left empty. The Federal Government eventually gave it to the Sydney City Council, complete with funds for its conservation. Architects Tonkin Zulaikha and Jackson, Teece Chesterman & Willis were commissioned to convert it into a cultural and information centre. The central feature is a glass atrium rising the full six storeys, topped with a glazed roof and computer-controlled louvres, designed to provide maximum levels of natural light. In a further change, three architecture practices transformed Customs House from an exhibition space into the City of Sydney Public Library, Function and Exhibition centre it is today. The architects were Lacoste + Stevenson; Peddle, Thorp & Walker Architects and Tanner Architects. The reconfiguration with its distinctive red colour scheme won much praise for design architects Lacoste + Stevenson and was recognised with a Royal Australian Institute of Architects architecture award in 2006.

ARCHITECTURE_TAKE A WALK

above
The interior of Customs House, featuring the award-winning restoration of Lacoste + Stevenson architects, and a model of the City of Sydney below glass panels in the floor.

photography
Peter Murphy

14

AMP Building
Junction of Alfred, Young and Phillip Streets, Circular Quay
Peddle Thorp & Walker Architects
1961

Completed in 1961 and designed by Peddle, Thorp & Walker, this was the first tall modern building in Australia. For the first time since 1912, the height limit of 150 feet (about 46 metres) was broken, with the resulting office building almost twice that. (The lifting of the height limit was a direct response to Melbourne's hosting of the 1956 Olympic Games. There was now more money to be made in Sydney!) Due to the novelty of such a high construction, a prototype was first constructed in North Sydney before the building was finally permitted. A decade later, the same firm built the smaller building behind the first. Heritage-listed in 1990, the AMP building dominated Sydney's skyline for several years in the 1960s. With its concave wall avoiding a box-like form, the building also accentuates the view from the harbour. Peddle, Thorp & Walker subsequently completed a considerable number of Sydney's post-war high-rise office buildings, and undertook a full refurbishment of the AMP building in 2004, together with architects Freedman Rembel and Architectus.

From here, take the lift to the viewing platform on top of the Cahill Expressway.

The platform provides an enlightening overview of the city and Circular Quay, as well as the Opera House and the Harbour Bridge. While here, spare a thought for the symbolic meaning that its opening in 1958 held for the city. Some say it marked the moment when Sydney chose to become Los Angeles, doing away with its large tram network and instead celebrating the car as king.

This is only the beginning! There are plenty more adventures where this one came from. The AAA runs hundreds of tours each year. While this one starts every Saturday morning at 10.30am at Customs House, Circular Quay, other walks focus on historical architecture, on harbour architecture and even on bar architecture. Also, the city's most prominent architects take tours to introduce visitors and locals to 'their' Sydney on the 'Architect's Choice' tours. Find out more on architecture.org.au or ring 8297 7283.

right
The AMP Building pushed Sydney to the forefront of international skyscraperism with only US and Hong Kong cities having larger floor-space ratios.

photography
Sharrin Rees, (Courtesy of PTW Architects in association with Freedman Rembel.)

Architectural adventures

right
Inspired by Chicago's 'Prairie School': the Griffins' homes in Castlecrag are uniquely connected to the landscape and constructed from local materials.

photography
Courtesy of the Griffin Society

There's always more to do and explore when it comes to architecture in Sydney. If you're an insatiable freak and need extra stimulation, strap on your boots and helmets and get yourself to the following destinations.

Meet the Griffins in Castlecrag

Castlecrag is an example of an early Australian urban planning experiment gone right. Ever since Chicago-born Walter Burley Griffin and his wife Marion Mahony Griffin arrived in Australia (in 1914) to implement their designs for Canberra, they had harboured a fascination with Sydney's spectacular natural landscape. Some years later, they tired of the politics surrounding their work in the capital and went to work in Sydney. Set up as a 'model suburb', Castlecrag's houses were built in harmony with the bushland and topography on an unusual layout of curvilinear roads that follow the natural contours of the leafy peninsula. Fourteen of the Griffin-designed houses are still intact. The Griffins had a unique vision that has inspired the country's architects ever since (especially those of the so-called 'Sydney School'). Burley Griffin said that there are 'no fences, no boundaries, no red roofs to spoil the Australian landscape'. The design also worked to promote a sense of community. It's a shame the idea didn't catch on further, inoculating us from today's plague of anonymous neo-Tuscan villas and McMansions. A self-guided tour is available through the dedicated Griffin Society (also check out their website for other Griffin-related events).
griffinsociety.org

ARCHITECTURE_ARCHITECTURAL ADVENTURES

Back to the Future at Rose Seidler House

Calling all architectural tourists: if you didn't miss visiting Rietveld's Schroeder House in Utrecht, then you must not miss the Rose Seidler House in Wahroonga. Completed in 1950, it is one of the most uncompromising residential modernist designs in the country. Set in the bush adjacent to Ku-ring-gai Chase National Park, the elegant box on stilts ignited an interest in modernism, and stimulated much social comment and debate, offering a way of living that was new and challenging for many on the clipped-lawn denizens of 1950s Australia. The furniture inside is one of the most important post war design collections in Australia. The house for Rose and Max Seidler was the first commission for architect Harry Seidler, who specially came to Sydney from New York (and never left). Guided tours are available on request, run by the Historic Houses Trust.
71 Clissold Road, Wahroonga
9989 8020
hht.net.au

Conquer the convicts with the Historic Houses Trust

This country's built history may be short, but that doesn't make it less interesting. On top of that, it's especially well-preserved courtesy of the Historic Houses Trust, which offers access to many important period and contemporary homes and estates around Sydney. Their exhibits range from the somewhat macabre Hyde Park barracks in the city, designed by convict architect Francis Greenway and erected by the prisoner inhabitants themselves, to the romantic surrounds of Elizabeth Bay House, once known as 'the finest house in the colony' and inhabited by the Colonial Secretary. Great supporters of design-related activities, the venues often hold interesting creative events. Check the website for more details.
Hyde Park Barracks
Queen Square
Macquarie Street, Sydney
Elizabeth Bay House
7 Onslow Avenue, Elizabeth Bay
hht.net.au

Scale that bridge

Zip yourself into a colour-coded jumpsuit, clip yourself to a strong rope and take the memorable walk across the superstructure of the iconic Harbour Bridge. The brainchild of Paul Cave, Bridge Climb is the corporate team building moment of the year, and an excellent chance to check out the sights of the harbour city. The walk has received many awards, including one for heritage conservation from the RAIA. The Harbour Bridge is particularly special to Cave because his late father-in-law lined up for two days from 19 March 1932, the day the bridge was opened, and purchased the first rail ticket across the bridge – ticket number 00001 – from Wynyard to Milson's Point Station.
bridgeclimb.com

View to the city

If you are out and about around Sydney Harbour it's well worth strolling up to the lookout at Georges Head in Mosman. Designed by Richard Leplastrier in 2006, there are also adjacent toilet facilities by the same architect at the site. A great place for a picnic lunch.
Suakin Drive, Georges Head

ARCHITECTURE_OLYMPIC EFFORTS

Olympic efforts

below
The Amenities Building, designed by Durbach Block Architects in collaboration with Neeson Murcutt.

photography
John Gollings

When every four years the world turns to one city to gape at super sports people, you'll often find that the record breaking is being done in venues designed by world-class architects striving to surpass previous achievements in their own field. In Sydney, a range of individual projects still make the visit to the Homebush site worthwhile.

While a number of large architecture practices took home the big gongs for their developments, a handful of smaller projects also stand out. Some of them have only been added to the site recently. Take the ferry out there and have a look around.

Sydney International Archery Park
Stutchbury and Pape

It's demountable and could be reassembled elsewhere, but the archery building remains where it has earned much admiration for its visual metaphors of strength, grace and flight, and abstract representation of the qualities associated with the sport of archery. The lyrical landscape of rippling grasses around the building came courtesy of Phoebe Pape. The simple yet dramatic linear pavilion stretches over 100 metres and is crowned by an enormous tilted and skewed canopy of corrugated metal over a long line of cabins. Peter Stutchbury, who now works on his own, is one Sydney's most reputable proponents of integrating architecture and landscape, believing buildings should reflect regional differences. (Archery Park has been likened to that simplest of forms in Australian architecture – the farm shed).

Amenities Building
Durbach Block Architects and Nicholas Murcutt

Glowing at night like a beacon, the dunnies designed by Durbach Block Architects (who teamed up with Nicholas Murcutt for the occasion) are among the quirkiest and most humorous designs around the Games. Situated in the car park on Edwin Flack Avenue to the west of the main stadium, the smoothly contoured structures have red, yellow and blue steel portals. Inspired by Japanese rice paper lights, the biomorphic shells are covered with translucent fabric that glows at night. Well-known in this town, Durbach Block are most noted for their residential buildings.

Brickpit Ring
Durbach Block Architects

First came the bricks, but now it's the frogs and the architecture that keep drawing people to this site at Homebush Bay. Opened in late 2005, the Brickpit Ring is a circular walkway that provides access to the site where hundreds of skilled labourers once produced the bricks for much of Sydney's suburban housing and many of the city's public buildings. Sitting more than 18 metres above ground, the 500-metre walkway allows access to the site from above while preserving the habitat of endangered frogs. The ring sits on top of a slender, steel-braced cruciform structure, which appears extremely thin

ARCHITECTURE_OLYMPIC EFFORTS

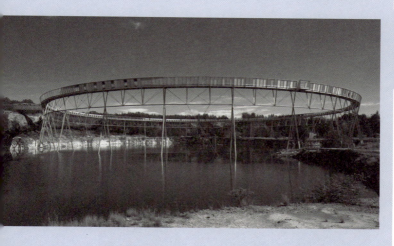

Above
Durbach Block's Brickpit Ring.

Photography
John Gollings

and allows minimal connections through its columns to the Brickpit floor.

Lighting Towers
Tonkin Zulaikha Greer and Hargreaves Associates

The Lighting Towers, a series of 19 pylons, each 30 metres tall, were a major feature among the architectural achievements of the Games. Uniting many functions in the one concept, the towers contain a variety of services and seating. For instance, a 5m-square facetted mirror reflects area lighting indirectly onto the Plaza for a glare-free night time ambience.

Shipwreck Lookout
Neeson Murcutt Architects

Completed in 2004, this project by small architecture firm Neeson Murcutt allows visitors a better view of three heritage-listed shipwrecks in the bay. Consisting of a path and three elevated platforms, using stainless steel and brick, as well as three large mirrors, the project is an interesting approach to using architecture as a viewing apparatus. Landscape elements consist of native ground covers, a gravel path and an inscribed cast-iron threshold.

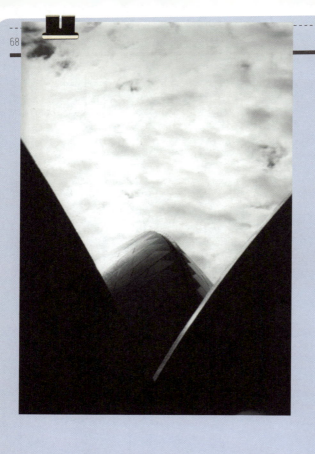

ARCHITECTURE_ THE OPERA HOUSE

Ten things you didn't know…

Left
According to architecture folklore, Utzon's design was inspired by the billowing clouds he had seen in a promotional video about Australia. It was, more or less, his only impression of this faraway place at the time.

photography
Eoghan Lewis

Its image is constantly beamed around the globe and, arguably, no other city boasts as prominent an architectural symbol. On the following pages, we cast a new look at the icon.

Sydneysiders and visitors alike are familiar with the story of the Sydney Opera House, but its place in popular culture overshadows its significance to Sydney and 20th century architecture in general.

Its design was awarded to young Danish architect Jørn Utzon in 1957. Over nine years, much of Utzon's time was spent finding structural solutions to the complex geometries of the shells and interiors with structural engineer Ove Arup. Then, mounting pressure to complete the project and an uncompromising new state government led to Utzon's forced resignation. In 1966, his masterwork half-finished, Utzon left Sydney, never to return. A committee of local architects was cobbled together to complete the building, and Utzon's intentions for the interiors never materialised. The controversy over this development was as monumental as the building itself, and ensues to the present day.

Utzon's influence on contemporary Sydney architecture is subtle but runs deep. Many of Utzon's students, including seminal figure Richard Leplastrier and, through association, Peter Stutchbury and Glenn Murcutt, talk openly about his influence. For a contemporary take on Utzon's legacy, check out Renzo Piano's Aurora Place buildings 800 metres away up Macquarie Street, which plays 'mainsail' to Utzon's 'spinnaker'. Read on for new insights …

ARCHITECTURE_THE OPERA HOUSE

There are many untold stories and surprising facts surrounding the Australia's most iconic building. We've unearthed ten.

Prior to winning the commission for the Opera House in 1957, Utzon had only built houses. He ran a small architecture office outside Copenhagen and worked on competitions while his kids were asleep at night. In this way, he designed the Sydney Opera House.

The enduring image that inspired Utzon in his design came courtesy of a promotional video he was given by the Australian consulate in Copenhagen. It was to lure migrants to Australia. Utzon remembered only the billowing clouds over the harbour.

Legend has it that Utzon's winning design was initially not among the ten schemes selected for closer consideration. Finnish-American architect Eero Saarinen, who arrived for his judging duties four days late, is credited with retrieving the scheme from the reject pile and encouraging his fellow judges to look again. Saarinen's futuristic TWA Terminal in New York was under construction at the time.

Look at it a little closer and you'll recognise: the Sydney Opera House is Sydney's Acropolis; a temple built at the threshold of the city atop a great stone base. You'll also find some elements of Gothic Cathedrals: soaring concrete vaults, dematerialising as they rise, where the structural ribs are the architecture. You might even see a Mayan temple, each step transporting you into the realm of the gods (the only time you ever walk down in the Opera House is when you leave, or when you find your seat). The platform might be a Greek or Roman amphitheatre, doubling as the city's great ceremonial gathering place.

Originally, the Opera House was to feature both a specifically commissioned Pablo Picasso mural, as well as a tapestry by Swiss architect and über-modernist Le Corbusier. While both works were commissioned and the artists had accepted,

above
Original model of the Opera House, also showing Utzon's original designs for the interiors, which never materialised.

Collection of the Powerhouse Museum, Sydney.

photography
Marinco Kojdanovski

these works never materialised. Utzon himself had spent his £5,000 prizemoney for winning the competition on a Le Corbusier tapestry.

NSW Labour party leader John Joseph Cahill – who's said to have had a soft spot for whisky – instigated and championed the Sydney Opera House competition. As he was dying from cancer, he knew he would not see 'his' building, but hoped it would become his legacy to the city. Unfortunately for him it is the bland two-storey Cahill Expressway that stretches around Circular Quay that bears his name. Some still refer to the Opera House as 'Taj Cahill'.

The announcement of the winning design attracted a mixed reaction around the globe. Sydney's great modernist Harry Seidler, then a young man and winner of one of 16 commendations for his own competition entry, wrote in a newspaper article that Utzon's design was 'poetry, spoken with exquisite economy of words'. Across the Pacific, America's greatest architect of the time, Frank Lloyd Wright, had a different opinion. He wrote: 'God help us all. I suppose this reckless design was chosen … because it exhibits neither rhyme nor reason for its purpose. This circus tent is not architecture … [but] absurd efflorescence. An inorganic fantasy that confirmed the folly of competition.' His compatriot, German émigré and modernist master Mies van der Rohe had a similarly strong opinion; he described the Sydney Opera House as 'diabolical, the work of the devil!' Late 20th century modernist Louis Kahn wrote that 'the sun did not know how beautiful its light was until it was reflected off this building.'

ARCHITECTURE_THE OPERA HOUSE

8

In fact, Utzon made a pilgrimage to Chicago to visit Mies van der Rohe. The first time they had met was in 1949 when Utzon was on his way to South America to study the Mayan ruins in Columbia and Mexico, and the master was amicable then. Yet when Utzon returned to Chicago 20 years later, folklore has it that Mies came to the reception, saw the Dane standing there, folded his arms and turned his back until eventually, Utzon walked away.

9

Between 1960 and 1966, with construction on the platform well under way, Utzon turned his attention to the interiors. During these years, he designed every knife and fork, every light fitting and all the furniture for the foyers of the Minor and Major Halls, which he described as perched like 'two exotic birds'. Then he left. Now almost 90, he says the six years he spent designing these interiors, none of which were realised, were the most productive of his life.

10

Since 1998, Utzon has been working with Richard Johnson of Johnson Pilton Walker (formerly of Denton Corker Marshall) on new Opera House interiors. Alterations to the Hall, Todd & Littlemore interiors (who took over after Utzon left), have been appearing since 2000. Check out the new colonnade to the western platform foyer and the new lighting washing over the 'folded concrete slabs' under the platform. The public lavatories have also been renewed and none of their light sources turn to the visitor directly, but instead wash up the structure to render a more sculptural effect. Also complete is the Utzon Room with its 14-metre-long tapestry, Utzon's first public artwork.

Curious? A full two-hour tour of the Opera House will reveal many more pieces of the puzzle. The Utzon Walk is part of the offerings of Sydney Architecture Walks, led by our collaborator Eoghan Lewis. Starting every Saturday at the Museum of Sydney at 10.30am, this 2.5 hour walk explores both the Opera House and Utzon's influence on Sydney architecture. There are many more tours on offer. For an overview, go to sydneyarchitecture.org

Books & buildings

above
Recent additions: Next Wave shows up-and-coming architecture practices, four of them from Sydney the new Burley Katon Halliday monograph by Thames & Hudson.

There is so much to discover about Sydney's architecture, particularly when it comes to the abundance of residential design this city is famous for. A little book like this one can't begin to do it justice, so we asked an expert to recommend some bigger ones …

<u>Anne Proudfoot</u> has managed the Royal Australian Institute of Architects' Architext Bookstore for over 15 years – not that it's made her job any less exciting. So passionate about architecture books that she says she's actually considered moving her living quarters into the store, she certainly knew what to pick out when we asked for a few new and classic publications about Sydney's built environment and its protagonists.

ARCHITECTURE_BOOKS & BUILDINGS

BKH
Heidi Dokulil (ed)
Design by Fabio
Ongarato Design
Photography by Sharrin Rees
Thames & Hudson, 2007

October 2007 marked a rare occasion: the launch of an Australian architecture practice monograph. And what a stunning book it is! Sydney's Burley Katon Halliday pioneered a particular approach to Sydney modernism, grounded in style and gushing elegance. Edited by Heidi Dokulil of the prolific design communication studio Parcel, the book features over 60 projects from waterside apartments, grand interiors of signature buildings, dramatic restaurant and retail spaces, corporate headquarters and harbourside homes. If you're into monographs on residential work in this town, it's worth also checking out the one's on Tonkin Zulaihka Greer and Durbach Block Architects.

Building a Masterpiece: the Sydney Opera House
Anne Watson (ed)
Powerhouse Publishing, 2006

This new addition to the literature on Australia's most iconic structure explores some of the untold chapters in the long history of the Opera House's gestation, development and completion. It looks at the individuals whose careers were made or broken by the Opera House, the pioneering construction methods, the workers on site, the politicians, architects and members of the public who championed it and its often beleaguered architect.

New Directions in the Australian House
Anna Johnson
Pesaro Press, 2006

This book focuses on residential architecture all around Australia, but notably features a house by respected Sydney practice Durbach Block on the cover. This book is in contrast to publications that focus on Australian residential architecture as distinguished by its respect for climate and surroundings. The author notes that the new directions she focuses on have 'a marked emphasis upon the theme of the monumental – a return to the idea of architecture as object.'

Next Wave
Davina Jackson (ed)
Design by Studio Round
Photography by
Shannon McGrath
Thames & Hudson, 2007

Written, designed and photographed by an all-female team, this very recent book looks at Australian residential architecture in a new light and, in doing so, presents four up-and-coming Sydney practices, namely young architect Adam Haddow of SJB architects, Terroir Architects, Turner Architects and Marsh Cashman Kooloos. Great for learning about the here, now and future.

Richard Leplastrier:
Spirit of Nature Wood Architecture Award 2004
Petri Neuvonen & Kristiina Lehtimaki (eds)
Rakennustieto Publishing, 2004

While Glenn Murcutt may be the man who catapulted Australian architecture into the international limelight, visitors should know that there's a whole 'School' associated with the cultural and environmental sensitivity that Murcutt espouses. Richard Leplastrier is a seminal figure in this circle. In 2004, he received the Finnish Spirit of Nature Wood Architecture Award for his (mainly residential) buildings that are very much the flavour of this city. The book, published in honour of his win, is a popular buy with international visitors, architecture students and lucky participants of the annual Glenn Murcutt master class, where Leplastrier (a one-time student of Utzon) is an educator.

Sydney Architecture
Paul McGillick & Patrick Bingham-Hall
Pesaro Publishing, 2005

From *Indesign* editor Paul McGillick and eminent Sydney photographer Patrick Bingham-Hall, Sydney Architecture is an all-encompassing volume that provides a great sweeping overview of both public and residential architecture. It's a good read, looks grand on the coffee table, and readers will close the covers with an understanding of the city's past and its present, and – most importantly – how it got here.

Sydney Architecture
Graham Jahn & Patrick Bingham-Hall
Watermark Press, 1997

This seminal book is a decade old. No doubt a monumental effort, it may be a teeny bit out of date as far as more recent architectural developments go, but is great for visitors who want some insight into historical architectural aspects. You can't go past this one.

ARCHITECTURE_SWIMMING POOLS

Making waves

left
Bathing history revamped. Built over the harbour in Woolloomooloo, the Andrew 'Boy' Charlton pool received a makeover courtesy of Ed Lippman in 2002.

photography
Willem Rethmeier

Beaches, glorious beaches – Sydney is all about the wonderful sand, sun and surf its denizens love to enjoy, but there's been some impressive man-made construction around the precious element too.

Whether they're of the open-water variety, taming a little piece of ocean, or of the chlorine kind, bringing the pleasure of the beaches to the inner city and suburbs, Sydney swimming pools come in all shapes and forms, and are a great source of pride for their architects and visitors alike. Here's a hit list of the six most talked about.

ARCHITECTURE_SWIMMING POOLS

left
Harry Seidler's legacy. The curvaceous Ian Thorpe Aquatic Centre is the latest addition to Sydney's collection of swimming pools.

photography
Dirk Meinecke

The boy wonder

When it opened to great fanfare in 2002, the Andrew 'Boy' Charlton pool (or ABC for short), was lauded as the most spectacular swimming pool the city had ever seen. It's no exaggeration. Named after a record-breaking Olympic swimmer, the history of this swimming spot stretches back to way before the First Fleet.

The design incorporates the historic and heritage aspects of the site by using old stone walls as well as the sea wall running along the water's edge. As you walk through, you'll be able to see down to the water through the timber decking suspended over the harbour. And while you admire the saltwater pool and dramatic view of Garden Island, and indulge in a healthy meal at the poolside cafe, you'll know why Surry Hills-based architect Ed Lippmann beat a competition of 150 firms for the design of this heavenly spot.
1c Mrs Macquaries Road,
The Domain
9358 6686
abcpool.org

The legacy

It's called the Ian Thorpe Aquatic Centre, after Australia's great Olympian, but if it seems weird to go to a pool named after someone who hasn't even hit 30, think of it as the Harry Seidler pool, since this was the last building the legendary architect designed before he died in early 2006, never to see its opening in 2007. This centre is considered the crown jewel of Sydney's regal collection of swimming facilities. It has been adapted to meet stringent environmental standards, incorporating rainwater collection systems and hydraulic roof vents. With its signature wave-like roof, spectacular city views, sun-drenched main pool and state-of-the-art aquatic and fitness facilities, this pool will no doubt play a major role in the making of future champions.
Harris Street,
Cnr William Henry Street,
Ultimo
9518 7220
itac.org.au

ARCHITECTURE

above
A backstroker's paradise. Featuring distinctive art deco plasterwork and superb views, the North Sydney Olympic pool is nestled between the Harbour Bridge and Luna Park.

photography
Patrick Bingham-Hall

The classic

When it opened in 1936, the North Sydney Olympic Pool was hailed as the 'wonder pool of Australasia'. If you believe the historical records, the high standard of its facilities and its sophisticated filtration system were among the most advanced on the planet. Of course, the pool isn't short of an impressive sporting history, with 86 world records broken here. In 2001, architecture firm Hassell were responsible for the award-winning addition of a 25-metre indoor pool, which celebrates its spectacular setting with a view through the walled glass front.
4 Alfred Street South,
Milson's Point
9955 2309
northsydney.nsw.gov.au

The concrete paradise

Completed just prior to the 2000 Olympics, the ribbed concrete and glass structure of Cook and Phillip Park Aquatic and Recreation Centre sits beneath the park of the same name. It includes an Olympic-sized pool, gymnasium, basketball court, cafe, wave pool and hydrotherapy pool. The centre was designed by one of Sydney's largest architecture practices, Bligh Voller Nield, in conjunction with Spackman & Mossop landscape architects. It's been the subject of much controversy since its inception, but continues to draw crowds, making for a sublime paddle as the afternoon sunlight filters through the glass ceiling.
4 College Street,
Cnr William Street, Sydney
9326 0444
cookandphillip.com.au

ARCHITECTURE_SWIMMING POOLS

The star

More famous than any other pool in town, the iconic Bondi Icebergs complex straddling the cliffs of South Bondi unites two ubiquitous Sydney stereotypes: barrel-chested leathery men in speedos and skimpily clad, equally tanned but hopefully less leathery starlets. While the former have been taking their infamous wintery swims in the saltwater pool since 1929, the latter came courtesy of the ritzy multi-million dollar refurbishment of the clubhouse in 2002, which now houses the fancy Icebergs Bar and Dining Room. The question remains which of the two prestigious groups is harder to join; to become an Iceberg you must be a resident and join a long waiting list, to sip cocktails with the starlets on the gelato-hued cushions and wicker furniture, you have to make it past the burly bouncers at the door. The good news is the alternative: the down-to-earth RSL squeezed between them. And casual swims are ok too.
1 Notts Avenue, Bondi
9130 3120
icebergs.com.au

The national treasure

Just a few hundred metres away from the British backpacker haven that is Coogee Beach, Wylie's baths were the first of the seaside pools that are now synonymous with this city. The historic wooden structure houses simple changing sheds and a cliff-hugging deck with steps leading to the 50-metre tidal ocean pool. The baths were built by Henry Wylie as a training facility for yet another Olympian, Wylie's daughter Mina, who competed – and won a medal – in the Stockholm Games of 1912. In the early 1990s, when they had become extremely rickety, community action saved them from closing down. In 1995, a careful restoration by architects Allen Jack and Cottier won the prestigious Greenway Award for Conservation. The architects decided to retain the essential form and spirit of the place, ensuring that the pool will remain at the heart of Sydney seaside culture for many generations to come.
Neptune Street, Coogee
9665 2838
wylies.com.au

OBJECTS_CONTENTS

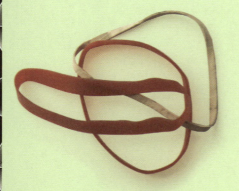

OBJECTS_CONTENTS   83

Products & Objects

86	To be objective_introduction
88	Take a walk_products & objects tour
93	Objects of desire_designers
108	Design across time_feature
110	From acorn to oak_wood
117	Shiny, pretty things_jewellery & metal
129	Thrown, cast, slipped_ceramics
131	Buffed & polished_glass
134	Stitched & woven_textiles
136	Print directions_textiles_feature
138	Stocks & shares_stores

PARTNER_TOP3 BY DESIGN

australia's design store 24/7

top3 by design is an edited collection of up to 3 products per kind, deemed best in the world by merit of design

top3.com.au
1300 top 333

To be objective

In his role as curator, writer and man about town, Associate Director of Sydney's Object Gallery Brian Parkes has helped to launch many a design career. He is perfectly positioned to give us a glimpse of what's moving in the realm of products and objects in his city.

'Sydney retains its "casual cool" and remains obsessed with showy displays of excess wealth, but the maturing design culture is finally enabling substance to compete with style,' says Parkes, who suggests that the city's design scene has come of age over the last two decades and is now positioned as a significant global centre for design.

He believes that this maturing is to no small degree thanks to the city's two leading public design institutions: the Powerhouse Museum and Object Gallery, but also feels that a supportive and nurturing environment is further evolving as leading showrooms actively promote local designers among their high-end imported offerings.

'Through continued critical and commercial success, a number of important Sydney design brands have emerged. Their common characteristics are inventiveness and entrepreneurship,' says Parkes. The local success stories? He suggests you keep your eyes peeled for Korban/Flaubert, Dinosaur Designs, cloth, Schamburg + Alvisse and Norman + Quaine. If you're after independent furniture and product designers, check out Charles Wilson, Caroline Casey and bernabeifreeman.

OBJECTS_INTRODUCTION

above
The Ken Woolley-designed, Sam Marshall-transformed Object Gallery building.

Object Gallery

The Australian Centre for Craft and Design at Object is a passionate supporter and showcaser of Australian products, and is basically the place to go if you want to know anything about the state and future of object design in this country. Object Gallery exhibits Australian product overseas, publishes *Object Magazine*, and is the home of the Bombay Sapphire Design Discovery Award exhibition from September through to November.
417 Bourke Street, Surry Hills
9361 4511
object.com.au

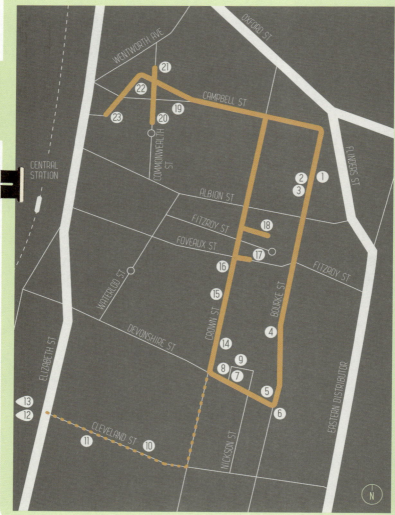

Take a walk

Once a notorious slum with an abundance of brothels, Surry Hills is no doubt Sydney's most creative area. It is the home of Sydney's design scene and the origin of the city's rag trade. Furniture and object makers have settled right into the heart of Surry Hills, with their studios and the stores they supply often only a block apart. We've asked Peter Salhani, long-time contributor to *Vogue Living* and now Editor of design mag *Monument*, to show you the best addresses in object and furniture design, with a few favourite art spots along the way.

Get yourself in the mood for Sydney design with the edgy mix of home objects and fashion at BOTI (Beautiful on the Inside) (see p. 139). The experimental feel of the store comes from not stocking the usual suspects. Across the road, Object Gallery (see p. 87) showcases Australian talent with handmade textiles, ceramics, glass, metal, jewellery and furniture. Collect (p. 141), is the street-level gallery store. A few blocks down, COTA (Courtesy of the Artist, see p. 121) is the newly opened retail space for handmade collections by Metalab and other designers, including metal by Robert Foster, glass by Ben Edols and Mark Vaarwerk's wearable plastic-bag art. Time to stop for a coffee. Bourke Street Bakery (see p. 312), on the corner of Devonshire, has the best pastries and pies in town – coffee's good too. Over the road awaits Ici et là ('here and there' in French, 588 Bourke Street), stocking a kooky collection of Francophile bric-a-brac; it's not design, but it is a nice distraction. Just up from the Bourke Street Bakery, Ray Hughes Gallery (270 Devonshire Street) is always good for contemporary (sometimes off the wall) exhibitions.

(8) Next door at Gineico (276 Devonshire Street), see classic architectural lighting and Australian designer David Knott's Lotus range. A sign just outside in Esther Lane points to the (9) Brett Whiteley Studio (2 Raper Street). This eminent artist's spirit is palpable in the site where he lived and worked. As we approach the intersection of Devonshire and Bourke, all those in a hurry turn right to head straight to stop number 15 on this journey, while those with stamina and a penchant for quirk, turn left. We're off to Cleveland Street and in for a retro and vintage bonanza. (10) Davidmetnicole (382 Cleveland Street) consists of a British-modern mix of old and new rejuvenated furniture, vintage industrial lighting and contemporary designs by co-owner David Page. (11) Glory Design (357 Cleveland Street) has mid-century tables, seating and storage with 60s lamps, made-to-order lamp shades and timber screens. (12) Further down is Mao & More (567 Cleveland Street) – a chaotic treasure trove of vintage and kitsch from China with furniture, lighting and lacquerware. Nearby (13) Vampt (268 Cleveland Street) has vintage Danish and art deco furniture and lighting with the occasional Memphis or modernist throwback, which makes it a fun fossick.

Now, it's time to head back to Crown Street. A coffee stop under the sunny awning of (14) Coffee Tea or Me? (536 Crown Street), revitalises the senses. A little further up the road, (15) Planet Furniture (see p. 146) is a truly local store, selling Australian textiles, ceramics, glass and tableware with an organic sensibility, along with the sustainably produced hardwood furniture by owner Ross Longmuir.

(16) Not far from here, Chee Soon & Fitzgerald (see p. 139) offer a seamless blend of old and new with fabrics, vintage tribal textiles, kimono silks, wallpapers, iconic glass, ceramics and tableware. Up on Foveaux Street, the newly opened (17) Format (see p. 142) showroom brings contemporary European furniture to Sydney along with classics by Panton, Prouvé and Vitra. Tucked in a tiny lane off Crown (18) Street, Metalab (see p. 121) is a collaborative studio making

OBJECTS_TAKE A WALK

handmade jewellery, glass and objects. Co-owner Cesar Cueva makes sculpture, runs workshops and hosts exhibitions here while wife Nina has just opened Courtesy Of The Artists, (see stop 4) nearby on Bourke Street as the retail arm.

Heading up Crown Street, turn left at Campbell for Koskela (see p. 143). They stock their own designs, sustainable contemporary furniture, goathair rugs, bedlinen, Aboriginal weaving and more.

Take the next left at Commonwealth Street for Planet Commonwealth (see p. 146), Ross Longmuir's larger store, where his full range of finely crafted Australian hardwood furniture is on show. A few blocks in the other direction on Commonwealth is Living Edge Studio (see p. 145) for classic Eames designs and local designers Charles Wilson, bernabeifreeman, Norman + Quaine and Jon Goulder.

Back up to Hunt and then left into Foster Street, Spence & Lyda (see p. 146) stocks contemporary European homewares like those of Missoni Home and iittala. Time for a rest. In nearby Mary Street, Published Art (see p. 290) specialises in the latest books and magazines on architecture, art and design from publishers worldwide – often ahead of other stockists.

right
Frag Woodall's Mr Stickley light and Ilium chair, available through Beautiful on the Inside.

above
Alessi loves Sydney: Abi Alice's design for the Italian giant.

(Resonance Centrepiece in 18/10 stainless steel; production Alessi Spa Italy)

right
The much-loved Zaishu stool by Matt Butler and his many associates.

Objects of desire

While some sprout from back shed to market, and others from computer-aided technology to rapid prototyping, all the product designers featured here germinated in the same promising environment – Sydney. If diverse perspectives can be a unifying trait, that's what connects these designers. Here's a selection of people and their specimens, from A to W.

Abi Alice

This woman is a true hybrid. Both an artist and a designer, she applies her creativity across many disciplines, including product design, sculpture, painting and photography. In 2006, she struck up a fortuitous collaboration with Italian homeware giant Alessi, designing her Resonance centrepiece, made of a thin sheet of stainless steel. Alice continues to develop new projects with Alessi alongside her divergent creative interests. Curious? That's easy. Her piece is waiting for you in Alessi stores across the globe.
abialice.com

Lana Alsamir-Diamond

Part owner and founder of the – dare we say revolutionary – product store Beautiful on the Inside (BOTI) in Surry Hills, Alsamir-Diamond is also a designer in her own right. Who would have thought a lamp could look as delicious as her Sugar Mamma piece, made of acrylic sheeting that looks like jelly? Naturally, it comes in strawberry or peaches & cream. She has also produced a range of silicon vessels emulating the aesthetic of crystal – through this one can bounce off the floor. Lana is busy holding the fort at BOTI, which is where you will find her products. Why not say hello?
322 Bourke Street,
Surry Hills
beautifulontheinside.com.au

above
Inspired by the childhood memories of searching for coins down the back of the couch: the Loose Change Chair, courtesy of DesignByThem.

Matt Butler

Living between Melbourne and Sydney, Matt Butler is a true design nomad. Some would know Butler's past output under his Canberra-based label Bluesquare, which focused on commercial furniture pieces. Butler's showpony, that has carried him all over the world, is Zaishu, a simple laser-cut plywood stool that slots together. The project's principle was to provide a blank surface that allows collaborations with artists and other visual mediums. Since its inception a few years ago, the project has been prolifically exhibited by Butler and his business partner Helen Punton. To date, Zaishu has featured Florence Broadhurst prints, works by artists and children from Samparc (outside Mumbai in India) and various street artists, as well as illustrations and imagery by local design talent such as cloth. You can get your very own unique Zaishu stool at many design outlets.
zaishu.com

Compact Desk

The face behind this efficiently named brand is product designer Stefan Kahn, who tackles a problem so many Australian product people try to solve: how to overcome the limitations and obstacles faced by designers and makers in this geographically isolated country. He has very successfully completed this mission. Piece by piece, the Compact Desk collection grows towards a stunningly simple

OBJECTS_DESIGNERS

Above
Glows like a warm fire: the Tallguy fibreglass light by Matthew Conway.

contemporary design system of desk and personal accessories, bringing order and organisation to everyday life. The trained graphic designer's stylish aluminium stationery vessels have found their way into diverse markets, with great success in Japan and the US.
compactdesk.com

Matthew Conway

According to this man, design should challenge an individual's expectation of what a product can be, engaging users on a functional as well as a psychological level. Conway doesn't limit himself in terms of processes and materials – instead, he commences with an idea. He works on a commission and exhibition basis with key pieces being his Tallguy lights.
matthewconway.com.au

DesignByThem

Formed by the duo Nicholas Karlovasitis and Sarah Gibson, DesignByThem is a unique kind of design studio, offering both commercial products and design consulting. The products are all Australian manufactured, while the consulting side of the business covers industrial products, fashion and accessories, graphic and web design, packaging and branding, as well as exhibition design and medical products. Quite a spread!
designbythem.com

... continued p. 105

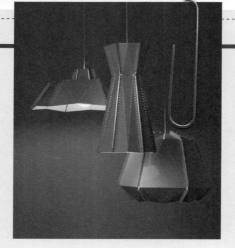

bernabeifreeman

above
The bernabeifreeman lighting series Seams was inspired by traditional archetypal cloth lampshades. Made from perforated and folded aluminium, the super light, thin metal gives them a paper-like quality.

The women behind the eponymous furniture brand bernabeifreeman love combining the qualities of handcrafted products with the possibilities of today's manufacturing technologies and industrial materials. The two combined their backgrounds in lighting and industrial design in 2002 and have since produced innovative contemporary lighting and furniture. Rina Bernabei and Kelly Freeman design and manufacture their products themselves, as well as create installations for exhibitions and work with architects and interior designers on custom projects. They are renowned for their use of punched and fabricated sheet metal for lighting pieces and furniture such as their Brodie table. Matching fresh materials with traditional models to create brand new types of products, bernabeifreeman products are quite collectable indeed. They're available from Living Edge.
bernabeifreeman.com.au

OBJECTS_DESIGNERS

Berto Pandolfo

Right
One of Pandolfo's latest projects, CRM, investigated a basic building material, sheet metal, as a means to create furniture such as this stool.

It's not just his Italian name that makes Berto Pandolfo a designer in the spirit of the Mediterranean masters. After graduating in industrial design at the University of Canberra, Pandolfo travelled to Italy and did a masters degree at the famed Domus Academy in Milan. Staying on in Italy, he became product manager for internationally recognised lighting company Flos, helping many significant designers resolve the manufacturing and production process for their pieces. No wonder he returned to Australia with a wide network of international designers and Italian manufacturing companies. He promptly turned this into the basis of his Ideas Agency, aiming to broker Australian products to Italian producers. Later, he formed the partnership R&D Department with fellow designer Michael Hoppe, developing and exhibiting household furniture and homewares. Pandolfo now teaches at UTS where he explores his interest in designs driven by new and emerging technologies, and is sincerely motivated to lead his students to international success. He is known to work on his designs in the workshop alongside his pupils, where they can observe his production methods. He also curates and exhibits regularly in Sydney, is an active member of professional awards and provides rigorous commentary through writing and curating.
bertopandolfo.com

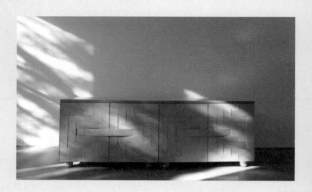

Caroline Casey

above
The Woven wall storage unit: doing with wood what others do with textiles.

Best known for her restrained and sophisticated wooden furniture, Caroline Casey dipped her finger into the fashion / textile pie before she moved to New York to study interior design. She returned to Sydney in 1995 to expand on the furniture range she had started developing in the Big Apple. Her work is essentially sculptural, with each piece starting as an exploration into form and working to achieve functionality. Casey's furniture is produced in modest batches by small-scale workshops in Australia and Germany, and pieces of her work are now held in major international collections in London, San Francisco and Canberra. In 2006, Casey formed the Casey Brown company with her architect husband Robert Brown. She creates installations and furniture sets within the residential homes Robert designs. Anibou stocks her work.
caseybrown.com.au

Adam Goodrum

above
Goodrum's multi-coloured flat-packed chair is a piece of simplistic form that integrates complex hinges to completely collapse.

Since completing his degree in industrial design at UTS in 1993, Adam Goodrum has become one of Sydney's most high-profile emerging designers, with objects ranging from large complex furniture to small witty pieces. He embraces both functionality and whimsy and his diverse work is united by its intelligence in execution, a degree of humour and a pragmatic view of the world. This includes the incredibly sensual stainless steel and leather Eve chair, the piece that won Goodrum the Bombay Sapphire Design Discovery Award (we'll subsequently refer to it as BSDDA) in 2005. Goodrum is conscious of the demand for space and portability and develops most of his designs into functioning prototypes to present to manufacturers. At the time of going to press, Goodrum was in serious conversation with some leading European manufacturers, including the granddaddy of Italian furniture makers, Cappellini. Stay tuned …
agoodrum@pacific.net.au

OBJECTS_DESIGNERS

Korban/Flaubert

below
The 2003 Cellscreen, made from anodised aluminium, and the 2003 bubble chairs, popular with kindergartens and ice cream parlours alike.

photography
Sharrin Rees

This dynamic studio of design and production is among Sydney's most original and successful, combining the skills of metal specialist Janos Korban and his architect partner in life and work, Stefanie Flaubert. Originally established in Stuttgart, Germany, in 1993, the two moved to Sydney two years later, setting up a workshop. Twelve years later, the exploration continues and has manifested itself in a complete range of furniture and lighting, all done from their Alexandria location. Their design – often focusing on roto-moulded plastics and metal – also extends to more ambiguous experimental forms and large site-specific sculptural commissions for commercial clients. Treating design as a process of discovery, Korban/Flaubert operate like a laboratory, with modelling and experimental materials, research and prototyping central to the methodological process. The duo has exhibited widely, from Milan to New York. You'll recognise their iconic pieces in books and magazines, and on back verandahs.
8–10 Burrows Road, Alexandria
9557 6136
korbanflaubert.com.au

Stefan Lie

below
Modelled on a caterpillar: Lie's 2004 Pila Seat.

After working and training as a toolmaker in Switzerland, Stefan Lie's design career in Australia began in 1998. Lie's designs range from large-scale installations and furniture to objects and jewellery. His work displays a cunning use of materials as well as the manipulation of traditional forms to create emotive outcomes. He is currently teaching at universities and design schools around Sydney, lecturing students in product, furniture and object design. If you want a piece of the action, his Ribs Bench – a wooden ribcage-like form – remains part of the Powerhouse Museum's permanent collection. If that still doesn't satisfy, go get your own Stefan Lie product from de de ce and his jewellery from Poepke.
stefan-lie.com

OBJECTS_DESIGNERS

Schamburg + Alvisse

below
Winner of the 2007 Australian Design Award: the eco-friendly, super-durable and colourful Smooth Tub chair.

In the mid 1990s, interior designer Mark Schamburg and architect Michael Alvisse made a decision. Rather than waiting around for an international talent scout to notice and consequently manufacture their work, they started to do it themselves – to a very high standard. Among the first to do so, the duo is now one of the country's most successful small furniture companies, producing tables, seating and lighting elements while adhering to their trademark triple-bottom-line business approach: using environmental, social and financial parameters to assess the value and viability of products and processes. This involves minimising waste, rationalising transportation, sourcing timber from well-managed forests and using only low-chemical glues.
And it's not just their environmental approach but also their smart marketing that makes the business so successful. Their first-floor showroom in Surry Hills, also their design headquarters, is well worth a visit.
116 Kippax Street,
Surry Hills
9212 7644
schamburgalvisse.com.au

Charles Wilson

above
The design for the Boulder Lounge and Ottoman was inspired by a grinding stone used for pounding grain, one of Wilson's childhood memories.

Merging a bold, sensual design aesthetic with expert technical knowledge of manufacturing and prototyping processes, Charles Wilson's work is well-resolved. Wilson believes it is the designer's duty to recognise opportunities for innovation. Though principally working with furniture, Wilson prolifically turns out stunning new designs that range from his recent two-part candelabra for Menu in Denmark to basic but beautiful vessels, from lounge settings including his Boulder range for Woodmark to commercial furniture. In 1994, Wilson's Swivel chair was among the first works of Australian designers manufactured by Sydney-based company Woodmark. While still enjoying physical exploration, he uses computer-based modelling to draw and test his design concepts, then creates finely crafted scale models to consider the work in three dimensions. Wilson was the 2006 winner of the BSDDA. His work is stocked at Living Edge and top3 by design.
c.s.w@bigpond.com

left, clockwise from top
Bowls even your granny over: the Topple lamp by Trent Jansen / Jo Philippsohn's Stripped Bare coat rack doubles as a light in the warmer months / Something old, something new: Trent Jansen's Sign Stool.

photography Alex Kershaw (Trent Jansen)

... from p. 95

Ella and Sofia

There's only one person behind the two names. It's Karie Soehardi who produces the eclectic range of limited edition handprinted wallpapers and screen-printed fabrics, cushions and accessories. The basis for the designs are her paintings, and thus complementing the wallpaper and fabrics is a range of artworks – oil paintings, framed illustrations and photographs. The two imaginary ladies are also available for commissions.
ellaandsofia.com

Michael Hoppe

Adelaide-trained industrial designer Michael Hoppe has a Bondi Beach studio (poor fella) by the name of Hop Design, which he set up in 1994. Creating consumer and electronic products, furniture and homewares, his work includes a highly successful watering can for Hortico, concept work on future transport (trains) and sports gear. Presently Hoppe is working on wireless computer equipment, office furniture and a hemp fibre resin chair.
hop-design.com

Trent Jansen

Part contemporary artist, part designer, Trent Jansen's cool profile suits his approach of reinventing traditional forms and mediums, and searching for new solutions in future design. Jansen imbues his work with an irreverent, slightly absurd quality inspired by the playful building blocks of childhood Lego sets. Making things from recycled bits and pieces, his most recognised work is made from discarded street signs, which he has, on occasion, constructed 'live' in stores.
trentjansen.com

Arthur Koutoulas

Part designer, part architect, all artist, Arthur Koutoulas is – pardon the jargon – a 'spatial sculptor'. Koutoulas' design work is recognised as being progressive and original: commercial interiors and product design meets experimental object installations. 'Design needs to speak to us,' he says. His work is stocked at Beautiful on the Inside.
arthurkoutoulas.com

Ruth McDermott

Lighting designer Ruth McDermott is inspired by the Australian environment and uses innovative materials and technologies. The trained industrial designer has designed for the NSW Department of Health and established Ovo Design with Rina Bernabei, one half of bernabeifreeman. Now flying solo, McDermott often produces lighting installations for high-end interior spaces. Exhibiting her designs internationally and throughout Australia at places such as Object Gallery, McDermott is well-known for creating a synthesis between light, material and technology. She also works as a lecturer at the University of NSW.
ruthmcdermott.com

Norman + Quaine

With a consistent output of soft furnishings, seating and table elements for residential and commercial interiors, interior designer Katherine Norman and industrial designer Caroline Quaine subtly reference the proportions and functions of mid-20th century furniture. The simple aesthetic of their versatile range, developed over the years, suits diverse interior styles and is stocked in Sydney through Living Edge.
normanquaine.com.au

Jo Philippsohn

In her idiosyncratically named studio, dwell by jo, Jo Philippsohn explores her penchant for simple forms and clever solutions. A product that makes this approach particularly visible is Stripped Bare, a coat rack especially designed for the mild, short Australian winters (in most of Australia, that is). The rack considers its redundancy for most of the year and therefore doubles as an oversized lamp for the sweltering summertime.
dwellbyjo.com.au

Elliat Rich

Born in Paris, raised in Burma and at home in Sydney, intrepid Elliat Rich is currently on temporary loan to Alice Springs, where she's been working on appropriate technology projects for remote Indigenous communities. For Rich, work always begins with the question 'what is it that we wish to sustain?' She finds her answers in the humble pleasures and moments of wonder throughout the day. Her products include the Lichen, a canvas piece

that, depending on the fold, forms either a tarp, swag or jacket; the Urban Billy, a seven-component glass piece that encourages sharing a cup of tea with someone special; and her Mycelium Pendant, nicknamed *Beauty & the Yeast*, where mould turns into jewels. She was shortlisted for the BSDDA 2007.
elliatrich.com

Amy Tang

Otherwise known as amzdesigns, Amy Tang recently secured a spot with local manufacturer Woodmark, joining a growing number of Sydney-based designers. The company will be producing her upholstered Flosion stools, comprising two sine-curved timber elements. Amy's influences are found in the form, texture and movements of nature.
amzdesigns.com

Frag Woodall

An ambitious young product designer, Frag Woodall was hardly out of university when he produced a range of designs covering a broad variety of typologies including spectacles, bicycles and furniture pieces – some of which are already in production with local design supporter Woodmark. He became the name around town in 2005, when he won the BSDDA Student Prize for his curvaceous Ilium chair. His fold-out bike, the Everglide, has made waves around the exhibitions circuit.
woodmark.com.au

Woodmark

Founded by designer Arne Christiansen in 1986, Woodmark is a family-owned company, and a highly valuable source of furniture and product design from Sydney. After importing furniture for over ten years, the company changed direction in 1990 to become a solid supporter of local furniture design. Among the first Australian designers taken under the Woodmark wing was Sydney's now-renowned Charles Wilson. Woodmark provides opportunities for Australian designers to have their work manufactured and distributed commercially – something most Australian furniture companies are yet to fully embrace. Designers also include Jon Goulder, Gary Galego and Frag Woodall and stockists are Anibou, Beautiful on the Inside and Living Edge.
woodmark.com.au

Design across time

The Powerhouse Museum's permanent gallery of decorative arts and design, *Inspired! Design across time*, showcases over 500 objects from the collection dating from today back to the 1700s. Australian and international furniture, fashion, textiles, graphic design, ceramics, silver, glass – and much more – demonstrate how social, technological and cultural change have impacted on design and shaped our taste and creativity over time. Above all, these diverse objects – from the unique to the mass-produced, the iconic to the everyday – reveal that design is a universal and continually changing language that is hardwired into the human condition. Powerhouse Curator Anne Watson shows a small selection from the gallery, illustrating that the 'stories' behind the objects can be as important as design quality in determining 'significance' in a museum context.

Marc Newson,
Lockheed Lounge;
aluminium, fibreglass, rubber; made by Eckhard Reissig, Sydney, 1988–90 (91/1309)

When Newson, as a young design graduate, launched the first version of the Lockheed in 1986 it created a sensation. Produced in limited edition since the late 1980s, it is now a highly sought-after international design icon.

Edols and Elliott,
Fallen leaf;
glass; Sydney, 2005
(2005/183/1)

Formed from hot glass and then carved and engraved, this beautiful shape was inspired by fallen palm leaves. Adjacent to its display is an interactive video giving a 360° view of the piece being made in the Edols and Elliott studio.

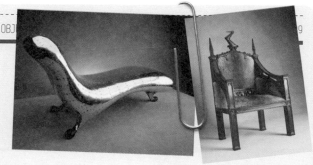

above left
The seat that started it for Mark Newson: the Lockheed Lounge. Collection of the Powerhouse Museum.

photography
Sue Stafford

above right
The seat that started it all down under: the gothic revival chair for Governor Macquarie. Collection of the Powerhouse Museum.

photography
Andrew Frolows

Bernabeifreeman, Peony chandelier; aluminium; Sydney, 2003 (2006/149/1)

The award-winning Peony adapts traditional textile patterns to modern industrial production, a synthesis between past and present that reinforces the 'connectedness' of design over time.

Jørn Utzon, Sydney Opera House sectional model, plastic, wood; made by Finecraft, Sydney, 1966 (B2309) Gift of Sydney Opera House Trust, 1978

This 1:128 scale model (see image p. 71) shows Utzon's final scheme for the interior of the Concert Hall of the Opera House. Made at the time Utzon 'withdrew' from the project under controversial circumstances, its dramatic red and gold plywood ceiling was never realised. Utzon is now revisiting the scheme for the planned redesign of the Opera Theatre.

William Kerr, Cricket trophy; silver, emu eggs, glass, wood; Sydney, c.1878 (A3221) Gift of W T Kerr, 1938

Designed as a table centrepiece this impressive silver trophy was probably inspired by the success of the first Australian cricket team to tour Britain in 1878. Its tableau-style format facilitated a degree of detail and craftsmanship unparalleled today.

John Webster & William Temple, Armchair; Australian rose mahogany, wallaby fur; Sydney, 1821 (H6862) Gift of the Vancouver Museum, Canada, 1961

This convict-made armchair is one of a pair produced for Governor Lachlan Macquarie (1810–1821). Its gothic revival style was fittingly regal, but it was also a style favoured by Macquarie and his wife Elizabeth for a number of early Sydney buildings.

From acorn to oak

Some are master craftspeople in the traditional sense while others experiment, developing new procedures and designs. What they do share are age-old ideals: a love for the material and a determination to produce high-quality works. They branch out, but share the same roots.

Matthew Harding

Yet another Canberra School of Arts graduate: sculptor, artist and designer Matthew Harding began his career as a carpenter and joiner. He's predominantly a furniture maker, but also a wood carver and sculptor. His career now spans over 20 years of sculptures, fine art exhibitions and lectures. He is also known to occasionally stray from working with wood to include metals, mosaics, textiles and plastics in his work. He embraces both traditional techniques and new technologies.
matthewharding.com.au

Johan Larsson

A Swedish import with Japanese sensibilities and a passion for the materials of his new home country, Johan Larsson's work is as interesting as his design biography, which includes stints studying and lecturing in design-related areas in Canberra, Kyoto and Lulea in Sweden. Now renowned for his SU1 flat-pack shelving unit and his commission work, Larsson stepped onto the local design stage in 1999 as the recipient of the annual Australian National University EASS (Emerging Artists Support Scheme) Award, and studied with the prestigious Wood Workshop at the ANU in Canberra. A year later, he won the DesignEx Award for his work and has since

... *continued p. 114*

Gary Galego

above
The sustainably made Leve chair was first conceived as an exploration into the steam-bending process. It's sold through Woodmark.

This designer is known for taking plywood to the next level with his award-winning Leve chair, manufactured by Woodmark Australia. The 30-year-old never completed his industrial design course at the University of NSW, instead moving to the Canberra School of Art's Wood Workshop to specialise in timber. After completing his studies, Galego swiftly developed some business skills and began selling the product he made as his final project at university. Fascinated with all incarnations of timber and earning a living from custom cabinet making, he was also a finalist in *The Sydney Morning Herald*'s Young Designer competition in 2002. Galego's furniture is distinguished by excellent craftsmanship, complete understanding of the materials used and the preservation of the functions of furniture in everyday life. Galego produces designs that transcend time.
garygalego.com

Jon Goulder

right
Goulder's unique approach to furniture making is widely recognised, such as his work with artisans in China to produce his latest creation, the STAK stool.

photography
Justin Malinowski

He may not be a household name, but when it comes to working with wood, Jon Goulder is one of the finest young designers this country has to offer. Now in his late 30s, Goulder began designing furniture in the mid-1990s after training as an upholsterer and furniture maker, and studying design at the Canberra School of Art. His big break came in the shape of the inaugural Bombay Sapphire Design Discovery Award in 2003. The product earning him this accolade was a sculptural fruit bowl inspired by a Glenn Murcutt-designed house in his neighbourhood. Early the following year, Goulder's showpiece the Leda Seat – a curved chaise-lounge-like piece formed from continuous parallel strips of birch plywood – went into production and is now retailed through Anibou. Fascinated with the flexible qualities of laminated timber, Goulder has developed an entire range of furniture and homewares (which he sells online) and is currently working with the Designing Futures project in Western Australia, an initiative that supports local designers in pursuit of innovating and fostering Australian design. Definitely one to watch.
jongoulder.com

...from p. 110

secured a reputation as one of Sydney's most promising young designers. While he has recently relocated his workshop to the countryside, his pieces are sold at Anibou and he is also represented by Scandinavium.
johanlarssondesign.com

David Muston

There is an unusual story behind how David Muston came to prominence. To complement the Alvar Aalto furniture in his Glenn Murcutt-designed home, Muston designed a slatted bed base. Furniture store Anibou was immediately interested in stocking it, and with the seal of approval from the late Aalto's furniture company Artek in Finland, the medical doctor began producing the Muston Bed. He now has a small workshop under his house where he investigates further furniture production and has produced the joinery for several of Glenn Murcutt's projects. His designs are sold through Anibou.

Leon Sadubin

Here's someone who has rocked Sydney's furniture boat for over 30 years. Now working from his home studio on the idyllic NSW South Coast, Sadubin was an influential player in the formation of the Woodworkers Association of NSW. A furniture maker and sculptor, he mainly works on private and public commissions and has designed a wide range of items for public spaces, such as ceremonial lecterns, public seating benches and furniture for places of worship. While Sadubin subscribes to traditional design techniques, he also sets the pace for succeeding contemporary designers to follow.
leonsadubin.com.au

Splinter Workshop

An old paint factory in St Peters, the Splinter Workshop is a collaborative studio set up in 1999 for ten creative wood-lovers to swap ideas, share expenses and engage with interesting products. All but one of the original founders are graduates of the Sturt School for Wood in Mittagong, in the Southern Highlands of NSW. With backgrounds as diverse as interior decoration and aerospace engineering, the output of the studio includes everything from wall sculptures to canoes and carved mirrors. Of course there are chairs and dining tables, stools and cabinets, but also

OBJECTS_WOOD

right
The torsion box construction of Johan Larsson's extremely popular SU1 shelf means that it is lightweight yet extremely strong.

lots of multi-disciplinary work, all of which is finely crafted with longevity in mind. One of the three founders of Splinter Workshop is designer and maker Julia Charles, who – prior to moving to St Peters – had shared a similar workshop with two others since 1996. Her influences range from Japanese architecture (undoubtedly inspired by a stint living in a Buddhist monastery in Kyoto) to Scandinavian furniture design and plant biology. Julia's designs are tactile and practical, and her favourite designers are greats such as Hans Wegner and the Eames'. You get the picture.
75 Mary Street, St Peters
9517 2212
splinterworkshop.com.au

Henry Wilson

Standing out from the latest crop of graduates from ANU's School of Art is newcomer Henry Wilson. Practising inventive ways of using traditional and sustainable material in domestic furniture design, Wilson designs clean-cut, simple furniture, particularly tables, chairs and stools, using lightweight resilient materials such as plywood and beech. After he was unable to find a simple, well-made, flat-folding table, he came up with his own, the Force of Nature table. Constructed as a laminated plywood and high-density foam sandwich with beech edging, the table is a dream, folding down effortlessly.
henry-wilson.com

OBJECTS_JEWELLERY & METAL

left
Alice Whish's Boronia pendants, from fine silver and gold plate on colourful silk thread, echo the brightness of spring.

below
Coloured bangles by Vanessa Samuels.

OBJECTS_JEWELLERY & METAL

Shiny, pretty things

You may find traditionalists batting up against technicians (the founding fathers and the fledgling folk), but Sydney's jewellery community is alive and kicking, turning out baubles that make music wherever they go.

Joung-Mee Do

Korean-born Joung-Mee Do uses the traditional Korean jewellery-making technique Iybsa (inlay). She spent some years perfecting this method under the tutelage of the master Kyo Joon Choi before moving to Australia. Here, she graduated from Melbourne's RMIT University with a Master of Arts and promptly moved to Sydney, where she incorporates traditional Korean textile patterns into metalwork using etching and metal-colouring techniques. Her stunning work is available from the Collect Store at Object Gallery and Workshop Bilk.
sydney_do@hotmail.com

Yuri Kawanabe

This jeweller's work is distinguished by its deceptive, papery appearance – her aluminium necklaces look like they've been simply snipped into shape with scissors. However, the detailing necessary to cause this effect is extremely labour intensive. Having moved to Sydney from Tokyo in 1987, Kawanabe's works have been selected for both Australian and Japanese major national exhibitions and were collected by public galleries and museums including the Powerhouse Museum in Sydney and the National Museum of Modern Art in Tokyo. Her work is more art-based than commercial, so the best place to see it is the Powerhouse Museum.

Sheridan Kennedy

A farm girl at heart, having blossomed on a sheep and cattle station in outback Queensland,

... continued p. 122

118 OBJECTS_JEWELLERY & METAL

Dinosaur Designs

left
From jewellery to homewares, Dinosaur Designs have made resin sexy all around the globe.

photography
Jason Loucas (Butterfly Choker)

Their story is now part of Sydney's design folklore, but tenacious trio Louise Olsen, Stephen Ormandy and Liane Rossler continue to draw crowds. The three former art students are among the most famous alumni of Paddington market graduates, where they began to sell handprinted fabrics and painted jewellery in 1985. They're synonymous with the rise of resin, the predominant material they still use to produce their colourful adornments and homewares that have now reached international acclaim. Navigating the divide between the handmade and the mass-produced, with dozens of creative assistants using complex casting techniques, the trio extended to New York in 2002, opening a small store. This came 12 years after establishing their two Sydney boutiques in the Strand Arcade and Paddington. It's not only the regular punters who love them. Their work frequently features in design exhibitions around the globe and luxury brands Louis Vuitton and Domain Chandon have knocked on their door for help.

339 Oxford Street, Paddington
9361 3776
The Strand Arcade,
412–414 George Street, Sydney
9223 2953
dinosaurdesigns.com.au

F!NK & Co

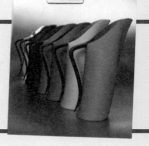

right
One of the most recognised contemporary Australian designs: the F!nk jug. Should you happen to pop into New York's Museum of Modern Art, you can even buy one there.

Possibly Australia's maestro of metalsmiths, Robert Foster has been hugely influential in developing the capabilities of small, innovative design studios to compete locally and internationally, primarily through his exquisite design and pioneering manufacturing processes. Expanding on a successful career in craft-based production, Foster founded F!NK & Co in 1994. His aim was to manufacture contemporary metal-based products in a collaborative environment. The company has since grown to become one of Australia's most prolific design manufacturing studios, producing an extensive range of homewares and personal accessories predominantly in metal, and authored by a diverse range of designers including Rohan Nicol and Oliver Smith. Foster's own work forms the mainstay of the studio's output and is globally renowned for its originality and craftsmanship. His first commercial product, the F!NK water jug, is one of the most recognisable pieces of Australian design, an iconic feature of many restaurants and museum collections. In addition to his craft-based production, Foster is an exceptionally talented toolmaker and manufacturing developer. His collaborative team pushes the boundaries of materials in the pursuit of new forms and finishes – he has even detonated explosives in aluminium tubes held within moulds to create unusually formed vessels. Most of this manufacturing process occurs in and around the F!NK studio, just outside Canberra, which has become a focal point for other talented designers. Foster has worked on projects with world-famous lighting designer Ingo Maurer and has exhibited extensively throughout Australia and internationally. Find his work at design retailers such as top3 by design, Metalab and Collect at Object.
finkdesign.com

OBJECTS_JEWELLERY & METAL

Metalab

right
A creation by young Sydney jeweller Sean Booth.

below right
The Multifacet Ring by the man himself, Metalab founder Cesar Cueva.

If you want to find Sydney's most interesting venue for local jewellery design, you can either ask dozens of curators, designers, editors and design lovers, or you can trust that we've done this for you and that the vote has unanimously gone to Metalab, the Surry Hills-based workshop and gallery run by metalsmith and industrial designer Cesar Cueva and wife Nina. Their hidden space is a treasure trove of Australian-designed jewellery and features a rotating exhibition schedule showing artists at work in the studio space and a wealth of emerging and established talent from around the country. September 2007 marked a new chapter for Metalab, as they opened a more retail-focused environment. This concept store, fittingly named Courtesy of the Artists, expanded their focus to homewares and glass, but predominantly shows jewellery. Always on the lookout for new and exciting pieces and ideas for exhibitions, Nina Cueva has also incorporated her background in hospitality into the space, so you can enjoy a cuppa while admiring the handmade tables you're sitting at.

10b Fitzroy Place, Surry Hills
8354 1398
Courtesy of the Artists,
547 Bourke Street,
Surry Hills
9331 5900
metalab.com.au

OBJECTS_JEWELLERY & METAL

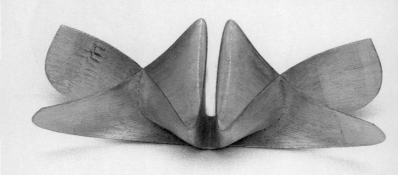

above
Merges traditional techiques with contemporary technologies such as computer-modelling: the jewellery of Gilbert Riedelbauch.

... from p. 117

Sheridan Kennedy is known for her highly original works that blur the boundaries between art, craft and design. (Perhaps she was inspired by farm machinery such as the Australian classic – the ute.) Sheridan explores widely varied approaches to making jewellery, creating one-off artworks for exhibitions as well as collaborating with leading fashion designers such as accessories queen Michelle Jank and Akira Isogawa. You can have a look at her designs in his store or at Collect at Object Gallery.
sheridankennedy.com

Elke Kramer

Graphic designer and illustrator Elke Kramer is a newcomer to the jewellery industry, and an original one indeed. Playing on an overtly nonsensical and frivolous nature, Kramer's pieces are abstract in form and hand-assembled from laser-cut shapes to give them a quirky but mysterious feel. Her second and most recent collection, *The Anti-Curse of Greyface*, is an assortment of wooden necklaces, pendants and earrings celebrating the notion of chaos and nonsense and is, she says, 'vaguely reminiscent of insect forms, Aztec motifs and clockwork mechanics'. You can buy her work at Orson & Blake, ksubi and Dobry Den.
elkekramer.com

OBJECTS_JEWELLERY & METAL

Bridie Lander

In 1995, *The Sydney Morning Herald* held its first Young Designer of the Year competition. The inaugural winner was young Bridie Lander. Her product, a light made from coloured gels, went into commercial production the following year. After taking up her prize of a scholarship in Milan, Lander went to work with one of the quirkiest and most innovative design ensembles on the planet, Droog Design in the Netherlands. Twelve years on, Lander is busy producing work that explores the relationship between the body, objects and technology. Making vessels out of metal and slip-cast models out of perspex, Lander uses a variety of materials, including plastics and found materials such as non-precious stones, shells and horse hair. One of her most recent series of semi-sculptural jewellery, stocked at Metalab, focused on an investigation of the olfactory, auditory and tactile senses. Lander also lectures and is Co-Coordinator of the Jewellery and Object Studio at the Sydney College of the Arts.

Larsen & Lewers

Darani Lewers and Helge Larsen are sometimes referred to as the 'founding fathers' of jewellery design in Sydney, as they've spent the last four decades nurturing and supporting the industry. They began working together when Danish-born Larsen joined Lewers in Australia in 1961. His penchant for Scandinavian simplicity hasn't worn off, and is reflected in their work, which usually includes abstract sterling silver forms. Often using the designs and patterns of cities and buildings, the duo believes that a piece of jewellery must become a sculptural part of the wearer's body and personality. Their inclusion of stone, wood and shell speaks volumes about their relationship with the natural environment. Having held over 60 exhibitions in the past 45 years, their work is bound to show up again soon. Gig gallery in Glebe is the venue of the moment.

70a Glebe Point Road, Glebe
9552 1552
giggallery.com

Cinnamon Lee

Sydney born and bred, designer Cinnamon Lee made her decision to study jewellery and object design early – a fortuitous move that has seen her career established between two capital cities. After some time furthering her studies in silversmithing at ANU in Canberra, Lee returned to Sydney. With a focus primarily on light and illuminated objects, she then embarked on a mentorship grant with Sydney furniture and lighting designers Korban/Flaubert. Returning to metal accessories with designs such as her *Squared Lime* collection (rings made of anodised aluminium), Lee now teaches at the Gold and Silversmithing Workshop in Canberra and exhibits nationally and internationally, with a recent inclusion in the National Gallery of Australia collection. Her work is available through Metalab, Collect and Worskhop Bilk.
cinnamonlee@hotmail.com

Rohan Nicol

Especially concerned with the application of his craft to industrial design processes, Rohan Nicol works in jewellery and metalsmithing. From his home in Wagga Wagga, NSW (where he also teaches), he designs ranges of handmade prototypes in materials and forms that lend themselves to eventual production elsewhere. Nicol has worked collaboratively with Robert Foster of F!NK & Co to design the F!NK bracelet, a press-cut and jig-formed piece in hard-anodised aluminium (still available from F!NK stockists). His work draws reference from diverse contexts – recent pieces relate to the theme of the tote bag, resulting in a range of bags made from hand-formed anodised or spun aluminium, with integral press-moulded, carved and formed polymer resin components, as well as a series of exquisite aluminium wallets for the urban aesthete. Aside from his metal-based pieces Nicol has also produced a series of brooches made from animal bone and takes time to explore design opportunities through computer-modelled renders and rapid prototyping.
rohannicol.com

Gilbert Riedelbauch

Part of the team that established the Digital Art Studio at the ANU in Canberra, Gilbert Riedelbauch began his career as a toolmaker back in Germany, before undertaking a degree

OBJECTS_JEWELLERY & METAL

above left
Bridie Lander's most recent semi-sculptural jewellery creations focus on an investigation of the olfactory, auditory and tactile senses.

above right
When is a knife a knife? Oliver Smith's cutlery.

in silversmithing. In the spirit of combining hands-on, three-dimensional design with the latest equipment, his current work focuses on creating 3D objects using CAD technology. Merging old and new processes calls for innovative design solutions so Riedelbauch runs Virtual Territory, a blog dedicated to issues big and small that arise from such a practice. Working as lecturer in Computer Aided Design at ANU, he also exhibits his metalwork and is represented in collections in the National Gallery of Australia. His work is stocked by Workshop Bilk in Canberra.
virtualterritory.wordpress.com

Vanessa Samuels

Vanessa Samuels is an established maker and exhibitor of jewellery and objects, working principally out of design studio and showroom Metalab. Teaming up with others to create a diverse and highly collectable series of works, using contemporary materials such as silver, resin, diamonds and enamel, she has also made some pretty pieces from silver and gold, mostly rings and pendants with names such as Love on the Horizon + Grenade, My Upside-Down Heart, Leaf and Half-Hearted.
vanessasamuels.com

above
Reinventing the Australian opal: the Venerari jewellery business.

Oliver Smith

This designer's pedigree in jewellery and metalsmithing stretches back through many generations to medieval armour makers. A skilled silversmith, specialising in hot forging, he has developed a particular interest in putting his one-off items of silver cutlery into commercial production in stainless steel and other materials. His work ranges from unique handcrafted pieces, special commissions and collaborative projects, to design for production. Originally from Canberra, Smith spent time studying in Sydney, followed by a period of work experience alongside significant silversmiths and metalworkers around the world. He now combines a vigorous craft and design practice with lecturing at the Sydney College of the Arts. Look for pieces at Collect, Metalab and Workshop Bilk.
oliversmith.com.au

Mark Vaarwerk

A magician of sorts, Mark Vaarwerk is a most resourceful jewellery designer, and can transform the most basic material into a precious jewel. Vaarwerk rejuvenates disposable and discarded plastic containers, shopping bags, shampoo bottles and their ilk to give them a second chance as bright brooches with concentric rings of colour. In this way, nine three-litre strawberry ice cream topping bottles from Wendy's turned into the wonderful Wendy's Bracelets. Other resources used in the five-piece bracelet series include Paul's milk bottles (white), Barambah milk bottles (blue), Wella Biotouch conditioner containers (yellow) and Only Juice Company bottles (orange). Find them at Workshop Bilk, Metalab and Collect at Object Gallery.
vaarwerk.com

OBJECTS_JEWELLERY & METAL

Venerari

Genevieve Lilley is at once an architect, a jewellery designer and one of the two faces behind Sydney's new jewellery brand Venerari (with partner Kingsley Wallman, an ex-corporate lawyer turned gemmologist.) After some time overseas, where Lilley worked extensively with internationally renowned architect David Chipperfield, the duo returned to Australia to 'reinvent the opal', bringing contemporary design to Australian gemstones, building on the many similarities between designing buildings and jewellery. With her architectural clientele including Dolce & Gabbana and Phaidon Press, Genevieve has still found time to design VenerARIs first store in the Strand Arcade, well worth a visit both for the intricate interior and to fall in love with Australia's most famous stone.
The Strand Arcade, 412–414 George Street, Sydney
9222 9797
venerari.com

Alice Whish

Although she describes herself as a contemporary jeweller in the traditional European sense, mainly using precious metals, Alice Whish also likes to incorporate less traditional materials such as wood, metal wire and shells into her delicate, intricate jewellery. She has worked with women from north-east Arnhem Land to raise the profile of their craft and, aware that many jewellers only have the opportunity to sell their work through temporary exhibitions, Whish decided to create a more permanent platform for selling her own and others' jewellery online. Her site is particularly popular with busy professionals who shop online for wedding jewellery, then work with the maker to suit their particular needs. Go for a browse yourself on definitestyle.com.
alicewhish.com

above
Ceramic brooches by Ruth McMillan.

right
David Edmonds' coveted handmade bowls.

Thrown, cast, slipped

Sydney's ceramicists take to many forms and come in many incarnations; there are those who produce entire homeware ranges, those who make one-off sculptural work and those who find themselves somewhere in the middle. Here is a selection that will help you get your eyes and your hands on some of the most prominent, promising and coveted pieces – for your kitchen or for something a little more special.

Rob Bamford

Already a renowned and respected Sydney ceramicist, Rob Bamford was approached in 1998 by owner of Sydney restaurant Bel Mondo to custom-design a suite of contemporary coffee cups and a range of tableware. Bamford made prototypes by hand and in digital format, after which designs were taken to porcelain and ceramic factories in Thailand and Bangladesh. He has since combined his interests in art, design and industry to make tableware for contemporary Australian cuisine. Since 1994 he has worked with Janine Brody at their Cone Nine Design studio on the NSW central coast to develop distinctive ceramic design ideas. tactile.com.au

Jane Barrow

Working out of a studio on the Hawkesbury River in NSW, Jane Barrow affords no boundary between nature and her working space. The effect is reminiscent of the woven fabrics she used to produce. Now, she has her hands deep in the claypot, spending six years in Japanese potteries where she often wedged up to 100kg of clay in a morning. In accordance with Japanese traditions, surface became very important to Barrow's work, the unglazed pieces often decorated in the form of inlay, using different types of firings and fluid finger

markings – an informal and spontaneous aesthetic that belies the skill with which it is applied.
janebarrow.com.au

Janet de Boos

An eminently collectable ceramicist, Janet de Boos was once head of the Ceramics Workshop at the Australian National University, yet she has always maintained her work as an artist in her own right. Since retiring in 1980 to run a production pottery, she has written three books on ceramic glazes and continues to exhibit regularly both in Australia and overseas. More recently, de Boos embraced manufacturing in China as a means to reduce the cover price of her products and open up newly viable creative avenues. This has given de Boos an opportunity to dramatically expand her market.
janet.deboos@anu.edu.au

David Edmonds

According to David Edmonds, a plate is only partially realised without food. Not surprisingly then, he describes his objects as 'tools for living'. A potter for over 20 years, Edmonds works closely with other sectors of the industry; his designs were the prototypes for the award-winning Sunbeam Ceramic Series Kettle. However, most of his time is spent producing a selection of beautiful, earthy, modern ceramic pieces. You will find them at Orson & Blake, Macleay on Manning and Duck Egg Blue in Sydney.
davidedmonds.com.au

Mud Australia

It's not surprising that this company's tactile, organically shaped bowls, platters and dishes in myriad colours are favourites of food stylists and homeware magazines around Australia. The simple, modern range perfectly combines a minimalist aesthetic with a handmade finish. Founded in 1994 by Shelley Simpson, who has no formal training in ceramics, Mud Australia products come from her studio factory showroom in Marrickville, where the signature mud look is created using a clear glaze applied to the interior of each item, while the exterior is left with a vitrified stone-like surface that is smooth and easy to handle. Mud is also stocked in several outlets across Sydney, and throughout Australia, as well as in the US, Japan and Europe.
15 Sloane Street, Marrickville
9519 2520
mudaustralia.com

Buffed & polished

above
Designed in Australia, manufactured in Mexico, released in New York: Johnathan Baskett's 2007 range of glasswares.

Hardly a fragile industry in this shiny city, glassmakers here run a blazing trade. You'll find age-old techniques generating cutting-edge design, and divine talent melding with scientific progress to produce everyday items as well as works of art.

Jonathan Baskett

Here's a young man who has made Australia the bellybutton of the world by fully embracing the possibilities of a global market. Connecting an age-old craft to modern mass-market strategies, Baskett is currently working on a project that sees him sending his designs as digital files to Studio Nouvel in Mexico City, where the glass products are manufactured before being distributed to international markets. Baskett forges connections to manufacturers while continuing to make his minimalist utilitarian glassware through traditional processes.

Baskett's savvy approach has won him and his functional, original and affordable glassware many fans across the globe. Baskett cut his glassworking teeth as an assistant at Isle of Wight Glass in England in 1992, and completed a Master of Arts in glass production design at ANU. His work is available through the studio, as well as Object Gallery and Powerhouse Museum stores. jonathanbaskett.com

Edols and Elliott

A partnership between two graduates of Canberra Glassworks, the pieces of Benjamin Edols and Kathy Elliot are simple and elegantly accentuated by colours. Blowing glass together since 1993, the two launched their joint careers in the US. Using traditional decorative-arts methods, their aesthetic direction is inspired by artists and designers such as Japanese sculptor Isamu Noguchi, free-former Ingeborg Lundin and Venetian

glassblowing maestro Lino Tagliapietra. They practise several different techniques – reticello, murrine and cold working – in their dedicated studio, which opened in 2001. Their pieces can be found in a number of galleries including Sabbia.
edolselliott.com

Andrew Lavery

One of the country's most promising young glass artists, Andrew Lavery is inspired by regular pilgrimages to the glass hotbed of Murano, a Venetian island. Perfecting his technique since the mid 1990s, Lavery produces glassworks mainly for exhibitions around the country and internationally, while also teaching at Sydney University's College of the Arts. Much of his work creates visual effects that are reminiscent of futuristic scenes or a skyline on the horizon. The inspiration is often derived from mid-20th century Italian and Scandinavian glassworks. Stocked at the Glass Artists' Gallery.

Denizen Glass

Originally a country kid from rural Victoria, Robert Wynne studied ceramics before becoming captivated by the dynamic process of glassblowing via a fellow student. Excited by the visual splendour of the material, he relishes the choreography of glassblowing, particularly the immediacy and risk that the substance demands. He established Denizen Glass in 1991 and now works in his studio in the beachside suburb of Manly, where he produces a range of handblown glass including smaller product work and large, one-off sculptural pieces. As a pioneer of studio glass, Wynne has provided a launching point for many of Australia's well-known glass artists.
robertwynne.com

Peter Minson

As part of the third generation in a family of glass blowers, Peter Minson began his career making scientific tools from glass. Before setting up his own practice, he managed the family business, which produced, among other things, those pipettes we all used in lab class at school. Minson now works out of a studio in Binalong, a small village 95km north-west of Canberra, where he continues to teach his craft. His work is available through his online store.
minsonartglass.com

Klaus Moje

Aficionados count Klaus Moje as one of the world's most visible and distinguished contemporary glass artists. German by birth, Moje has spent a good part of his prolific career in Australia, founding the Canberra Glass Workshop and inspiring a generation of makers in kiln-formed glass. Through his work and teaching, Moje has helped many artists realise new possibilities for the medium of glass, using traditional processes first established in Ancient Egypt. Look for pieces at the Powerhouse Museum and Object Gallery.

Keith Rowe

Primarily a glass blower, Keith Rowe also works with sand and kiln casting. From his studio in Blackheath in the Blue Mountains, he produces a large range of pieces for private and public collection and also runs glass-blowing classes. Rowe's groovy, mouth-blown glass creations are often distinguished by striking colour and visual form. His work has been exhibited widely and he also works with much-loved Sydney jewellery and homeware brand Dinosaur Designs.
krglass.com

Emma Varga

Grandiose glass pieces are Emma Vargas' staple. Since migrating from Serbia 10 years ago, she has mastered an unusual technique of glass shaping, which uses thousands of splinters of glass, akin to forming a mosaic, to create three-dimensional sculptures. Her signature pieces carry the bright colours of the sky and the ocean and the burning horizon of the sunset. They are appropriately named Lagoon, Ocean, Before the Storm and Red Sky Burning.
emmavarga.com

Richard Whiteley

British-born Aussie Richard Whiteley is current head of the prestigious Glass Workshop at the ANU in Canberra. First working as an apprentice in a commercial stained-glass studio, he has since developed an internationally recognised practice focusing on cast glass. His work is held in corporate and public collections including the National Gallery of Australia and the Powerhouse Museum, as well as significant private collections around the world. His work is available for sale at Workshop Bilk.
richardwhiteley.com

Stitched & woven

Old meets new as digital technology and traditional techniques unite in the work of Sydney's textile community. Design studios are respond to the demands of the fashion sector, while craft-based practitioners explore the growing array of production processes available to them. Their work is cross-disciplinary, often influenced by the nature surrounding them, intelligent and quirky. Here's a cross section of key players.

Cecelia Heffer

Alongside her work in the Fashion & Textile Program at UTS, Cecelia Heffer's vibrant studio practice integrates new technologies with hand-generated techniques. Crucial to Heffer's process is the connection to textile history. A main theme of her work is exploring the idea of linking people to history through the integration of memory, pattern and technology. She predominantly works with silk organza, georgette and shantung, as well as velvets and lace. Heffer was recently commissioned to design a set of contemporary lace curtains for the refurbishment of the staterooms at Government House in NSW, while a UK distribution agent plans to launch her catalogue, *LACED*, based on exhibitions and recent textile work in the near future. Her series of textile lengths and scarves retail at Planet Furniture and Planet Commonwealth in Surry Hills.
ceciliaheffer.com

Zoe MacDonell

Often using recycled knitted fabrics, Zoe MacDonell's designs are innovative and unique, which explains why her work continues to be featured in high-profile exhibitions such as Object's *Sydney Style* at the Opera House and *Workshopped* at the Strand Arcade. The textile artist and designer's pieces often involve

sketching, photocopying and photography over silk, calico and a variety of other textures. She draws on imagery of everyday items such as discarded objects and botanical specimens. Alongside her own design, she is also the author of the online course Textiles: Tradition and Contemporary Technology, run by the University of NSW's College of Fine Arts and exhibits in Australia and internationally.
zoemacdonell.com

Sixhands

As the name suggests, textile design trio Anna Harves, Alecia Jensen and Brianna Pike are all hands-on. Combining fashion, textile and graphic design backgrounds, the three women are print and fabric surface treatment specialists, who create exclusive bespoke designs for a broad range of visual applications. Promoting environmental sustainability and Australian-based production, Sixhands produce distinctly edgy design out of their studio in Surry Hills. Using fabric and wallpaper, printed, flocked, appliqued and embroidered, these six hands have designed for fashion, interiors, wallpapers, soft furnishings and more.
sixhands.com.au

Liz Williamson

For several years, this designer's studio-based practice has been concerned with an investigation into cloth and memory and the meaning embedded in fabric. Making woven wraps and shawls on floor looms, Williamson interlaces fibres that react differently to washing after weaving. As a lecturer at the UNSW College of Fine Arts, Williamson's research interests focus on fabric that has already been altered through wear and tear, darning and mending. She has held several exhibitions at Object Gallery and was also part of the recent *Smart Works* exhibition at the Powerhouse Museum.

Print directions

According to Sydney textile specialist Cecelia Heffer, two Sydney-based textile studios are underpinning a not-so-quiet print revolution in the fabric world.

'Virtually any image can now be printed onto a range of exquisite silk, organza, cotton and wool. Even hemp is coming to the digital print party,' enthuses Heffer as she describes the work of two leading players in Sydney's textile world: Think Positive Designer Prints and Longina Phillips Designs. Heffer suggests that due to the more affordable prices of these once expensive technologies, even the smallest local design studios can now produce unique collections without compromising on quality.

Leading the digital vanguard are the business partners behind Think Positive Designer Prints, becoming famous for their colour accuracy in one-off design work. The business is expanding to Tokyo and Melbourne. Another digital leader heads Longina Phillips Designs, translating designs onto cloth with an acute attention to detail. 'This digital capability affords unlimited artistic expression on cloth,' says Heffer. Designers can now print as little as one metre of fabric for a one-off piece. A revolution is under way!

Think Positive Designer Prints,
14–16 Kent Street,
Millers Point, The Rocks
9251 2233
thinkdesignerprints.com.au

Longina Phillips Designs,
425 Elizabeth Street,
Sydney
9212 3750
longinaphillipsdesigns.com.au

cloth

below
it's all hand-printed, designed and produced in Sydney: the cloth showroom.

A small company with a staff of five, cloth is a local designer-maker success story. Begun by designer Julie Patterson in 1995 and launched with her business partner Penny Simmons in 1997, cloth's signature hand-printed linen and hemp textiles have gained huge popularity with interior designers and the general public alike. Having migrated to Australia in the late 1980s, UK-born Patterson is inspired by the local landscape. She paints on wood for the design development, and some of these paintings are then translated into printed prototypes, forming the basis for new designs. Her permanent range, designed in her idyllic beachside studio in Clovelly, includes over 20 designs, printed on an array of products. Recently, Patterson has been working on a new fabric collection called *In The Shed*, possibly referring to the tiny shed in the Blue Mountains where her designs are made. This work strongly emphasises her creative process and was launched at the Object Gallery retail store Collect. Cloth now distributes throughout Australia, Asia and Europe, but it is at their great new retail space, which they share with Porch outdoor furniture in Surry Hills, where you can catch of the whole cloth range, peruse product and sift through selected one-off samples.

35 Buckingham Street, Surry Hills
9699 2266
clothfabric.com

OBJECTS_STORES

Stocks & shares

We went on a quest to uncover Sydney design retailers who focus on local design or present a local angle alongside their international content. Here's what we found.

All Hand Made Gallery
This is the best place for quality contemporary ceramics, domestic and fine art collectables, as well as textiles for the table. The gallery has an excellent reputation and acts as a touchstone in the evolution of the Sydney ceramics world. Established in 2001 by Helen Stephens, a walking encyclopedia on all things ceramic, the gallery represents over 40 artists. They include Keiko Matsui, Marie Littlewood and Rob Bamford, who recently launched two unique tableware products – the Sonic Loop and Serpentine bowls. A full list of stock and artists represented by All Hand Made can be viewed on the website, but that certainly won't replace a personal visit.
252 Bronte Road, Waverley
9386 4099
allhandmadegallery.com

Anibou
A true institution in the Sydney design world, Anibou has been one of Sydney's key retailers of contemporary design for nearly 20 years. Its directors, Ute Rose and Neil Burley, focus on a mix of local designers and international brands such as Artek (the company that makes and distributes the iconic designs of late Finnish architect Alvar Aalto) and UK brand Isokon Plus, as well as classics by masters like Marcel Breuer. Anibou also have a soft spot for local produce, and have garnered a reputation for fostering alliances with talented furniture makers. Take a look at the CV of many of Sydney's more established designers, and you'll find that at some point or other Anibou was backing their work. These include Caroline Casey, Jon Goulder, Gary Galego and Johan Larsson, who all make contemporary Australian wooden furniture.
726 Bourke Street, Redfern
9319 0655
anibou.com.au

OBJECTS_STORES

above
Since Beautiful on the Inside opened its doors in 2006, Sydney is home to an entirely new breed of product store.

above left
This sculptural vessel by Adam Goodrum is inspired by the Boab tree and sold at Vert Design.

Beautiful on the Inside
A stunning little newcomer to the world of furniture and product outlets in Sydney, Beautiful on the Inside (BOTI) opened in September 2006 as a design and lifestyle store whose collection is carefully edited by designers Lana Alsamir-Diamond and Arthur Koutoulas. The focus is on young designers and their new and fresh creations. All pieces are hand-picked according to BOTI's philosophy of choosing 'pieces with soul'. That means they look at the story behind each piece, its design process and its quality.
322 Bourke Street, Surry Hills
9360 7733
beautifulontheinside.com.au

Chee Soon & Fitzgerald
A pair of avid collectors passionate about furniture and decorative art opened this store in 1996. Chee Soon & Fitzgerald has evolved into a legendary space that stocks well-designed contemporary interior furnishings, including fabrics, wallpaper, lighting and multi-functional furniture pieces by both Australian and overseas designers. Their focus is on colour, form and sensibility of product, which can be seen in designs such as those by local lighting designer Marc Pascal. Other pieces include Marimekko fabrics, vintage Japanese kimonos, woven grass wallpaper and African tribal pieces inspired by painters of the 1930s and 40s.
387 Crown Street, Surry Hills
9360 1031
cheesoonfitzgerald.com

Collect
With a philosophy of 'finely crafted objects for life', the renowned Object Gallery's retail space, Collect, is the place to go for jewellery, glass, ceramics and general homewares of great design

OBJECTS_STORES

above
A must-see when exploring local design is the Anibou Showroom, representing many of Sydney's talented designers.

right
Very sensuous: Jonathan Ingram's Yoga Sex Lounge.

far right
The Rod Bamford Serpentine Bowl from All Hand Made Gallery.

OBJECTS_STORES

and collectability. Grab your gifts and things, then head upstairs to the gallery.
417 Bourke Street, Surry Hills
9361 4511
object.com.au

Corporate Culture
As the name implies, Corporate Culture know their business. Under owner Richard Munao, the well-established retailer stocks a diverse range of designer furniture and products. These are predominantly leading European imports, including Belgian furniture giant Bulo and traditional Danish furniture house Fritz Hansen. However, one of the business' philosophies is to nurture and support emerging Australian design. These include arnoldlane with their curvaceous rolled Chest, Ben McCarthy with his Tilt Light and the lights of Melburnian Thomas Seymour, to name a few.
21 Levey Street, Chippendale
9690 0077
corporateculture.com.au

de de ce
Dedece is a vat of fabulous furniture features. A business owned and run by the Engelen family, this razor-sharp furniture shop is located in a Darlinghurst warehouse. Elevated display platforms show products by international greats such as Cappellini, Minotti, Map, Knoll and Depadova alongside a sprinkling of local talent. It's no wonder the client list is littered with the interior designers and architects du jour. Recent projects and magazine articles can also be found regularly updated on the de de ce website.
263 Liverpool Street, Darlinghurst
dedece.com.au

Euroluce
As the leading lighting distributor in Sydney, Euroluce represents iconic Italian brands such as Flos, Oluce and Luceplan as well as Japanese brand Yamagiwa in a contemporary environment. The Euroluce showroom also acts as a gallery, presenting regular exhibitions and installations, and including ongoing projects alongside Sydney's Italian Chamber of Commerce and the Italian Trade Commission. If you are into lighting, this is a must-see site, with an extensive array of contemporary decorative and technical lighting

systems. The staff demonstrations of different types of lighting are always popular.
99 Flinders Street, Darlinghurst
9380 6222
euroluce.com.au

---

fy2k
Last year, established design store fy2k moved to its current Redfern location, bringing along its large collection of sleek and modern design furniture and lights by Australian and international designers. Run by Michael Manos and Julie Angland, fy2k imports modern classics from Europe (mainly Italy), but there are also a few local products by Australian and New Zealand designers. In particular, there's the Meri chair by Michael Goldsmith and the versatile range by Nico Design.
17 Thurlow Street, East Redfern
8399 1644
fy2k.com.au

Format
This new Sydney arrival, which originated in the laneways of Melbourne, is the lovechild of furniture aficionado John Parker. It is set to stir modernists and minimalists with its avant-garde designs by famed British furniture house Established & Sons and celebrated designers e15 from Germany. Its wonderfully eclectic range also includes the well-known Vitra Home collection. Local talent represented includes Samantha Parsons' innovative floorscapes and Suzie Stanford's tea-towel-upholstered chairs, which must be seen to be believed.
146 Foveaux Street, Surry Hills
93315050
formatfurniture.com

Glass Artists' Gallery
Originally established in Paddington in 1982, the Glass Artists' Gallery has been an institution on Glebe Point Road for over three decades, showcasing a comprehensive collection by Australian and New Zealand artists.
70 Glebe Point Road, Glebe
9552 1552
glassartistsgallery.com.au

Hub
Another new addition to the swelling ranks of design stores in Surry Hills is the Melbourne export of Hub Furniture, run by sisters Jaci Foti-Lowe and Sandra Foti. Hub presents a range of international brands to drool over, arranged alongside leading Australian pieces. International brands include Moroso and Sawaya & Moroni, while local works include Sam Robinson ceramics,

furniture by Tim Collins and Lowe Furniture. Expect great detailing, passionate visual merchandising and lots of design events.
66–72 Reservoir Street,
Surry Hills
hubfurniture.com.au

InDestudio
Furniture produced by designer Jonathan Ingram's InDestudio tends to transcend fashion; his many pieces rely heavily on quality materials and finishes, so that they exude that much-desired contemporary yet classic flair. Ingram's refined, uniquely detailed, and subtly innovative furniture pieces are exhibited through shows such as the annual furniture incubator Workshopped, and are the darlings of restaurateurs and those who fit out corporate interiors. He recently opened a showroom space in Surry Hills – well worth a visit.
119 Kippax Street, Surry Hills
indestudio.com

Interstudio
Opening just over five years ago, Interstudio mainly stocks fresh, contemporary business furniture and focuses on pieces from both local and Scandinavian designers. Closer to home, the small selection of local products includes the contemporary angular designs of Ross Didier, the detailed wood pieces of Melbourne-based Tony Basile and Matt Butler's ubiquitous Zaishu stool.
693 South Dowling Street,
East Redfern
9360 9377
interstudio.com.au

Koskela
Opening in 2000, this homely first-floor showroom was set up by designer Russell Koskela and his partner Sascha Titchkosky. Furniture maker Koskela graduated from the renowned Sydney Institute of Technology interior design course and learned much about his work on travels throughout Scandinavia and the UK. Koskela furniture is equally loved by those specifying pieces for commercial use as it is by those looking for a piece for their home. The simple, well-made wood, steel and upholstery pieces are designed with the environment in mind. One of Koskela's primary

OBJECTS_STORES

right
Do not miss this one. Ross Longmuir's Planet stores in Surry Hills mix the owner's wonderful furniture designs with that of other Australian (mainly Sydney) talent.

photography
Ernest Fratczak

below
Feel at home in Koskela's lofty showroom.

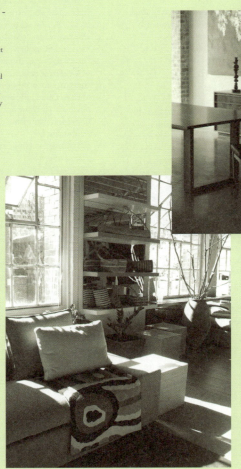

objectives is to promote Australian furniture, so the store sells homewares and furniture by local talent, including Indigenous makers.
91 Campbell Street, Surry Hills
9280 0999
koskela.com.au

Living Edge
A dinosaur in the furniture game, Living Edge has been selling to the trade and residential market for almost ten years. Representing local designers such as Norman + Quaine, Charles Wilson, Matt Sheargold, bernabeifreeman and Jon Goulder, international designs on the floor include those by Ray and Charles Eames for Herman Miller. The commercial showroom in Alexandria is complemented by another space, dedicated to residential applications, in Surry Hills.
74 Commonwealth Street, Surry Hills
9640 5600
111 Burrows Road, Alexandria
8596 8888
livingedge.com.au

MCA Store
While the store at the Museum of Contemporary Art is more of a gift and bookstore, you can certainly pick up some great little pieces here, including those of local designers. Stock is often based around the current exhibition, like bags designed by artists from Buenos Aires or lights by Dutch designer Tord Bootje.
West Circular Quay, The Rocks
9245 2458
mca.com.au

Orson & Blake
Mother and son partnership Orson & Blake is a 'lifestyle emporium' of eclectic items, including a range of local produce. While their Queen Street store focuses mainly on soft furnishings and accessories, the three-level Surry Hills location also includes a cafe and downstairs fashion store, while the furniture section includes larger pieces such as couches and tables.
83–85 Queen Street, Woollahra
9326 1155
483 Riley Street, Surry Hills
8399 2525
orsonandblake.com.au

right
Style on a grand scale: the Space Furniture showroom in Surry Hills.

Planet Furniture
& Planet Commonwealth
Showing work from over 70 different local makers, Planet favours beautifully made pieces from materials such as solid Australian hardwoods, ceramic and textiles. Ross Longmuir, the man and furniture maker behind the store, has a strong environmental approach to design. His first of two showrooms opened on Crown Street in 1998. Known to feature Sydney's most defining designs, Longmuir opened a second store early in 2007 to focus predominantly on hardwood furniture – most of it designed by himself – as well as the fine-art end of ceramics and textiles.
419 Crown Street, Surry Hills
9698 0680
114 Commonwealth Street,
Surry Hills
9211 5959
planetfurniture.com.au

Sabbia Gallery
This is the place to check out contemporary glass and ceramic artists from Australia and New Zealand. With its high ceilings and original timber floorboards, Sabbia creates the perfect gallery space. Directors Anna Grigson and Maria Grimaldi represent key artists such as Edols & Elliot, Klaus Moje and Richard Whiteley.
72 Campbell Street, Surry Hills
9281 4717
sabbiagallery.com

Space Furniture
Under the watchful eye of design industry protagonist Kevin Jarrett, Space Furniture launched its first showroom in Sydney in 1993, quickly establishing an extremely high benchmark for retailing design in Australia. With over six levels of interiors in the Sydney showroom designed by Nik Karalis, Space showcase a range of product from high-calibre international and local designers. Space are proactive in their engagement with the design sector and regularly run design workshops (even for kids) and talks. For more insider knowledge, sign up for their quarterly *More Space* magazine, described as the 'best branded mag available in Australia' by *Vogue Living* editor David Clark.
84 O'Riordan Street, Alexandria
8339 7588
spacefurniture.com.au

OBJECTS_STORES

Spence & Lyda
Fiona Spence's store is eclectic and full of interest – a mandatory stop for those interested in the dynamic collection from Missoni of Milan. Spence also works with local designers, offering an exhibition space and a retail outlet. Spence & Lyda also manufacture their own line of furniture in Sydney.
16 Foster Street, Surry Hills
9212 6747
spenceandlyda.com.au

Tibet Gallery
What sounds like a Buddhist temple is actually the home of Sydney's most interesting designers and makers of hand-woven rugs. In its ritzy Queen Street environs, Tibet's interior was designed by well-known Brisbane architects Donovan Hill. Inside this haven, owner Tim Linkins and partner Diki Ongmo, who live and work in their studio in Kathmandu, show that weaving a rug also means creating a story. Through the texture, colours and traditions of their work, they create clashes of futurism and antiquity, Orient and Occident, and connect cultures and images.
22 Queen Street, Woollahra
9363 2588
tibetsydney.com

OBJECTS_STORES

top3 by design

Nurturing design is very close to the heart of Australian design store top3 by design. Terri Winter, who opened its doors in 2001 has quickly gained international recognition for the unique concept in retailing. Global trend forecasters regularly report on the unique top3 retail approach of cherry-picking a small selection of the world's best-designed products. The top3 customer offering is in stark contrast to the traditional flogging of anything and everything a brand happens to produce. Buyers benefit from knowing where their product has come from and who designed it, made it and why. All top3 staff, Winter included, have a stylist or design background. Her passion for well-made, ethically produced design is just as strong when it comes to the local design community. Stocking a range of Australian-designed-and-made product, including that of several Sydneysiders, has brought about a lot of community and industry engagement and feedback. The large following that the website has developed is testament to that, and an indication of much bigger things to come from top3 by design in the near future.
391–393 Pacific Highway, Crows Nest
Westfield Bondi Junction, 500 Oxford Street
1300 867 333
top3.com.au

Vert Design

Owned and run by Sydney-based industrial designer Andrew Simpson, Vert Design combines the expertise of master glass blowers with a commercial design practice. Designing everything from medical and sporting equipment, electrical and consumer goods and furniture for leading Australian and international manufacturers, Vert also produces commissioned glass works for galleries, collectors and commercial spaces around the globe. Part of the glorious range is the Boab by Adam Goodrum, a sculptural vessel inspired by the Boab tree.
262 Annandale Street, Annandale
0418 768 892
vertdesign.com.au

OBJECTS_STORES

right
International classics meet local style at top3 by design.

150 INDUSTRIAL DESIGN_CONTENTS

Industrial Design

152 Industrial strength_introduction

153 Industrial design_the talent

Industrial strength

Since the first industrial design consultancies began business in Sydney in the 1960s, the sector has grown into a highly competitive community, writes <u>Angelique Hutchison</u>, Curator of Product Design at Sydney's Powerhouse Museum.

Today, Sydney's product designers are making their mark with products ranging from highly advanced medical devices to the branding on your water bottle. Their work generally fits into the categories of consumer goods, medical devices and business technologies. Situated in inner-city offices and industrial warehouses, they work in consulting groups or directly for manufacturers, taking on all aspects of a product's life cycle. With their clients, makers and end-users all across the globe, the designers' efforts have been rewarded with a swag of national and international awards.

Familiar products designed in Sydney include the Mount Franklin water bottle, Victa lawnmowers, Sunbeam and Breville appliances, Energizer torches, ResMed sleep apnoea devices and FCS H-2 surfboard fins.

Many of these locally designed products are held in the Powerhouse Museum collection, which constitutes the first collection of contemporary Australian industrial design. The Museum acquires into the collection selected products along with records, drawings, models and prototypes. Thus, we aim to record the nature of industrial design in Sydney and across Australia – providing inspiration for the designers of today and a rich resource for the researchers of tomorrow.

INDUSTRIAL DESIGN _ THE TALENT

The talent

right
Salvation for housewives: the Sunbeam Mixmaster Professional

photography
Sotha Bourn, Powerhouse Museum

We dug deep to find some of Sydney's most influential industrial design practices. Here's who – and what – we unearthed.

Bang Design

Industrial designers Bryan Marshall and David Granger founded Bang Design in 1989. Producing mostly furniture, they are famous for their cool, free-flowing forms – as seen in their Pli series, a most progressive range of eco furniture.
bangdesign.com.au

Breville

For all those non-natives: when you hear an Australian refer to a 'Breville', they're most likely referring to a toasted sandwich. Such is the success of this true-blue business that they've managed to brandmark an all-American snack with their name. That success dates back to 1974. The company itself, however, made its name in the days when the family gathered around the radio at night, not the box. Bill O'Brien, a radio salesman, and Harry Norville, an engineer, invented the Breville Radio, earning near-instant success with their fledgling product. Now they produce an 800-product-strong catalogue of consumer goods including the accolade-riddled Ikon series of household goods.
breville.com.au

Caroma

Caroma's toilets are the most water-efficient dunnies you'll ever sit your sweet toosh on. Handy during a drought, their H2 Zero urinal, is – as the name suggests – a super saver and completely waterless.
caroma.com.au

Cube

Based in Watson's Bay, Cube specialises in the design of plastic moulded components, plastic injection mouldings

... continued p. 156

INDUSTRIAL

BlueSky Creative

above
Flaming success = cash in the pocket? Bluesky's Dosh wallets and Olympic Torch.

Probably Sydney's most prominent design firm, BlueSky Creative entered front-page territory with its Olympic torch in 2000. The torch received recognition around the country, even bagging an Australian Design Award. Founded by Mark Armstrong in 1984, BlueSky Creative produces industrial, graphic and environmental designs. The 12 designers in the Sydney studio (and a smaller office in Melbourne) create products for local and international companies including Victa, Sunbeam, Electrolux and Philips (Mark's former employer and part-owner of BlueSky until 2003). Recently, they took on a true-blue Aussie icon when working on a range of lawnmowers with Victa. They have also started creating their own products, one of which has only just been released. It's the Dosh wallet, a durable and stylish pouch for those who normally burn holes in their leather ones.
blueskycreative.com.au

above
The Crinia wireless audio conference system.

Design + Industry

Another big player, the 20-year-old company Design + Industry now provides the daily bread for 35 designers and engineers in studios in Sydney and Melbourne. This accumulated brainpower is behind the electronic funds transfer machines (aka the Eftpos terminal), and even if you're more a cash kinda guy, it won't be hard to stumble over a product from the Design + Industry stable. They include outdoor weatherproof multimedia payphones and internet access terminals, as well as the electronic multibay parking meter. From axial field generators for the treatment of cancer to high-performance flippers for body boarding, they do it all. More than half of Design + Industry's business goes to clients outside Australia. They have also recently begun producing a range of furniture and homewares under the name Dandi.
design-industry.com.au

INDUSTRIAL DESIGN_THE TALENT

...from p. 153

and toolmaking. Through an intercontinental collaboration with their associates in China's Shenzhen, Cube have produced products such as the Breeze therapeutic facial massager, a blood-alcohol reading device and Blue Eyewear – sunglasses with interchangeable polycarbonate lenses. Cube teamed up with Breville on their award-winning Ikon range which is, well, iconic.
cube.net.au

D3 Design

This is the design group behind the packaging for Mount Franklin water, one of the most popular brands in Australia (it won't take long til you spot someone taking a swig from a bottle on the street). Run by Clive Solari, currently President of the NSW branch of the Design Institute of Australia, D3 have recently released their own range of products called Mint.
d3design.com.au

Design Resource

Founded in 1980 by John Brown, Design Resource is responsible for pretty much every Energizer torch on the market. They also do boats and public transport systems. Spare a thought for them when you enjoy the ride in one of the new millennium trains.
designresource.com.au

Electrolux

In 2003, Swedish company Electrolux established a Design and Innovation Centre in Sydney. With a design team of 14, they develop concepts for locally made appliances under the Westinghouse, Simpson, Hoover, Electrolux and Kelvinator brands.
electrolux.com.au

Ideal Industrial

This design consultancy in Surry Hills adds a special twist to their traditional industrial design practice by producing stunning structural branding and packaging design. Founded in the early 1990s by Oliver Kratzer, an active member of Sydney's design community, Ideal Industrial was recently awarded with a Gold Medal in the Australian Packaging Council Awards.
ideal-industrial.com

Konstrukt

When it comes to sports design, Konstrukt may just win the race. Based in Sydney, with offices in Shanghai and Milan, Konstrukt designed the Quantum Stadium Seating found in many sports

right
ISO table by
Bang Design.

photography
Andrew Frolows,
Powerhouse
Museum

stadiums and other large arenas. Recently, they came up with the award-winning Barracuda Predator Swimming Goggles, which have an oversized aesthetic designed specifically for triathlon and open-water swimming.
konstruktdesign.com

KWA Design

For a peek at the portfolio of the KWA Design Group, peruse the infrastructure of the City of Sydney. The street furniture includes Smart Poles that feature a whole raft of technological and functional elements, commissioned for the Sydney Olympics. There's something for everyone: they make spray-on tan applicators, too.
kwadesign.com.au

Neoz Lighting

Peter Ellis and Anne Gothe formed Neoz Lighting in 1983 to cordlessly brighten things up. Neoz now illuminates restaurants and bedside tables in over 50 countries, and has produced the world's first rechargeable lamp using lithium ion cells. They also make illuminated furniture.
neoz.com.au

Nielsen Design Associates

This was one of the first design consulting studios in Sydney, established in 1961. Now, the director heads a team of ten, developing products ranging from telephones to medical devices and laudable sink plugs. One of Nielsen Design's most innovative projects is a

INDUSTRIAL

above
Talon chair by Bang Design and Talon Technology.

inset
One of Design Resource's Energizer torches.

photography
Sotha Bourn, Powerhouse Museum

foldable carbon-fibre urban sports bike, based on sailboard manufacturing processes, for a Malaysian company.
9816 5566

ResMed

When Colin Sullivan, head of the Sleep Disorders Unit at the University of Sydney, developed a mask to treat sleep apnoea over 20 years ago, he had trouble finding a company to commercialise the device. ResMed pocketed the job, and have since helped loads of people around the world sleep better. They've also developed diagnostic devices for lots of other human body parts, organs and fluids – you name it.
resmed.com.au

INDUSTRIAL DESIGN _ THE TALENT

Sunbeam

This US company has made products down under for almost 90 years, and crossed the Pacific permanently in the 1980s. Their initial designs, such as the Sunbeam Mixmaster, quickly became beloved benchtop babes. Since then, their industrial aesthetic has steadily infiltrated the international and national domestic markets.
sunbeam.com.au

Tiller + Tiller

The Mixmaster Compact has provided salvation to hundreds of housewives, househusbands and housesingles. Developed in collaboration with Wilson Product Development and Sunbeam, this food-mixing device can be used while resting on the stand or in the hand. Other products include the modular emergency vehicle light-bar system used by police, ambulance and fire services, life-saving headbands for motor vehicle drivers and a mining cap lamp.
tillerdesign.com

4design

Not even five years old, this company of four industrial / graphic designers has already achieved considerable standing. Their mission is to study international trends in design, architecture, fashion, material research and technology before embarking on new product development. So far, they've entered into serious business with products that analyse skin cancer, Xbox consoles and the bullet-proof transit TV, and complemented the range with fun things such as chocolate fountains and the design and branding for an energy drink containing flower essences.
4design.com.au

Charlwood Design

We couldn't let you go without giving the man himself a credit. Paul Charlwood is the founder of this Design Guide series. He is a very distinguished industrial designer himself, with a history as wide and varied as designing high-tech gadgets like the Queen's Baton for the 2006 Commonwealth Games (he received a coveted Premier's Design Award for that one) and household cleaning equipment for Oates Clean, as well as sophisticated medical and banking devices. His office is in Melbourne, but his designs are universal, of course.
charlwood.com.au

FASHION_CONTENTS

FASHION_CONTENTS 161

Fashion

165 Introduction
166 Tides of fashion_history_feature
168 Take a walk_fashion tour
173 Fashion's next generation
184 Influential neighbours
188 The graduates
192 By the beach
196 The Sydney style
206 Established & sons
208 Green threads
209 Frocks, frills & fancy_boutiques
220 Have shop, will travel_out of town designers_boutiques
222 Vintage_boutiques
224 To market, to market!

Introduction

left
The Willow lingerie launch, titled *Homage to Newton* in honour of the late photographer.

The Sydney fashion scene is as celebrated as the design talent in it. It's impossible to separate the two. The city's outdoor lifestyle, beaches and love of a party influences its designers, writes <u>Edwina McCann</u>, Fashion Editor at *The Australian*.

Melbourne fashion design tends to focus on artistic and intellectual expression; Sydney's is often just about the expression part – and making lots and lots of noise.

Those who are loudest are heard, which doesn't mean there is less original talent blossoming in Sydney but rather that those who have it have to learn how to market it, often from a very tender age. The majority of the national fashion media is based here, and this tends to draw interstate designers to the capital. It also gives a business focus to the city's designers as they vie for column space and glossy pages with international names.

I believe the competitive and international nature of the city is constantly improving its design talent, but it can make it difficult for newcomers to get a foothold.

And still, there is a constant stream of exciting and original talent emerging. In this guide you will find them – old and new, artistically challenging and commercially minded. Their diversity makes Sydney's fashion energetic and fuels my passion for it.

Tides of fashion

right
Experimenting with motifs of native flora: Jenny Kee's Wattle dress of the 1980s.

inset
Early Australian dressmakers obtained fabrics from Asia, rather than Europe; the 1822 ballgown of Ann Marsden, made from Indian muslin.

Collection of the Powerhouse Museum

photography
Courtesy of the Powerhouse Museum and Jenny Kee

Once upon a time, a remote colonial outpost looked solely to Europe for inspiration and quality in fashion, but Sydney's thriving design community has slowly come into its own, writes <u>Glynis Jones</u>, Curator of Fashion and Textiles at Sydney's Powerhouse Museum. She glances at the milestones in the city's fashion history.

From the beginning of European settlement in 1788, the small colonial elite of Port Jackson were anxious to establish their superiority over the convict population by maintaining a fashionable appearance. At first, however, shortages of even the most basic clothing supplies made such distinctions difficult to maintain. The colony's clergyman Samuel Marsden and his family, who had arrived in 1794, frequently sent letters to friends and family in England asking to ship them back the latest styles, due to the lack of local shopping facilities, dressmakers and tailors. More reliable supplies of dress and fabrics were also traded from closer ports in India.

By the 1880s, the situation was much improved. Sydney boasted a thriving shopping hub with several large department stores including David Jones and Farmers, offering dressmaking and tailoring services and a wide range of ready-made garments and accessories both local and imported. There were also large numbers of professional dressmakers, while home dressmakers created their own garments with the help of mass-produced paper dress patterns and sewing machines.

Nearly 100 years later, in the mid 1970s, Sydney-based designers Jenny Kee and Linda Jackson began to forge a unique vision of Australian dress, one that did not look to trend-driven international fashion for inspiration but drew on Australia's cultural and natural landscape. It wasn't a purist expression of Australian identity but melded an eclectic assortment of elements drawn from colour theory, art history, theatre, Chinese opera and European haute couture as well as dress and textiles from other cultural and Indigenous groups.

Over the last decade, the speed of global communications has ensured fashion news and images reach a worldwide audience within days. Rather than homogenising fashion, however, it has had the opposite effect: the market is no longer dominated by 'big' trends but has fragmented into seasonal series of smaller trends alongside a more volatile, eclectic and individualistic range of styles sold through increasingly specialised markets. Sydney has witnessed the rise of a new generation of designers such as Akira Isogawa, whose signature style has earned accolades in this international marketplace that constantly seeks innovative designs.

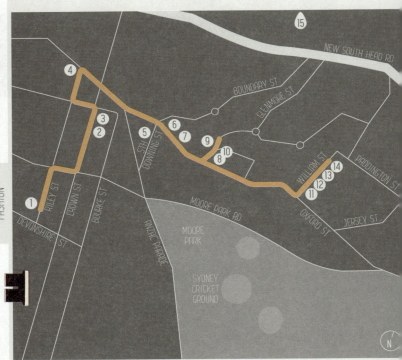

Take a walk

We've asked two professional shoppers to lead the way for those fashion fiends short on time or impatient to hit the racks. Who would know better than <u>Clare Buckley</u> and <u>Kym Ellery</u>? The two work as stylists and Kym has recently launched her own label, Ellery, to great acclaim. She also works as Market Editor for Sydney's own fashion bible *Russh*, where Clare was previously Fashion Editor. Starting from their shared abode in designer district Surry Hills, let the two take you on a rambling stroll though the frock highlights of that suburb and Paddington. No heels for this one.

Right next door to our house on Riley Street is <u>Orson & Blake</u> (see p. 213), a sensory shopping experience. You can browse books, leaf through the local fashion and try out the garden furniture, then head off after spending three dollars — or maybe a bit more.

All the way down Crown Street is the <u>Dobry Den</u> (see p. 211). Streetwise and casual, go there for the best emerging talent such as Friedrich Grey, My Pet Square, China Heights tees and Kate Hurst. Hoodies with a sense of humour stand out, as does the clientele with their directional hairstyles.

Almost next door is <u>Zoo Emporium</u> (see p. 223). We've found some life-defining vintage clothing in here. The neighbours, Puf'nStuf and the great C's Flashback, are equally full of opportunities to replenish your wardrobe.

4 Back on Riley Street is a brand new store, named after its own address, 32 Riley Street, which brings a Melburnian vibe to the inner city. The store's industrial style and lighting is reflected in the clothing – it's a breath of fresh air in the Sydney fashion scene.

5 Up Oxford Street and just to the right in South Dowling Street is clever and kooky Capital L (see p. 210), the doings of the lovely Lou Iselin. Her eye and ability to pick up new labels bound for the top is amazing. She attracts a cool crowd of fashion-following shoppers and feeds them exactly what they want. Lamps and stuffed animals, vines, graphic wallpaper and odd props all add to the love-vibe in the space. The ever-changing painted shop front is one of the best bits – a form of 'artist in residence' for local fashion talent.

6 Skipping up Oxford Street, one store stands out among the rest, that of Melburnian Lisa Gorman (see p. 220), who recently opened up to offer a different aesthetic for the indulgence of Sydneysiders. The charming and friendly interior feels a bit like a Swedish log cabin – don't be afraid to have a yodel.

7 For inspiration and trend direction before you spend the big dollars, the Ariel Booksellers (see p. 289) Paddington store outdoes itself with a great fashion, art and photography book selection.

8 Further up Oxford Street, standing tall on the corner of the shopping district fondly named The Intersection, the Scanlan & Theodore (see p. 221) store is superb. You can spend hours picking out clothing you'd trade your left arm for. Gary Theodore and his team also scour the globe to bring us the best international accessories from outside the mainstream. Did we mention Stefano Pilati, Head Director of YSL picked up some pieces here when in Sydney recently? That's how good it is.

9 Not far from here, ksubi (see p. 204) screams Sydney and vice-versa. Directional, modern and wearable, this brand represents the strength of Australian fashion with international appeal. Watch out for the new collection, where the ksubi boys teamed up with Think Positive (see p. 136) to create printed designs set to freshen the market and stir up the most weary shopper. The store has seen the likes of Erin Wasson, Brittany Murphy and the woman herself – French *Vogue* Editor Lady Carine Roitfeld – popping through when in town. Roitfeld even picked up a pair of ksubi fluoro spray-painted jeans on her last visit to Sydney, making them hot property around the globe.

Also in the Intersection cluster is Zambesi (see p. 221), a perfect example of New Zealand's idiosyncratic fashion. Adhering to the dark mood of its native land, there's deep mystery embedded in the clothing.

Back on Oxford Street, make your way to another fashion enclave, William Street. Belinda and The Corner Shop (see p. 212) collectively hold the wares of the entire Francophile fashion elite, spiced up with a few avant-garde Belgians and Brits, and of course Australian designers.

On the same street is Poepke (see p. 216). Shop here for more intellectually guided voices with a quirkier nature. Showcasing collections from Ann Demeulemeester, Dries Van Noten and Bernhard Willhelm, Poepke highlights key pieces of the chosen collections to demonstrate the strength and vision of the designers. Just don't eat any icecream sundae inside.

Just a few doors down, Melvin & Doyle (see p. 222) is the place for those allergic to dust but inspired by fashions from previous decades. Its slick, chic interior showcases hand-selected clothing by owner Bianca Doyle. A stylist's cream sundae, Annie Hall would have been at home here, as would any style icon with a penchant for masculine tailoring.

Here ends our little walk, but there's one more destination you don't want to miss when unearthing the best fashion in town: Blood Orange (see pp. 209-210) in Elizabeth Bay. Store owner and buyer Loren Abood displays chic, classic yet fashion-forward pieces from the likes of Lover, Youth World and Ellery, which will leave you better dressed than you've ever been.

FASHION_NEXT GENERATION

above
Simple and sophisticated with just the right amoung of quirk: Rittenhouse.

photography
Max Doyle

left
Not-so-average menswear for not-so-average males: the doings of FrisoniFinetti.

photography
Terence Chin

Fashion's next generation

This lot are the trailblazers of Sydney's fashion community. Eschewing conventional processes, materials and styles, the next gen breaks away from the frilly frock, jeans and T-shirt labels the city is famous for. Some are freshly hatched, others have reputations that precede them, all are defined by the brand-spanking new approach they bring to the design process.

The Cassette Society

One of the funkiest streetwear labels to emerge from a sea of nondescript denim and T-shirts, the Cassette Society is on a full-speed, fast-forward roll into the pop charts. Its designer, ex-Brisbanite Katie Boyd, fuels the brand with her two major interests: her love for fabric of all kinds and passion for pop culture inspirations that range from Broadway dance studios to Japanese anime. After showing her first collection in 2004, the then 25-year-old swiftly secured a deal with high street fashion empire General Pants. Now teamed up with Tania Rickarts, the funky collection for summer 07/08 piled on the metallics and screamed colour – no wonder they called it *Technicolour Love*. Another cool trick from The Cassette Society's repertoire: joining forces with local illustration and art talent to work on fabric designs for their unitards, chunky parkas, micro-mini sundresses, spliced playsuits, three-quarter leggings and T-shirts. Local artists Elke Kramer (who's featured elsewhere in this book) and Briony Russell were the first ones to take up the pen.
General Pants,
112–116 Campbell Parade,
Bondi Junction
9319 7380

Ellery

One-woman show Kym Ellery is Sydney's newest kid on the block, but also one of the hottest. She launched her first collection, *Robocrobat* (guess what

top right
Shakuhachi interchanges between opposites: work boots and chiffon dresses, sweatshirts and corsetry.

photography
Akila Berjaoui

bottom right
Silence is Golden's blend of Riviera and revolutionary peasant chic.

photography
Lucas Dawson

it was inspired by) at artist-run initiative China Heights in 2007, but being a fashion designer is only one of her incarnations. The other two are Market Editor at Sydney's own fashion mag *Russh*, and fashion stylist. Young Ellery herself wasn't even around when her 1970s showgirl muses were stepping it up, but the retro-futuristic creations she sends down the catwalk are nonetheless a convincing display of her individual and eclectic style – in the shape of dresses, leotards and bustiers adorned with tassles and ropes, studs and eyelets and specially printed fabric designs. All of it is available at Blood Orange in Elizabeth Bay.

FrisoniFinetti

A Teutonic, wearable style reminiscent of *A Clockwork Orange*, this label is for the ultra-stylish city dweller. The brand draws on the design experience of veteran Nicola Finetti (who's sought-after women's label is featured elsewhere in this book, see p. 199) and the critical eye of fashion journalist Fernando Frisoni, who's originally from Brazil but made a name for himself in Australia writing for daily newspapers such as the *Sun Herald*. The collaboration takes an intellectual approach to clothing design, segmenting their latest collection into *Black Story*, *White Story*, *Grey Story* and *Blue Story*. Each of their pieces, available through David Jones and Orson & Blake, combines classic with contemporary, such as metallic suiting with a sportswear lining. In the words of *Men's Style*: 'Casually smart, not smart casual.'
frisonifinetti.com

Friedrich Gray

Slouching onto the fashion stage in the months before this book's release, Ben Politt's label Friedrich Gray is a freshly hatched beast. His bogan-slash-minimalist *Stranger than Darkness* collection debuted at Fashion Week 07 in an abandoned church. With monochrome hoods, bat pants and slumpy cardigans for fiends, with goth-punk tops and vintage plaid for the fiendettes, the label is a clash of styles that hint at two famous characters that may or may not have inspired the name, Friedrich Nietzsche and Dorian Gray.
friedrichgray.com

Rittenhouse

More enclave than empire, Rittenhouse must be the best-kept secret in Sydney's celebrity-riddled fashion world. They don't show at Fashion Week, don't generate celebrity headlines and aren't featured in the weekend papers showing off their latest home renovations. Yet Sally McDonald and Micah Hamdorf traverse the globe with the most wearable and original style that is Rittenhouse. The first thing the small team did after finishing their first collection was circle the globe to find stockists. Now into their seventh collection, the label includes both women's and menswear with a twist, ranging from slouchy T-shirt dresses to beautifully crafted parkas and sculptural tops. Yet despite its extensive network that captures Sydney, LA, London and Japan, Rittenhouse stays firmly rooted in Sydney. Truly glocal. Get it at Orson & Blake, Poepke and The Corner Shop.
9281 0644
rittenhouse.com.au

Michelle Robinson

No website, no store, not a huge profile, but lots and lots of fans – the eponymous Michelle Robinson label is stocked in all the right places (Capital L, Blood Orange, Orson & Blake) and attracts the right crowd. Former East Sydney TAFE student Michelle Robinson launched her label in 2004 and now dresses the most fashion-conscious clientele around Australia with her intelligent and quirky detailing, keen sense of colour and unique silhouettes. Inspired by pop icons and artists, Robinson also honours more technical references, like exposed zips that honour 1950s design.

Shakuhachi

A small, simple-looking and very delicate instrument, the Shakuhachi flute is painstakingly hard to learn. It is also a major inspiration of Jessie White, the self-taught fashion designer who named her label of intricately crafted garments after it. Relying on zip and pleat detailing and angular lines, White's latest collection features lots of metallic, high-waisted pants and playful patterns, available at Capital L and David Jones. Shakuhachi is a little bipolar, just like its hometown. But it works beautifully.
shakuhachi.net.au

Silence is Golden

Don't be fooled by the name – Silence is Golden created a resounding echo throughout the fashion crowd on its launch in 2005. Founder and designer Kelvin Tam was a practising architect before he threw himself into fashion and has managed the transition, well, seamlessly. From architecture, he transposed to his clothes his predilection for structure and fluid lines. With 'silence' standing for subtlety and calm, and 'golden' suggesting treasure and charm, Tam has wowed his audiences, winning the Mercedes Start Up Award during 2005 Australian Fashion Week with a collection inspired by the film *The Pianist*. This larrikin take on tailoring is vailable at The Corner Shop, Incu and Paris Texas, among others.
silenceisgolden.com.au

Youth World

If you happen to be in Moscow, drop in at local boutique Cara & Co and admire the new Youth World collection, entitled *Cake Fight*. Or if you're in New York, ask Elisabeth Charles to show you their wares in her store. The label, launched in 2005, is another globetrotting Australian creation, with almost as many stockists internationally as on its home turf. Perhaps the reason is founder Therese Rawsthorne's international fashion pedigree (acquired during stints with Issey Miyake and Oswald Boateng). Her own garments (available in this town at The Corner Shop and Blood Orange) range from the sculptured Strapped Up Swing Tank in lime-yellow silk to the metallic Wonder Dress Deluxe. Using garment archetypes as inspiration (the pencil skirt, the cigarette pant), Rawthorne isn't interested in anything retro. She likes to look forward and – like we said – across borders.
thisisyouthworld.com

18th Amendment

Here comes the youngest of Sydney's denim labels, but there's already a celebrity following including Gen Y frock ambassadors Mischa Barton and Sienna Miller. The label was set up by friends Rachel Rose and Rebecca Dawson, who have created a diverse collection with styles ranging from spray-on to flare. Stocked at Parlour X and instantly recognisable by its embroidered wings logo on the back pockets, this might just be the next ksubi or sass & bide. We warned you!

FASHION_NEXT GENERATION

Josh Goot

above
Clean lines, bold cuts: the New Line Dress.

If Sydney fashion ever sheds its heels-wearing, bottom-baring and cleavage-staring reputation, rest assured Josh Goot will have had a major part in it. Urban sportswear and bold patterns with an undercurrent of minimalism is what comes out of Goot's studio. Although he's spending much of his time globetrotting between fashion capitals and following exactly the lifestyle you'd expect from a young frock celebrity, the media and communications graduate initially didn't set out to enter the rag trade. In late 2004, however, his time had come. His comfortable, casual – yet clingy – dresses, made from 100% cotton jersey, were celebrated as the latest, biggest deal in Australian fashion and barely a year later the designer – in his late twenties – found himself showing at New York Fashion Week. As his career picked up, so did the volume of designs pumped out of his small office. He forged a partnership with Australian Wool Innovation to collaborate and develop unique fabrics from Australian Merino Wool and produced collections for four fashion shows within 12 months (two in Australia, two overseas). His latest, shown at CarriageWorks during Australian Fashion Week 2007, was one of the biggest on the bill with more than 40 designs. Another 2007 milestone was his capsule range for Target, where he joined a line-up including Stella McCartney and Tina Kalivas in presenting upmarket wear with a downmarket price tag.
joshgoot.com

FASHION_NEXT GENERATION

Kirrily Johnston

above
The silhouettes of Johnston's well-constructed garments often stand in contrast to feminine fabrics like satin and chiffon.

photography
Brad Hick,
Six Photography

Toying with a fashion career after leaving the Melbourne Institute of Textiles in 1999, Kirrily Johnston's first collection debuted in the Victorian capital two years later. Her big break, however, only arrived when she ditched her earlier moniker, überchic, moved to Sydney and launched her first collection under her own name. That was in late 2004. Although the glamorous mid-30s Sydneysider has got all the right contacts in the glitzy set of the city, her output couldn't be described as the ubiquitous frills-and-all Sydney frock. Muted pastel, grey and white hues are interspersed with bouts of screaming colour: orange and blue in 2006/07 and canary-yellow and Shrek-green for the following Spring/Summer collection. Apparently, her design process begins with colour, at Mitre 10 hardware store of all places, where she selects wall paint samples and takes them back to the office to experiment – legend has it her staff wear them on their foreheads to make sure they complement various skin tones. The collections themselves draw on pop-culture references that are laudably unpretentious, with *Ben Hur* and *Desperately Seeking Susan* among past muses. These resulted in fleshy silk-chiffon tank tops embellished with a Swarkovski-crystal-beaded black crucifix, and the Rosanna dress framed with big black beads on the neckline.

6 Glenmore Road, Paddington
9380 7775
kirrilyjohnston.com

Lover

above
Beautiful overall: the Lover *One Plus One* collection.

photography
Stephen Chee

The people behind this label are indeed lovers. Their creations are clever, but not too clever, feminine, but not frilly, simple, but with mindblowing attention to details, hems and necklines. Contradictory concoctions? No, just two opposing but complementary natures. One, Nic Briand, loves anything loud and irreverent (think AC/DC and comic heroes) the other, Susien Chong, is into ethereal and feminine (think ballet and *Picnic at Hanging Rock*). No wonder they choose equally ambiguous heroes and heroines as inspiration for their twice-yearly collections. Muses have ranged from Patty Hearst (the two aimed to chart her journey from heiress to guerrilla in their Spring/Summer 2007 collection) to Marianne Faithfull, Woody Allen and Jean Luc Godard. What we see on the racks (at Blood Orange, Incu, Capital L and The Corner Shop) is not at all controversial. And the verdict is unanimous. We want that.
loverthelabel.com

FASHION_NEXT GENERATION

Mad Cortes

above
A love affair with the dress: Mad Cortes' panelled dress with neck tie.

photography
Terence Chin

With a sailor-adventurer for a godfather and a Bosnian couple as parents, Mad Cortes truly marries European sensibilities with a little bit of Australian cheek. Creator Mira Vukovic, who started the business with her graphic designer husband Ameli T Orman, moved to Sydney from Sarajevo in 1996 and promptly enrolled in Fashion Design at East Sydney TAFE. Upon forming her label (named after her childhood comic-book hero Corto Maltese) four years later, it was Sydney boutique Capital L who snapped up her first designs: thickly draped swagged dresses with wavy, spliced panels. In 2005 she was celebrated as best emerging designer at Mercedes Fashion Week. Girly without being frilly, her trademark feminine, playful yet well-proportioned and textured garments are made from silks, satins, jerseys and printed cottons. Like so many small fashion businesses Mad Cortes emerged from its owner's lounge room, though it is now incorporated into the Lisa Ho empire. From here, it continues to make many sophisticated ladies happy.
madcortes.com

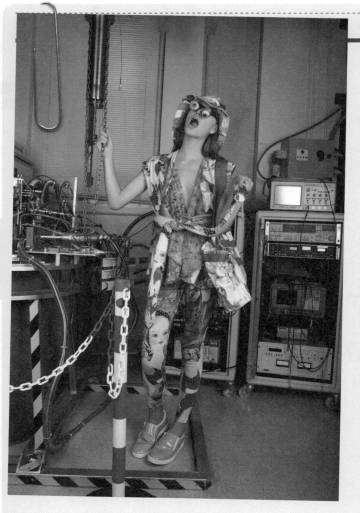

Romance was Born

left
Fashion for rockstars and crazy professors: the *Mad Science* collection.

photography
Tanja Bruckner

If you listen to the fashion editors around town, Romance Was Born is the most interesting young design team Sydney has to offer. No wonder that the creatives, who graduated from East Sydney TAFE in 2004, turned down international allure to focus on their own turf. When internships at the Paris atelier of John Galliano beckoned, the two decided against the city of romance for a very own romance of their own.

By their own accounts, the team behind the quirky label, Anna Plunkett and Luke Sales, has only produced one 'serious' collection, *Weird Science*, shown at the 2007 Rosemont Australian Fashion Week. But that was enough for them to make serious waves across Australian fashion circles (not least by adorning their bride with a giant wedding cake for a hat).

You could say that it was Björk who brought the two together, as they found themselves united by fantasies of creating her dresses. Indeed, it seems utterly likely that their super-loud shiny leggings or other items of their trans-seasonal stagewear for the street will one day make their way into the Icelandic singer's wardrobe.

In the meantime, the two aren't faring too badly on the rockstar front, having started their label in 2004 to design stage outfits for the Yeah Yeah Yeah's singer Karen O as the band was touring Australia.

Interested in 'creating a story, rather than a fad', the renegades take inspiration equally from native birds and Australian sports starts, as seen in their 'bloody legends' singlets. Drop by at Capital L if you want one.

Influential neigbours

Paris, London and New York? How about Kyoto, Kuala Lumpur and Chitral? For the designers described here it's our closer neighbours who inspire the creative process. Drawing from the cultures of atypical fashion centres, here are three labels that illustrate Sydney's connection to the East, whether that be Far, Middle or just Newcastle …

Caravana

How is Caravana different from all the other labels you'll find around the country? Let us count the ways. For starters, the two ladies behind the much-loved label, Kirsten Ainsworth and Cath Braid, don't actually manufacture and live in Australia. While that's not so unusual, they have set up a unique production scheme that involves employing 400 local women in the northern Pakistani village of Chitral, where the duo also lives for much of the year. Then there are the techniques used to produce the collections – traditional local embroidery is heavily featured in the colourful skirts, blouses and of course in the coveted handbags. These patterns are then complemented with the skilful designs of the Caravana team, so that every catwalk the two populate with their work seems illuminated and the audience is enchanted. The childhood friends moved to Pakistan in 2003, after Braid completed her studies at London's famed Central St Martins College. Producing up to four collections a year to be shown on international catwalks, legend has it that Braid once walked five hours across a snow-covered pass with 16 suitcases and seven porters in tow in order to make it to Sydney Fashion Week, guaranteeing her employees' wages for the next season of work.
caravana.com

FASHION_INFLUENTIAL NEIGHBOURS

above left Melding their heritage with their very own style, High Tea with Mrs Woo produce sartorial, feminine garments in bold colours, defined lines and decorative patterns.

above right Patterns and embroidery from Pakistan paired with designs from Sydney and London: Caravana.

High Tea With Mrs Woo

Newcastle isn't just steel and coal. It's also theatrical and East-meets-West. That's thanks to the three sisters of Chinese-Malaysian descent who are behind High Tea With Mrs Woo, their womenswear label founded in 2004. Still based in Newcastle, where the three have lived since migrating to Australia from Malaysia in 1988, the label now has a worldwide fan base, with the trio increasingly focusing on markets in Europe and Asia. After completing their degrees at Newcastle University – with the two older sisters, Rowena and Juliana, emerging as graphic designers and the youngest, Angela, with a degree in finance and economics – the three became fixtures in the Australian fashion landscape with a gig as part of the start-up group at Australian Fashion Week. Their earliest forays were at Glebe Market and they still run the label from their Darby Street shop and studio in Newcastle. Get their wares in Sydney at the Von Troska stores and Strelitzia, among others. None of the sisters is called Mrs Woo, but they say the fictional name honours the matriarchy that has influenced and inspired them: their mother, auntie and grandmother. highteawithmrswoo.com.au

FASHION_INFLUENTIAL NEIGHBOURS

Akira

left
The otherworldly creations emerging from Akira's 'science lab'. (Clockwise from top left: Akira Resort 2008; Akira Autumn Winter 2007; Akira Autumn Winter 2007.)

photography
Stephen Ward

While some fashionistas still cross swords over the identity of Australian fashion, Akira Isogawa is hailed by others as embodying exactly that, marrying the heritage of his homeland – which he left as a teenager to study fashion at East Sydney TAFE in 1986 – and Australian sensibilities in exquisite garments that have rendered him a couture genius far beyond our shores. Depending on who you listen to, he's described either as a de-constructivist (fusing disparate elements in ways alien to their original context, such as the kimono fabrics and vintage garments he collected on frequent visits home to Kyoto) or as a postmodernist, in that his subject matter is the creative process itself, as evident in his unconventional methods of dyeing and using fabrics in what he calls his 'science lab'. Since Akira opened his first store in Woollahra in 1995, his fan base has been enraptured with his delicate, hand-finished garments. By the late 1990s, Akira was not only commercially successful, but was also embraced by many other arts sectors. As a consequence, we've admired his work in productions of the Sydney Dance Company and in the halls of the National Gallery of Victoria. He was the first Australian fashion designer the Gallery devoted a solo exhibition to. More recently an Akira-designed shampoo has appeared, as well as a postage stamp, delivered to even the most remote areas of this country.
Akira Boutique, 12a Queen Street, Woollahra
9361 5221
The Strand Arcade, 412–414 George Street, Sydney
9232 1078
akira.com.au

The graduates

With tentacles stretching deep into the fashion industry, these designers all have a history of work, under many different guises, for fashion houses and fields across the globe. Their experience and insight ensured success when these singular creatures finally set out on their own, ensuring they were almost instant hits.

Jayson Brunsdon

Illustrator-cum-stylist-cum-fashion designer Jayson Brunsdon is a fervent subscriber to glamour. Launching his womenswear label in 2004, his search for the perfect dress is far from over. He learned the ropes of the fashion business in a decade as the creative director for fashion brand Morrissey, and now flavours his oh-so-Sydney creations with a twist of cinematic drama and artistic reference. His Audrey Hepburn and Coco Chanel-inspired creations have attracted the attention of Our Mary and further royalty – fashion and otherwise. Only three years after his debut, Brunsdon now retails to almost 50 stores in seven countries. Yet he is firmly anchored in Sydney, especially since opening his flagship store in the fashionable Strand Arcade in 2006. UK *Vogue* has labelled him 'the toast of Sydney' – his dresses are certainly the perfect frocks for celebrations.
The Strand Arcade,
412–414 George Street, Sydney
9233 8891
jaysonbrunsdon.com

Jessie Hill

Yet another truly international Australian, Jessie Hill started at the top, launching her namesake label into the global arena in New York in 2005. Perhaps she felt compelled to retrace her ancestry (the glamorous ex-stylist is related to Woody-Allen muse and actress Mia Farrow). Hill juzh-ed up bands like No Doubt and the Red Hot Chilli Peppers in LA before channeling all her creative energy into a new job as Head Designer of cult label Buddhist Punk in London (where compatriot and fellow Sydney design legend Alice McCall also acquired many of her skills). Finally deciding on Sydney as the hometown of her own label, Hill set about creating feminine fashion for the everyday, including asymmetric knits and printed leggings, but also featuring the odd piece of haute couture in her first collection, *Broken Windows*, which was greatly anticipated at Australian Fashion Week 2007. The inspiration for the collection came courtesy of *Blade Runner*, very LA of course. jessiehill.net

fashionassassin

He's been called 'the busiest man of Australian fashion' and must be the country's suavest networker. Alex Zabotto-Bentley launched his streetwear label fashionassassin in 2003 after a successful career as a stylist and as Men's Fashion Director for *Vogue*. Having styled the likes of Holly Valance, Danii Minogue and Human Nature, the arts and science graduate certainly knows the value of celebrity branding. When he finally assaulted the world with his own brand, it wasn't to anyone's surprise that he sent out 'care packages' to many a starlet, containing pieces of the label's first collection. Some months down the track, Beyoncé Knowles was donning his frocks. Always the wheeler and dealer, he is a resident fashion critic for *Who Weekly* and broadcasts from the red carpets of the Logies and the Oscars. As Zabotto's ever-expanding fan base procreates, the thrifty marketer has thought ahead and caters to the minis with his Assassino Bambino range. fashionassassin.com.au

above left
Glamour on Jayson Brunsdon's catwalk.

right
Backstage at fashionassassin. The designer's inspirations range from paratroopers to pineapples, and manifest themselves in jeans and T-shirts complemented by – depending on the season – tailored jackets and crocheted minis.

Alice McCall

left
McCall's style is far from the ballgown line of many Sydney fashion fellows.

photography
Courtesy of Alice McCall

Here's another fashion veteran who's taken a punt and come out on her own. And the way things look, Ms McCall will have no regrets. She spent her teens watching her fashion designer mother, her twenties dressing stars like P Diddy (aka Puff Daddy), Natalie Imbruglia and Destiny's Child, as well as working as a designer at UK label Buddhist Punk and Sydney's own sass & bide, and just before hitting thirty she shed her past and sewed her own. Her first collection of sexy clown-print dresses and lurex party numbers was hailed by fashion critics across the nation, and she joined the exclusive troupe of first-time fashion designers who were immediately approached to sell their wares at David Jones. Her stockists list includes the coveted Corner Shops and Alfie's Friend Rolfe in Darlinghurst. Her signature style stands out from the jeans and denim crowd by a mile. There are retro references and psychedelic gestures, skinny jeans, liberty print blouses and chiffon dresses, and above all there's absolutely no boredom. In 2006, McCall was one of three Australian designers who created a range for Target. Her *Welcome To The Dollhouse* collection of 2007 was infused with flouro and included a collaborative jewellery collection designed in a joint effort with brother and sister team Pete and Amanda Zuitton. It was inspired by – what else? – *Alice in Wonderland*.
alicemccall.com

By the beach

It's true: Bondi Beach holds the record for the most bikini-clad babes in one place. In September 2007, just over 1000 women donned their itsy-bitsys to claim the Guiness World Record title. With so much pride for the sweet little nothings and some of the best-dressed beach-bums around, it's no wonder there is a thriving scene around beachwear. Here are some of the most interesting makers, old and new.

Anna & Boy

This new label provides an exciting and refreshing take on designer swimwear for both the beachy beaus and the lapping ladies. Plunging head first into the fashion industry at the 2006 Mercedes Australian Fashion Week, Anna & Boy are certainly one of the most exciting new swimwear labels in the biz. The duo behind the label, Anna Hewett and Lill Boyd, draw on fond memories of their childhood, with those endless summers and carefree ease of holidays by the beach. Anna & Boy was the result of the founders' years on the editorial team at Australian *Vogue*, where the pair first recognised the dearth of decent swimwear in the Australian market. Their debut collection mixed retro floral hipster bikinis with printed cover-ups, and included 1970s pool-boy shorts for men, all adorned with their signature gold peach trinket. In subsequent collections they've relied on high-quality fabrics in bold prints as well as precision detailing, mixing sporty bikinis with sexy one-pieces.
annaandboy.com

Issla

The brainchild of Simona Krom, Issla is a newcomer to the swimsuit arena, but she's making waves. The design ideas started coming to Krom as she sat on the beach in Sicily, and there's a distinct Riviera feel to

FASHION_BY THE BEACH

the cozzies the little label turns out. The prints as well as the wares themselves are all designed and manufactured in Australia, with inspiration drawn from bazaars, watercolours, snippets of vintage Parisian textiles and – you guessed it – mischievous Italian girls.
isslavoyageur.com

Mambo

There was a time when thousands of Australian teenagers made their mothers cringe by wearing Mambo 'farting dog' T-shirts. Today those kids are all grown up but still treasure their old shirts, and Reg Mombassa,

clockwise from far right
Girly and sexy Oscar & Elvis / Anna & Boy look after girls and boys (2 images) / Rivieria-inspired Issla.

the artist responsible for the flatulent canine, is a national treasure. A huge success story in the Australian surfwear business, Mambo was always just that little bit different. Where other surf companies focused on the surf, the chicks and the Hawaiian tradition in their apparel, Mambo founder Dare Jennings concentrated on strong designs with political, religious or humorous themes for the clothes, swimwear and surfboards his company whipped out. Founded in 1984, Jennings began to commission artists for those designs, among them Mombassa (who was also a founding member and guitarist of the band Mental As Anything), as well as ceramicist and jeweller Gery Wedd and cartoonist Matthew Martin. Other Mambo motifs include surreal suburban landscapes populated by vomiting dogs, horned bulls, boxy fibro houses and Australian insects such as Bogong moths. Still hugely popular, Mambo has two stores in Sydney and a bunch more around the country.
80 Campbell Parade, Bondi
9365 2255
80 The Corso, Manly
9977 9171
mambo.com.au

Oscar & Elvis

Barely three years old, Oscar & Elvis was launched by friends Stefanie Colman and Indhra Chagoury the moment they got out of fashion school. Frilly, girly and influenced by European fashion, they have gained international buyer attention and are now stocked at David Jones.
oscarandelvis.com

Tigerlily

Named after the character from *Peter Pan*, Tigerlily is the first in the 'new generation' of small swimwear labels originating from Sydney's sandy beaches. From its early days it was destined for fame, wealth and glamour thanks to its media-friendly pedigree. Founded and designed by ex-swimsuit model and ex-media-mogul-wife Jodhi Meares, the weeny bikinis are inspired by vintage wallpapers and a bit of baroque, as well as (now signature) leopard prints and 1970s nautical themes. There's also further beachwear and party accessories. Perfect for that poolside party.
tigerlilyswimwear.com.au

FASHION_BY THE BEACH

Zimmermann

right
Go perfectly with that perfect tan: Zimmermann bikinis.

With the influx of new swimwear labels over the last decade, we must not forget that sisters Nicky and Simone Zimmermann are the godmothers of Sydney designer swimwear. It was sometime in the early 1990s that Nicky, recently graduated from East Sydney TAFE (the same place that was alma mater to Akira and Mira Vukovic of Mad Cortes), began to design her small range in her parents' garage to sell it to the public at – again, note the parallels to Akira et al – the Paddington Market. Soon recognising the potential of her cozzies, Nicky teamed up with sister Simone who took over the business side of the operation, and the two officially launched the label at Australian Fashion Week 1996. While the pair is now most noted for the skimpier elements of their business they've also found fame with their regular garments (Madonna has been seen parading around in a pair of Zimmermann jeans).

The two launched their first store in 1999 and before they knew it, the famed models of the *Sports Illustrated* calendar were donning their creations; now they sell at places like Saks and Bloomingdales. At the time of going to press the sisters were making a splash in the US, where Gwyneth Paltrow was spotted in one of their new resortwear pieces, which promptly sold out via the internet.

Westfield Bondi Junction, 500 Oxford Street
93875111
387 Oxford Street, Paddington
9357 4700
The Strand Arcade, 412–414 George Street, Sydney
9221 9551
zimmermannwear.com

The Sydney style

This city is Australia's capital of party, beach culture and glamour. Translate that into fashion, and what you get are snappy, glamorous cocktail frocks and heels that morph into strapless barefoot outfits for sunsets on the deck; sharp city suits and sneakers that glide into weekend boardies and designer thongs. Here are a few labels that set the scene.

Bec & Bridge

This crafty little label, established by friends Becky Cooper and Bridget Currer, who met on their first day as fashion design students at UTS, is the latest addition to Sydney's booming denim and T-shirt stable. It all started when friends began requesting makeovers for their neglected jeans. The ladies sprayed, printed, dyed, stitched and scratched so that old, tired-looking denim became old, fancy-looking denim. Most importantly, they left their mobile numbers on their works of art, so others could contact them. It's paid off for the pair. Showing in Mercedes Australian Fashion Week's New Generation Show 2005 – the label also joined the exclusive local fashion lineup of retailer David Jones. Their range now includes lots of dainty details, perfect beachwear for the young and the young at heart. becandbridge.com.au

Bowie

Before Hong Kong-born fashion designer Bowie Wong conquered the Sydney fashion set, he had already gathered impressive credentials as a costume and stage designer. The son of an opera singer, his fascination with elaborate costumes was later supported by degrees in drama and costume design in Canada. He then traveled the world working on productions like *Phantom of the Opera* as well as Paul McCartney's and Madonna's

right
Bec & Bridge's creations for the beach and beyond.

world tours. It's not surprising that when he finally settled down in Sydney in 2000, he began to design each of his collections as a production, inspired by a story and highlighting the styles and intricacies of the narrative. These days, Bowie sends Shanghai-inspired collections down the runway – embroidered dresses contrasted with inspired and wearable menswear.
The Strand Arcade,
412–414 George Street, Sydney
9232 22 92
bowie.com.au

Camilla & Marc

Not so long ago Marc Freeman was a graduate engineer and his sister was almost off to Italy where she had won a scholarship to complete a Masters degree – four years ago to be precise. But then came Mercedes Australian Fashion Week 2003, where Camilla Freeman-Topper launched a small collection as part of a graduate show, and no one anticipated its success. The phones didn't stop ringing while department store David Jones snapped up the line faster than a model makes it down the runway. Now, the siblings continue to wow the fashion crowd with pieces that are both elegant and understated, reflecting the Freemans' frantic and perfectionist search for the highest quality fabrics. New: the flirty and fun swimwear range, which is utterly wearable, even if you don't spend your working hours on the catwalk.
camillaandmarc.com

Cohen et Sabine

Natalie Cohen once listed in an interview what she loves. Among her favourite things were: antique embroidery, beading, her grandmother's style, Brigitte Bardot in *Contempt* and Jean Seeberg in *Breathless*. Now take all these things and imagine them as a fashion label. What do

… continued p. 200

Collette Dinnigan

right
The legacy of Dinnigan's historical techniques is still alive and kicking in her latest, more casual, collection. (Metallic Honeycomb Lace / Jewelled Bodice Lace Dress / Collette Dinnigan shoes)

photography
Kim Weston Arnold

On a bad day, some fashion cynic might tell you that alongside Melbourne couture prodigy Toni Maticevski, there is only one truly international Australian designer. And that's Collette Dinnigan. You are not to believe it – there is plenty of talent in this country's big pool of designers, but the point illustrates the iconic status of this South African-born, New Zealand raised designer. After studying in Wellington and taking a job in the props and frocks department of the ABC, Dinnigan launched a collection of lingerie under her own name after being confined to bed with an injury in 1990. She didn't so much skyrocket to fame as slowly trawl there, pounding the pavement and lugging a suitcase around the world until, some five years down the track, New York department store Barneys popped up on her stockist's list.

Her first Sydney store opened in 1992, where fabrics were dyed in the studio above. Dinnigan owes much to her costume-design past and all that period-frock expertise. A combination of these construction techniques and her signature material, lace, found its way into her collections of art deco-inspired, feminine pieces, often using fine wool as the base material. Soon, Hollywood celebs were queuing up to walk down the aisle in a Dinnigan gown, or at least wear one down the red carpet. Most recently, for the first time, Dinningan has shown a collection that was explicitly (so she says herself) inspired by her adopted home country. She said the colours she used were inspired by Australian nature … She's 'our' Collette, after all.
33 William Street, Paddington
9360 6691
collettedinnigan.com

FASHION_THE SYDNEY STYLE

Willow

right
Willow continues to wow audiences with her feminine silouettes.

'The most exciting label to come out of Australia in years!' gushed UK *Vogue* when Kit Willow Podgornik showed her eponymous range at London Fashion Week in 2004, one year after she had caused a sensation among fashion fiends and buyers in her home country. She's been known as Australia's lingerie queen since her first collection in 2003 was devoted mainly to luxury underwear with an unusual twist, but the true bestseller was a capsule collection of jewelled and sequinned dresses and tops that Podgornik had added to her range at the last minute. The sales of her collections – ditching the lingerie after the first year – continually doubled or tripled within the first few years of her existence, and today 70% of her buyers live outside of Australia.

The Melbourne-born 31-year-old, who's recently become a mum, uses inspired production techniques such as embedding Victorian corsetry in hourglass tailored jackets. Having spent ten years in the fashion business – first in sales, then in PR – Podgornik also knows how to promote her work. In 2006 she collaborated with high-street fashion store Portmans to design a handful of dresses, then at least half the production run sold online before even hitting the racks. In 2007, Willow again showed lingerie, this time with a more feminine, flowing aesthetic, incorporating luxurious silk, cotton, lace and tulle. Contrary to her first range she also included black, but held onto her firm 'no-G-string' policy. willowltd.com

... from p. 197

you see? Right, there are delicate and floaty pieces, luxurious fabrics carefully finished in appliqué and embroidery, lace and ribbon ... you get the picture. Her garments are more Sunday school than frou frou, more old-worlde bohemian elegance than fake-tan territory. Not a trained fashion designer but a fine arts graduate, Cohen spent five years slowly growing and refining her label, participating in a fashion week parade for the first time in 2005. Her creations, stocked at David Jones and Orson & Blake, now enjoy a well-deserved reputation for 'comfortable glamour'. So Sydney.
cohenetsabine.com.au

Ginger & Smart

Made for today's Bonnie Parkers (chic but slightly disheveled, the ultimate creative professional), this label extends to accessories and luxury spa products, and the pieces are built for travel: the Shanghai dress, the Waldorf bag, the Compass belt. Sisters Alexandra and Genevieve Smart launched in 2002, but both had previous lives with considerable fashion cache: Genevieve spent time at the design helm of Lisa

below left Camilla & Marc's fine tailoring.

below right One of Nicola Finetti's distinct silhouettes.

above
A Fleur Wood creation floats down the runway, (it's Tallulah of Scene Model Management).

Ho and at Zimmermann, and Alexandra left a publishing career that included a stint as Editor of fashion mag *Oyster*. The year 2007 was a big one for the sisters, securing a deal with David Jones; the two will be joining the likes of Akira and Willow at the upmarket department store.
7 William Street, Paddington
9380 9966
gingerandsmart.com

Nicola Finetti

First training in architecture, Nicola Finetti takes a conceptual approach to design and aims to create pieces that enhance individuality. His range is mainly produced in Bali, where the man himself spends much of his time. Both mothers and daughters love his muted palette, vintage lace and fine beading in incredibly flattering garments, available – among others – at Capital L. A man of many talents and interests, Finetti has also recently launched contemporary menswear label FrisoniFinetti, and runs a directional diffusion line, the more casual NylonFlocks.
nicolafinetti.com
nylonflocks.com

Fleur Wood

The roots of this eponymous fashion label lie deep in the Indian Himalayas, where Fleur Wood, a trained visual merchandiser, worked on a culture-preservation project for the exiled Tibetan Government. A couple of years later, with a bundle of Indian fabrics on her back, Wood moved back to Sydney where she began importing these pretty silks, making a small range of slips and camisoles in 1999. Inspired by vintage wear, Wood's delicate, floaty evening dresses now flitter down the red carpet adorning Hollywood celebrities and the local glamour set alike.
464 Oxford Street, Paddington
9380 9511
fleurwood.com

sass & bide

right
Now beyond denim: sass & bide glam chic extends across the entire wardrobe.

In true-blue Sydney style, it started at a market. Sarah-Jane Clark (sass) and Heidi Middleton (bide) started selling their scandalous denim with a zip that – at two inches long – barely band-aided a Brazilian at London's Portobello Market. Like the length of their zippers, they have kept growing and are now among the handful of top earners in the fashion business in this country. Theirs is a fairytale that couldn't be more Sydney-esque. It features some celebrity endorsement (Elle McPherson was one of their most ardent early admirers, and then there's the legend of the two slipping one of their denim jackets to a security guard on New York's *Sex and the City* set, only for Sarah Jessica Parker to don it in the next episode). It also has casual glamour (think sequinned and studded denim, animal print chiffon dresses, fringed minis and a general glam-trash rockstar feel), an exclusive deal with a department store (David Jones devotes an entire section to their wares), overseas success (their huge following in the States was one reason why they stopped showing at Australian Fashion Week and have, since 2003, sent their wares down the runway only in New York) and of course dedicated stores (Sydney and Brisbane have theirs, Melbourne's is in the making). With the two being so devoted to both their business and their friendship that they wrote 'must have baby' in their business plan (only to give birth within three months of one another), the fairytale also contains the necessary quirk that ensures its bestseller status.

132 Oxford Street, Paddington
9360 3900
sassandbide.com

Tina Kalivas

right
The Mondrian jumper makes an appearance on the runway.

She first explored her formidable couture skills at the London School of Fashion and then moved on to work at Alexander McQueen and London costume house Angels & Berman, but Tina Kalivas has been applying her talent for making a statement in Australia since 2002, and her wares are now available at the best fashion addresses, like The Corner Shop and Parlour X. Kalivas is noted for her emphasis on structure, applying panelling, corsetry, pleats, zips, snaps, buttons, pockets, solid stitching and manipulated graphics to create a futuristic vision that could be termed 'op-art touched by an android'. Fish-tailed bodice dresses, geometric shirts, stick-figure trousers, cuffed and belted triangle coats are all ultimately wearable thanks to Kalivas' innovative tailoring techniques. Kalivas fans are creatures of the universe – the extremely hip who don garments based on the day's plan, whether that be marching against Neptune, seducing the Galaxial Emperor or flitting off to the moon for an afternoon's star-gazing. And they'll be well-dressed to boot.
tinakalivas.com

ksubi

right
No it's not a an android wet T-shirt competition – Ksubi just loves a scandal.

photography
Kane Skennar

When the boys from ksubi released live rats onto the catwalk at one of their first fashion parades, they created an instant furore. While the outrage over the rodents initially got more publicity than the denim and streetwear they were showing, the label was in for a meteoric rise similar to their female counterparts and contemporaries sass & bide. Dan Single and George Gorrow, who famously met in an LA bar brawl, have backgrounds in graphic design and modelling, and began to sell distressed jeans and printed T-shirts alongside a range of sunglasses they were importing at the time. Quickly developing a reputation as fashion's bad boys, the two have never fallen short of orchestrating an impressive spectacle alongside their exponential label. Shortly after starting out in 2001, the two showed in an abandoned tube station in London, where the mob was quick in taking to their surfwear / urban-bad-boy cross, easily distinguished by its painted label.

For the last three or so years ksubi has been branching out, creating entire fashion collections with the help of prodigy designers like their former creative director Michelle Jank. Ksubi is more of a subculture than a jeans label, and its two owners have always maintained their interest in art and scandalous displays (not always in that order). While their latest collection picks up political themes, earlier stunts include throwing late-night booty bar parties and creating sculptures for the famous Burning Man Festival. At the time this book is going to print, ksubi is making headlines again; this time for having entered the *Business Review Weekly* rich list.

16 Glenmore Road, Paddington
9361 6291
86 Gould Street, Bondi
9300 8233
ksubi.com

FASHION_THE SYDNEY STYLE

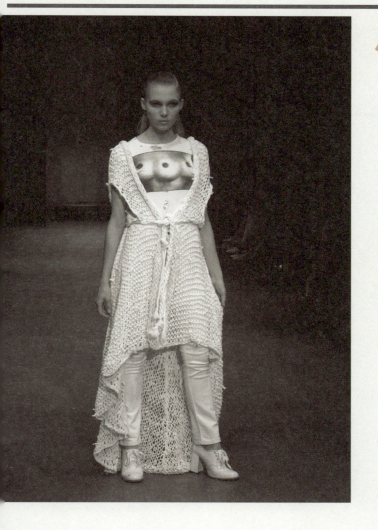

Established & sons

These local success stories turned global empires are the rocks of Sydney fashion, batting into the wind back when the rest of the world thought of Oz as a fashion backwater.

Wayne Cooper

London-born Wayne Cooper originally thought he'd be a lawyer. Then he realised his strong sense of style and love of clothes was much more suited to the fashion industry. Cooper moved to Australia and, in 1996, decided to go it alone, launching his own signature garments that are inspired by muses such as Faye Dunaway and Michelle Pfeiffer. And with two boutique stores in Sydney and another handful across the country, it seems the East London lad is an import we won't be giving up in a hurry.
Westfield Bondi Junction,
500 Oxford Street
9387 5855
The Strand Arcade,
412–414 George Street, Sydney
9221 5292
waynecooper.com.au

Leona Edmiston

Today producing lavish frocks under her own name, Leona Edmiston immortalised her place in Australian fashion history when her and Peter Morrissey's joint venture was, reportedly, the first antipodean label ever to be featured editorially in US *Harper's Bazaar* in 1994. (Apparently the Sydney fashion set wanted that day declared a national holiday.) More than a decade later, Edmiston is still going strong with her sexy frocks that exude classic femininity. Her kids' range, Little Leona, helps snotty toddlers grow up to be stylishly-clad ladies. Buy it at five boutiques across town.
The Strand Arcade,
412–414 George Street, Sydney
9221 7277
88 William Street, Paddington,
9331 7033
leonaedmiston.com

Lisa Ho

A vanguard of the Australian fashion industry for nearly 25 years, Lisa Ho began sewing at the age four and got her first sewing machine by the time she was ten. Years later, Ho started her career on a rickety fold-out table at Sydney's Paddington Market. Inspired by romanticism and vintage textiles, the label is now one of the most recognised in Australia, with a string of celebrity followers in tow. In 2004 she even gave the Commonwealth Bank staff a makeover.
2a–6a Queen Street, Woollahra
9360 2345
The Strand Arcade,
412–414 George Street, Sydney
9222 9711
lisaho.com

Alex Perry

As one of the veterans of local design, Alex Perry – never seen without sunglasses – has supplied red carpet celebrities with bottom-baring hemlines for over 15 years. As such, he has cultivated an impressive clientele to boot. Opening his first atelier in 1992, his fortés are racing gear, over-the-top cocktail dresses and plunging necklines as far as the eye can see.
The Strand Arcade,
412–414 George Street, Sydney
alexperry.com.au

Carla Zampatti

A true Australian fashion pioneer, Carla Zampatti has been in the game since 1965. In 1973 she was one of the first Australian designers to introduce swimwear into their collection, with a canary-yellow towelling T-bar maillot appearing on the cover of fashion magazine *Pol*. She designs up to eight collections each year, including the so-called 'cruise collection', which is usually only produced by European fashion houses who turn out summery garments such as swimwear in the thick of winter to cater for wealthy women on their Caribbean cruise ship adventures. Now running a chain of about 30 boutiques across Australia, Zampatti is also the Chairman of the Board of SBS Australia and has redesigned a car for Ford Australia especially for the women's market.
The Sheraton on the Park,
161 Elizabeth Street, Sydney
9264 3257
585 Military Road, Mosman
9960 2585
carlazampatti.com.au

FASHION_GREEN THREADS

Green threads

above
Sara Victoria's collection ranges from basics to ballgowns – so no one has to compromise ethics for glamour.

Fashion = sweat-shops, image-obsessed divas and a shallow, fickle, throwaway culture? You can now trade those terms for environmentally-friendly, ethically-motivated and community-minded. Here's how.

Sara Victoria

As far as fashion goes, the words 'green' and 'cool' have been sitting on opposite ends of the spectrum for as long as we can think. But Sara Victoria, the lady behind the eponymous label, is steadily working away at instilling some cool into organic fashion. Her pieces, ranging from underpants to overcoats, are all made from 100% organic cotton (or other eco materials such as hemp and tencil, made from tree fibres) and dyed only with natural colours. They are far from the hessian sacks you might have previously associated with eco fashion. Have a look at her entire collection on the website.
saravictoria.com.au

Sam Elsom

After running his label Funukolo for about three years, Central St Martin's graduate Sam Elsom called it quits in 2006 to start something a little more worthwhile. Launching a brand-new label under his own name, a pair of jeans made from organic cotton and sold on Net-a-Porter became a big hit. The young designer now works with suppliers and manufacturers around the world to ensure that the materials he uses are produced under safe and fair conditions for workers and the environment alike. Concentrating on age-old processes of hand tailoring, he now produces suits, dresses, organic basics and jeans in gelato-hued washes. No wonder David Jones signed him up quick smart.
elsom.com.au

Boutiques

Frocks, Frills & Fancy

The tastemakers of the city, boutiques are handmaidens to the fashion set. Delivering style on a platter for the delectation of their patrons, the stores listed here present the best in show of Sydney garment design.

Alfie's Friend Rolfe

This 30-square-metre shop on the ground floor of a typical 1930s Darlinghurst apartment building has now been open for six years. Co-owners Rob Street and Kyle Roxburgh continue to stock 'a tight collection of kick-ass labels' for both women and men. Among these are Lover, Alice McCall, ksubi, Kate Sylvester and Karen Walker for the ladies, and hem & haw, Franklin Marshall, Evisu, WMC and Duffer for the gents.
221 Darlinghurst Road, Darlinghurst
9361 0220

Arida

Situated on a corner at the stylish end of Potts Point, Arida is a strong proponent of international design in the city. Stocking both clothes (think Stella McCartney and Marc Jacobs, but also the new eco-label Edun, founded by Bono's wife Ali Hewson) and homewares, Arida portrays an entire lifestyle: the kind that involves you pulling up out the front in a brand new European car. Guaranteed you bump into the most stylishly dressed Sydneysiders here.
61 Macleay Street, Potts Point
9357 4788
arida.com.au

Blood Orange

After surrendering themselves to an inevitable change of vocation, Olivia Beynon and Loren Abood – both interior designers – fitted out their fashion store themselves. Dominated by a striking feature wall of pressed-metal panels, the store represents local designers such as Lover, Ellery and Michelle Robinson, as well as well-loved but little-known international labels such as French minimalists APC,

FASHION_BOUTIQUES

above
Since opening two years ago, Blood Orange has become a destination boutique thanks to its unique vision and fashion sense.

and the cool chic of Manhattanite Alice Ritter. It's a little out of the way from the fashion havens of Paddington and Surry Hills, but it's definitely worth the journey!
35 Elizabeth Bay Road,
Elizabeth Bay
9357 2424
bloodorange.com.au

Capital L
This is more than just a store! Capital L has cult status among all fashion fiends. For good reason. If it's a new label with a promising future, you'll find it here first. This was the case, for instance, with the line of Mad Cortes, revered today, but barely known in the early days when designer Mira Vukovic personally dropped off her gear. Dress models or watch short films, listen to music or gaze at work from up-and-coming local artists, it all happens in the one place that's refreshingly off the main drag. The long list of designer stock is something that'll keep you busy for hours, and along with the best of boutique Aussie and NZ booty, they also stock their own in-house label Please Louise. If you want your fingertips on this city's fashion pulse, Capital L is the place to go.
333 South Dowling Street,
Surry Hills
9361 0111

Christensen Copenhagen
Responsible for reintroducing Burberry back into the Australian fashion market, Christensen Copenhagen are certainly style-savvy, presenting the finest current season collection from Europe and stocking designers such as Paul & Joe, Matthew Williamson, Mayle and Missoni. But perhaps

FASHION_BOUTIQUES

most lavish is the store's layout – yet another reason to schedule a stop-over in Copenhagen.
2 Guilfoyle Avenue, Double Bay
9328 9755
christensencopenhagen.com.au

Dobry Den
When travelling in Eastern Europe, Keira Blue and Nicole Skilbeck fell in the love with the phrase 'dobry den', meaning 'hello' or 'good day' in Slovak. It's now been over a year that the two combined their love for the word with their love for fashion and quirky accessories and swung open the doors to their store in Crown Street. It's truly rock n' roll, with plenty of black and streetwear. That's why you'll find a lot of Melbourne labels here, like the eternally-brooding Claude Maus or Alpha60. They're paired up with funky accessories by fellow Melburnian Princess Tina and joined by New Zealander Cybele. The clothes and accessories on offer are ever-changing and rest assured the ladies are always looking for new and exciting wares from far-flung places with exotic names.
326 Crown Street, Surry Hills
0402 741 123
dobryden.com.au

Duck Egg Blue
Former fashion marketing executive Leanne Carter-Taylor escaped the London rat-race just in time for the new millennium and, three years later, opened this wonderful Balmain homewares and fashion store, which brings a slice of London chic to Sydney town. In doing so, she has also become a supporter of the local fashion scene, stocking neighbourhood labels Ginger & Smart, Fleur Wood, knitwear line Jac & Jack and Cohen et Sabine, as well as Carl Knapp's beautifully tailored suits, now all the rage. The brilliant ceramics of David Edmonds are also on show as well as for sale in the online shop – we're certain some of them come in duck-egg blue.
246 Darling St, Balmain
9810 8855
duckeggblue.com.au

From St Xavier
This urban store couldn't be further away from the beach culture that is Bondi, even though you can hear the waves rolling in. Stocking mainly streetwear labels, the store offers a great selection of local and imported wares, and not always the usual suspects. You'll find Buddhist Punk clothes here, the label where both Alice McCall and Jessie Hill cut their teeth.
75a Gould Street, Bondi
9365 4644
… *continued p. 214*

Belinda

One of Sydney's chief arbiters of taste is neither a fashion editor nor a fashion designer, it's fashion retailer Belinda Seper. Fifteen years, twelve Australian stores (nine of them in Sydney) and a South African outlet, but not a single advertisement; yet her name is gold in Sydney's frock business. How she did it? Not only does this style predator have the best nose for sniffing out emerging talent, she's also got the shiniest coat when it comes to presenting, and the loudest bark when it comes to defending her empire. Her first store opened in 1992, at a time when Australia was known only as a place to export to, not from, and the country's fashionistas suffered an almost impenetrable cultural cringe. The former army recruit and model decided it was time to change that. While she personally selected international avant-garde designers for her store, she also took on the likes of Collette Dinnigan, Willow and Akira. And was surprised by the response. It wasn't until eight years later that her multi-brand boutique approach germinated The Corner Shop, the venture that truly put Australian design on the wishlist of Australia's frock elite. While her other stores catered to a more upmarket clientele, it was here that many a fledgling label found early fame and recognition, both through Seper herself and the clientele the store attracted. As such, Seper is known to have brokered many a successful fashion career. Catering to Sydney's obsession with unique finds, the Frock Exchange, now in Double Bay and Balmain, sells top-quality vintage clothes and allows loyal patrons to exchange their pre-loved Belinda frocks for the next generation.

FASHION_BOUTIQUES

right
The original Corner Shop in William Street.

Belinda
8 Transvaal Avenue, Double Bay
93286288

MLC Centre, 19 Martin Place, Sydney
92330781

39 William Street, Paddington
93808721
belinda.com.au

The Corner Shop
43 William Street, Paddington
93809828

The Strand Arcade,
412–414 George Street, Sydney
9228 1788

Belinda Shoe Salon
14 Transvaal Avenue,
Double Bay
93278199

The Frock Exchange
see pp. 222-223

FASHION_BOUTIQUES

above
One of the best addresses for Sydney-designed fashion: Capital L.

… from p. 211

The Graduate Store
Ever the fashionable location, the Strand Arcade isn't home only to established frock folk. Thanks to the initiative of the Fashion Design Studio at TAFE NSW and the support of the Strand Arcadians themselves, the Graduate Store offers new designers the opportunity to display and sell their collections to the public, and gives punters the chance to snap up some one-off and interesting designs for an affordable price. It's what you call a win-win situation. And who knows, you might just discover the next Akira here.
The Strand Arcade,
412–414 George Street, Sydney
9233 4413

House of Capulet
Far from the usual fashion destinations, this is an exclusive boutique located in a loft in Cronulla. While it's not classic drama, it's still a story of kinship, owned by brothers Matt and Daniel Hart, who stock exclusive ranges from Australian and international designer and streetwear labels such as The Cassette Society, the revered My Pet Square and Melbourne's Alpha60. Even if you don't find your Romeo in there, you'll know where he might be shopping.
28a Cronulla Street, Cronulla
9544 3886

Incu
In Korean, Incu means 'to inspire', and that they do. There are a number of stores around Sydney; the one in the city has a somewhat industrial feeling, while the one in Paddington also stocks one-off pieces. Designers represented by Incu are the cream of the crop of Sydney design, including newcomers Silence is Golden and Shakuhachi, but also some New Zealand talent like ever-popular Karen Walker and her lesser known – but not lesser talented – protégé Mala Brajkovic. There are art installations in here too. One of them was done by the boys from Astoria, who also customised a line of footwear for the shop.
500 George Street, Sydney
9266 0244
256 Oxford Street, Paddington
9331 6070

FASHION_BOUTIQUES

Orson & Blake
A veritable Sydney design institution, Orson & Blake is best known for selling homewares and furniture, but the basement of its expansive Surry Hills gallery is a paradise for local style hunters. Mixing Sydney and Melbourne labels with the international avant-garde, as well as displaying design books, designer baby gear and accessories, you can be absolutely certain that your wallet won't make it out of here unscathed. From Romance was Born to Rittenhouse, the styles represented here range from wonderfully weird to wonderfully wearable. Representation in this store is at the top of many a local designer's wish list.
483 Riley Street, Surry Hills
83992525
orsonandblake.com.au

Our Spot
Conceived as a cross between gallery and concept store, Our Spot was a bit of a secret destination when it opened in 2001 in a clandestine location down a lane off Crown Street. At the time, Darlinghurst was awash predominantly with vintage clothes stores, and this place was something new. Since then, however, the owners have refined their vision in a new store in Liverpool Street, just selling fashion. This includes men's sneakers and T-shirts mainly from Australia and the US, including stuff by local designers Beat Poet. Notwithstanding their success, Our Spot is still one of Sydney's best-kept fashion secrets.
221 Liverpool Street, Darlinghurst
8354 0300

Paris Texas
A relatively new addition to the Sydney fashion scene, Paris Texas is an offspring of local fashion agency Dollface. Opening in 2006, industry insider Annette Verrusio has assembled an invigoratingly eclectic mix in her Bourke Street boutique, which is a platform for young designers to springboard their collection into the fashion arena. This quirky, off-beat collection of Paris meets the wild wild West has cultivated a faithful following since it opened, catering to the most fastidious of fashionistas, the most selective of shoppers and the craftiest of consumers. Labels include Silence is Golden, Bec & Bridge, State of Georgia, Bless'd are the Meek, Life with Bird and Fleur Wood to name a few.
729 Bourke Street, Surry Hills
9319 2709

above
Incu stocks a variety of local and international design.

Parlour X

Back when Sydney's walls were still predominantly painted white, Eva Galambos opened her eclectically dressed boutique in Paddington's Five Ways. She furnished the classic Victorian terrace with antique chandeliers and cabinets, and papered it with a splashy baroque Florence Broadhurst print in deep red and cream. And although she emphasises that 'it's not just about the clothes, it's about creating that "parlour" feeling,' stock includes an array of stand-alone designers. There are international pieces by Comme des Garcons, Viktor & Rolf, Vivienne Westwood and Alexander McQueen, and on the home front, Willow, Camilla & Mark, Josh Goot and Tina Kalivas fill out the racks.
213 Glenmore Road, Paddington
9331 0999
parlourx.com.au

Poepke

After discovering their mutual love for Northern European design, and the lack thereof in Sydney, co-owners Nicola Lie and Annabelle Buchanan settled into this little terrace shop in one of the most popular, fashionista-friendly shopping district. With an evident French / German chic (think Bernhard Willhelm, the fashion wunderkind who's made dirndls look cool), brands such as Dries Van Noten, Vernique Branquinho and Christian Wijnants are only some of the Belgian labels that put the proverbial cream on the, er, waffle. But the ladies haven't neglected some antipodean representation. There's To Sire With Love, Bassike, Rittenhouse and New Zealanders NOM*D. The design focus extends to the interior, where vintage class, European style and local design meet. The poofs made from milk crates and recycled billboard vinyl are by local designer Stefan Lie.
47 William Street, Paddington
9380 7611

Pretty Dog

A slightly hidden gem among the bustle of Newtown's students and alternative scene, the store sits just off the main drag. Formerly a vintage clothing haven, Pretty Dog has now turned to showcasing the creations of upcoming

Australian designers. Cohen et Sabine, Tina Borg and Lover are just some of the homegrown labels stocked, and there's a separate section for men's apparel as well. The very best of New Zealand designers are here too, with names such as Karen Walker, Kate Sylvester and Deborah Sweeney featuring prominently. The pretty pooch also features jewellery by Moira Delaney.
1a Brown Street, Newtown
9519 7839

Reads

Reads opened up shop in 1976, first trading as Reads Town and Country Wear. Since then, owner Mary Read has developed it into one of Sydney's most comprehensive women's fashion stores. The interior, influenced by European styling, and redesigned by Sydney designer Dino Raccanello of Arclinea, helps customers view the garments in their best light. These include local labels Lisa Ho, Caravana, Trent Nathan and Carolyn Taylor. Imports from New Zealand and England are classically cut, simple fits by Trelise Cooper, Ashley Fogel, Nougat and Penny Black. From pure fashion indulgences to eclectic contemporary pieces, Reads has a strikingly stylish wardrobe full of glamourous garments to suit the lavish lady. Reads also donates profits to Cambodia in conjunction with established homeware outlet across the road, Cambodia House.
130 Queen Street, Woollahra
9328 1036

Riada

Mostly representing the European avant-garde, this store on a corner of fashion paradise Queen Street has been revving up the style of many Sydney fashionistas, including the local designers. Known for its individuality, this is the place to spot previously unknown international talent and ensure your wardrobe is always up-to-date with the latest trends and luxury garments.
Queens Court, 118 Queen Street, Woollahra
93630654

above
Pretty Dog holds the local fashion fort in Newtown.

Somedays
This must be one of the most coveted fashion destinations in Sydney. Its Nordic cool comes from the Scandinavian frocks this gallery-boutique hybrid has on offer. They hand-pick the Swedish fashion talent but have also added a couple of local designers they couldn't resist, such as Melbourne outfit hem & haw. The adjoining gallery in the loft-style space offers up-and-coming artists a chance to promote and sell their original artwork without the pomp and circumstance of many traditional galleries, whether they are seasoned professionals or fresh out of year 12 art class. Expect to see a lot of well-dressed, very hip, Nordic-accented folk at the openings every second week or so.
72b Fitzroy Street, Surry Hills
9331 6637

Strelitzia
This is one of the stalwarts of Sydney fashion, but after it's 22nd year, Strelitzia recently had a makeover. It's a wide space, with a black and white interior, carved columns and long lounges. But despite this European feel, owner Moyra Peach stocks predominantly local labels, and makes a point of scoping out the emerging local talent. There is a huge range of labels here, both from Australia and New Zealand, inlcuding Akira and Melbourne's Metalicus, plus Kiwi labels Verge and Zambesi. As such, the age of the clientele is wide-ranging. The pieces are quirky and unpredictable – you never know what you're going to find hidden among it all.
327 Darling Street, Balmain
9810 7290

above
Paris Texas is a platform for young designers to springboard their collection into the fashion arena.

Tuchuzy
This store has been at its sandy Bondi location forever, holding the fort for local and quirky international designs in a setting where surfwear tends to prevail. Among the labels on offer are shoes from My Pet Square, Nobody denim from Melbourne and the pretty frocks of New Zealand's Kate Sylvester.
90 Gould Street, Bondi
9365 5371
tuchuzy.com

Via Alley
You won't find too many frocks here, but everything to go with them. There's a reason why the word 'treasure trove' has become a staple in retail copywriting vocab – Via Alley shows you why. Its cave-like interior houses knick-knacks from local and international artists and makers alike. Lots of local T-shirt makers also sell through Via Alley.
289 Liverpool Street, Darlinghurst
93311119
viaalley.com

Von Troska
Like so many local labels, Von Troska had its humble beginnings in a small stall at Paddington Market. But, over 20 years later, the rickety tables are long gone, and in their place are five stores around NSW, four of them in Sydney. As well as their own label, 'Von Troska and Friends' also stock some pretty frocks by Sydney labels and New Zealand talent.
QVB, 455 George Street, Sydney
9269 0015
294 Oxford Street, Paddington
9360 752

FASHION

FASHION_OUT OF TOWN DESIGNERS_BOUTIQUES

Have shop, will travel

From interstate and across the Tasman come some not-to-be-missed designer labels that have set up shop in Sydney.

Alannah Hill
Flouncy, frilly, girly and very idiosyncratic – Alannah Hill's colourful label became a fashion icon when Melbourne was still drowning in a sea of black. Originally from Tasmania, Hill arrived in Melbourne as a penniless 17-year-old with no formal fashion education, but with her own style and vision. Over the years she has continously fine-tuned her range, opening nine glitzy stores throughout Australia, and Sydney's taken to her style like a duck to water.
118–120 Oxford Street, Paddington
9380 9174
The Strand Arcade,
412–414 George Street, Sydney
9221 1251
alannahhill.com.au

Gorman
About half a decade ago, a former nurse made waves in the Melbourne fashion pool by supplying folk with a wonderful selection of Thai fishing pants in beautiful fabrics not normally associated with this casual wear. A few years down the track, Gorman has developed her fledgling label into a veritable Australian womenswear icon, one which harmonises utilitarian styling with girlish overtones. More recently, an organic range of basics has hit the racks in Gorman's beautifully different store on Oxford Street.
30 Oxford Street, Paddington
9331 7088
gorman.ws

Body
It was while dancing in New York that designer Dainy Sawatzky decided to turn her rehearsal wear into everyday wear, and such was the birth of Body, flattering but functional effortless attire. Originally opening in Melbourne, now with two stores, Sydney now has its own flagship store.
32 Queen Street, Woollahra
9362 0930
body.com.au

Easton Pearson
Brisbane's most successful fashion label was set up by duo Pamela Easton and Lydia Pearson in 1989, who quickly became known for the crafted and delicate detailing of their evening frocks. Their luxurious and elegant, often hand-embroidered textiles enjoy a strong following in Sydney, so the pair operate an entire store here.
18 Elizabeth Street, Paddington
9331 4433
eastonpearson.com

above
The Gorman store on Oxford Street pairs a Swedish log cabin aesthetic with sensible womenswear from Melbourne.

Scanlan & Theodore
Feminine without frills, structure without stricture, and subtle without being slight, Scanlan & Theodore has been defining Melbourne style for nearly two decades. The label began with a tiny boutique in Chapel Street, Melbourne, in 1987, resolutely rejecting the boxy power suits of the time, and the garments are now highly coveted both here and overseas.
122 Oxford Street, Paddington
93809388
Chatswood Chase, 345 Victoria Avenue, Chatswood
94101711
scanlantheodore.com.au

World New Zealand
They call it a factory of ideas and environments, and they're not kidding. Established in Auckland almost two decades ago and now celebrated as royalty in their homeland (co-founder Denise L'Estrange-Corbet received an MBE from the Queen for her services to the fashion industry in New Zealand), they are equally as admired by Sydneysiders for their 'witty effrontery' (according to *Time Magazine* Fashion Editor Michael Fitzgerald). If fashion retail had a pole position, this would be it.
1 Glenmore Road, Paddington
93680442
worldbrand.co.nz

Zambesi
It's the antidote to much of Sydney's fashion, but it's so much loved! A Kiwi label associated with brooding sensibility and asymmetric cuts, it's perfect for fashion lovers who know how to express themselves through dress. Zambesi has established a devoted following in their home country, and the art crowd flocks to not only indulge in Zambesi's fine wear, but also in a raft of other moody Kiwis and the European avant-garde.
5 Glenmore Road, Paddington
9331 1140
zambesi.co.nz

Vintage

One-off finds and classic style mark the harvest of Sydney's coterie of old-world stores, where fashionistas locate that special something to set them off from the crowd.

Blue Spinach

This store supports local designers, and as such the ranges of home-grown labels such as Collette Dinnigan, Zimmermann, Alannah Hill and Scanlan & Theodore are on show. Alongside is their selection of recycled international designer labels, where you might be lucky enough to pick up a little goody such as a Chloe bag, a Christian Dior silk tie, a pair of Missoni shoes or a DVF frock. The shop is split into men's and women's – girls on one side, boys on the other.
348 Liverpool Street, Darlinghurst
9331 3904
bluespinach.com.au

Glamourpuss Emporium

The retro style of Glamourpuss is a dream for ladies who love to look pretty. Specialising in gorgeous handbags, dresses, gowns and skirts, Glamourpuss is all about beautiful, high-quality garments inspired by that exceptionally pretty time of the 1950s. They also stock silk wraps and beaded jewellery boxes for somewhere safe to store your trinkets. Glamourpuss has been open in Erskineville since March 2007, previously residing in Manly, but they also have a mail service for those who enjoy the excitement of a parcel arriving by post.
38 Swanson Street, Erskineville
9550 2275
glamourpuss.com.au

Melvin & Doyle

Specialising in the kinds of items that age like a fine wine, Melvin & Doyle stock chic classic vintage pieces handpicked from the most fashionable hot spots – Chanel, Gucci, Prada and YSL – as well as accessories that please every palate. Owner and local designer Bianca Doyle also stocks her own label, Notions of Legacy, made from vintage prints and fabrics. And while you'll find anything from stunning 1920s hand-beaded flapper gowns to Jackie O on vacation in 1970s Pucci, this vintage cache is worth visiting just for a peek at the wild pink walls and antique confessional box changing rooms.
59 William Street, Paddington
9361 4023

The Frock Exchange

This store is another brainchild of Sydney's fashion queen Belinda. In a town that's crazy about scouring

right
Belinda Seper's Frock Exchange is perfect for a city that's crazy about scouring vintage collections.

vintage finds, she's right on the money. Ever the businesswoman, she's even invented her own currency specially for this old-world haven. If you bring your pre-loved Belinda clothes to the Clovelly-based store or its much larger sister in Balmain, you're rewarded with B-dollars – cash to buy more Belindas. And you'll need them – the place is full of the finest fashion imaginable.
407 Darling Street, Balmain
98182066
221 Clovelly Road, Clovelly
9664 9188
belinda.com.au

Vintage Clothing Shop
It's been around since 1974, and with an unusual and eclectic selection of original vintage clothes and accessories complemented by a range of stylish costume jewellery, this small store in St James Arcade continues to be a vintage aficionado's dream. With antique lace pieces, beautiful brooches, smoking jackets, blazing ballgowns and shimmering shoes, all the stock is well-considered, in immaculate condition and extremely covetable. The interior is cosy and gorgeous with beautiful 1950s floral carpet and art deco showcases.
St James Arcade, 80 Castlereagh Street, Sydney
9238 0090

Zoo Emporium
Spurred on by a love for vintage treasure-hunting and a collective passion for things from bygone eras, this superfly funky vintage store is the longest standing on the Crown Street strip. As such, it holds a massive selection of accessories, bags, sunglasses, clothes and costume jewellery from the 1940s right through to the 1980s, with everything from retro rock-a-billy rags to flower-power flares. Even the shop fit-out feels like a glam 1970s disco. There are watermelon-pink walls, a restored keyboard counter and an installation of 20 mirrored disco balls that hang from the roof. Undoubtedly opulent in sensibility, Zoo Emporium, as the name suggests, is an eclectic mix of vintage goodies jam-packed with garments that will take you back to any decade you desire.
332 Crown Street, Surry Hills
9380 5990

To Market, To Market!

Fresh product is the name of the game in these little hubs that have helped germinate so much new talent and continue to deliver fashion finds. Here's the cream of the crop.

Balmain Market
It started as a working-class market, but there's hardly a trace left of ye olde ginger-beer days. With a lean towards second-hand books, homewares and jewellery, the market is also known as a testing ground for the ambitions of local designers, especially those who start up kids' clothing labels.
Saturdays, 7.30am to 4pm
St Andrew's Church, Cnr Darling Street and Curtis Road, Balmain

Bondi Market
This bazaar, open every Sunday on the grounds of Bondi Beach Public School, is becoming more and more popular with up-and-coming designers. This is the spot where the guys from ksubi flogged their first pair of jeans, which hints at the vibe of the place. Urban, cool and of course infused with beach culture, there's lots of vintage and second-hand gear on offer as Bondi residents spring-clean their wardrobes and garages.
Sundays, 10am to 4pm
Bondi Beach Public School on Campbell Parade
bondimarkets.com.au

Hope Street Market
Here's something completely different and probably Sydney's most exciting development as far as markets go. The stalls aren't actually erected on Hope Street, but are designed to bring hope to the street. Set up by the same-named organisation, the irregular weekend event invites designers and makers from all over Sydney to show and flog what they've got, donating part of the profits to the homeless projects the charity oversees. The turnout – and consequently the turnover – has been huge at recent events, with fashion and T-shirt designers setting up next to jewellers, craftspeople and other creatively minded individuals. Check the website for the next event.
182 Campbell Street, Surry Hills
hopestreetmarkets.com

Glebe Market
It may not be as stylish as some of the others, but Glebe market – like the place itself – has the bohemian vibe down-pat. You can stock up on pre-loved camel-hair jumpers for the kids, purchase some Sydney-made jewellery for yourself or take home some scented candles for grandma. Held every Saturday on the grounds of Glebe Primary School, the market is a true Sydney institution. People have moved here because of it.
Saturdays, 10am to 4pm
Glebe Public School,
Glebe Point Road

FASHION_MARKETS

Kirribilli Market
This neighbourhood fair is popular with the city's fashion designers and stylists, and great for picking up a second or sample from a big name. There's the ubiquitous bric-a-brac, homewares and handmade jewellery, as well as heaps of other stuff, including gourmet food and a beautiful view.
Last Saturday of the month, 7am to 3.30pm
Bradfield Park North, Kirribilli

Paddington Market
As far as fashion goes, this is the mother of all Sydney markets. Paddington Market has rocked the cradle of fledgling labels like Lisa Ho and sass & bide, who have since grown up into fully-fledged, super-sized adults. Among the many stalls of pre-loved and specially designed fashion, there are lots of crafty products and objects. Of course there's some typical marketplace mass-production, but rest assured among them are some future stars. The hugely successful Dinosaur Design crew also started here. And if you want to know who's going to make it big and who isn't, the clairvoyants are on site too.
Saturdays, 10am to 4pm
395 Oxford Street, Paddington
paddingtonmarkets.com.au

Surry Hills Market
Held once a month, the Surry Hills market is as cool as the crowd who shop there. It's been around for over 20 years and still retains its distinct community feel, with residents trading second-hand goods and the occasional handmade item, but it's definitely a place to be seen and take home some weird and wonderful bargains.
First Saturday of every month, 10am to 4pm
Surry Hills Neighbourhood Centre, Cnr Bourke and Mort Streets

---

Young Blood Market
This twice-yearly fete is held on the premises of great design supporter the Powerhouse Museum, and attracts fashionable crowds both behind and in front of the stalls. Peruse an array of jewellery, homewares, fashion and many other things on offer. As there's a rigorous selection process, it's quite a 'curated' show. Many of the designers are already quite successful and enjoy meeting customers and getting some feedback. Check the website for upcoming dates, it's a great chance to meet your maker.
Twice a year
500 Harris Street, Ultimo
powerhousemuseum.com/youngblood

226 ART_CONTENTS

Art

- 229 Introduction
- 230 Take a walk_artist-run initiatives tour
- 235 Artspace_profile
- 237 Museums & galleries
- 239 Things to see
- 242 Take a walk_galleries tour

Introduction

left
The Artspace residency studio.

There's a reason this book is called the Sydney Design Guide – because it focuses on design. But we are also quite aware that many a design freak has arty leanings, or at least draws inspiration from the worlds of sculpture, painting, drawing and so on (maybe literature and dance too, but that's pushing it a bit far here). And really, there's some amazing Sydney art stuff and goings-on that we just couldn't leave alone. So we asked our experts in the field to list a selection of major players, independent innovators and a few rebels doing it on their own, profiled herein. We've also included some pointers to major public artworks around Sydney town and most importantly a couple of walks for you, so all you have to do is follow and stare.

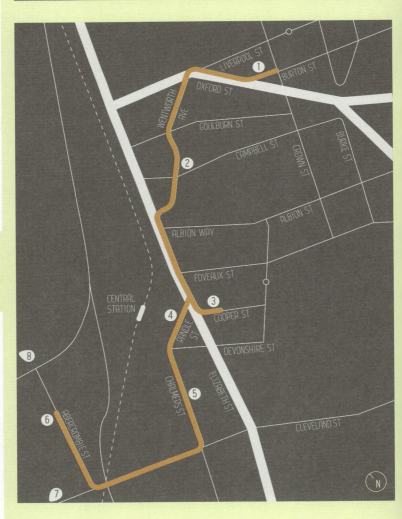

Take a walk: artist-run initiatives

Put simply, artist-run initiatives (or ARIs) are galleries run by artists for artists. They are often tucked away: down side streets, through unmarked doors and up rickety staircases. Artist and art critic Dominique D'Angeloro walks us through eight of the best from Darlinghurst to St Peters.

Finding an affordable space to lease poses the biggest problem for galleries in Sydney. ARIs are almost exclusively not-for-profit; fuelled instead by volunteers with a desire to explore, promote and expand new forms of art making. There is no single blueprint for these spaces and each usually bears the markings of the creative people behind it. It is also a challenge to get government funding unless the space has been up and running for a while. This means that Sydney ARIs are typically fluid spaces, shape-shifting in response to changes in rental prices or the circumstances of the directors. Since some galleries are here today but gone tomorrow, think of the following list as a snapshot in time.

Monster Children Gallery

Child of the street culture mag *Monster Children* (which spruiked a recent edition with the line 'Buy the issue and help another two million trees get chopped down'), this gallery deftly rides the territory between street art, skate / surf culture and design. Housed upstairs from a bunch of fashion boutiques since early 2005, Monster Children Gallery is the go-to space for work by local and international graphic designers.
20 Burton Street,
Surry Hills / Darlinghurst
monsterchildren.com

China Heights

China Heights has a reputation as the most streetwise of the Sydney ARIs. Located in a large Surry Hills warehouse, directors Edward Woodley and Mark Drew circulate word of their shows though MySpace and focus on very short exhibitions with very big openings. The exhibitions cut a mix of street art, photography, design and fashion, often showing local talent alongside international artists. With China Heights nearly five years old, Woodley and Drew have recently opened a sister-space called Oxford Art Factory. With a nod to Warhol's creative nest, the new initiative looks to be part gallery, part theatre, part social set.
16–28 Foster Street,
Surry Hills
chinaheights.com

Chalk Horse

Initially working on a roving model, the Half Dozen Collective were so-called because they organised six shows each year at various venues around town. However in March 2007 the group set up their own sweet home in this slick Surry Hills warehouse, consisting of two exhibition spaces. Chalk Horse continue to make their own rules, sidelining group shows in favour of showcasing work by solo artists and employing a full-time gallery manager to achieve smooth-as administration. The rise and rise of Chalk Horse sees them set to open a third space upstairs, while dedicating one of the downstairs galleries to new media arts.
56 Cooper Street, Surry Hills
chalkhorse.com.au

above
Art is everything; the launch of fashion label Ellery at China Heights in early 2007.

④ Gaffa Gallery

Refusing to become unstuck after a shaky start on Crown Street in 2006, Gaffa has recently relocated to large new premises elsewhere in Surry Hills. Run by a group of artists from an object-based background, they aim to provide a unique platform for artists and designers working with glass, metal, plastics, jewellery and ceramics.
7 Randle Street,
Surry Hills
gaffa.com.au

⑤ firstdraft

Celebrating its 21st birthday this year, firstdraft is the undisputed granddaddy of the ARI scene. The changing board of about eight directors – each on a two-year contract – ensures that the space is constantly fuelled by new energy and ideas. The gallery is made up of three spaces that are regularly filled to capacity at the monthly openings. Not content to rest on their old-timer laurels, firstdraft has instigated several new initiatives in recent years including an artist studio residency, an emerging curator's program and monthly artist talks.
116–118 Chalmers Street,
Surry Hills
firstdraftgallery.com

⑥ MOP

Opening MOP Project in a Redfern warehouse in 2003, directors Ron and George Adams displayed a keen eye for hard-edge painting practices. Run from the get-go with thorough professionalism, the gallery quickly became a favourite for artists to visit and exhibit in. In June 2007, MOP relocated to its slick new

above
More China Heights / An installation by Marita Fraser and Alex Lawler at MOP in 2007.

Chippendale premises, dropping the 'Projects' in its name. Long-gone too is the early focus on any one genre; the two-space gallery regularly plays host to video, sound and installation.
27–39 Abercrombie Street, Chippendale
mop.org.au

SNO Contemporary Art Projects

Run by a group of seven artists called SNO (Sydney Non-Objective), this gallery has eyes only for contemporary, non-objective art or what they describe as 'post-formalist activity'. The group opened the small gallery Factory 11 in 2004, but have since moved into their current SNO premises consisting of four spaces. The gallery is hooked up to networks of like-minded artists around the world, making SNO a kind of portal to the formalist art universe through exchange programs, international satellite shows and publications.
175 Marrickville Road, Marrickville
sno.org.au

May's Lane

While in cities like Melbourne graffiti art is around every street corner, Sydney's graffiti police seem determined to keep the bricks bare. In 2005, May's Lane sought to reclaim some artistic territory by erecting a wall of panels as a sprawling outdoor gallery space. Located down a side street in St Peters, May's curator invites local and visiting graffiti artists to realise ambitious large-scale works and exhibit them for a four-week period.
May's Lane, St Peters
mays.org.au

ART_ARTSPACE_PROFILE

Artspace

above
No longer the Gunnery, but still explosive: Artspace.

Across the road from the fancy Finger Wharf in Woolloomooloo, the historic Gunnery building is home to one of the city's most progressive art venues, Artspace. Before it opened in this location in the early 1990s (it was previously in Surry Hills), the three-storey building was home to squatters and penniless artists; today it aims to further art through state-funded residency programs and exhibitions. The focus is mainly on media art practices such as installation, video, performance and sound art. Artspace hosts visitors from around Australia and the world, who undertake both residential (live-in) and non-residential studio work. Building a critical context and fostering work relationships between Australian and international artists, curators and writers, Artspace presents up to 30 gallery projects each year. Long involved in the development of critical writing, Artspace also publishes a number of exhibition catalogues, books and artist monographs to accompany major solo projects.
43–51 Cowper Wharf Road, Woolloomooloo
9356 0555
artspace.org.au

Museums & galleries

top left
Old meets new: the historic site that is CarriageWorks received an overhaul courtesy of architects Tonkin Zulaikha Greer.

photography
Michael Nicholson

bottom left
The extension to the historic Art Gallery of NSW building was designed by Denton Corker Marshall.

photography
John Gollings

A day out in Sydney's galleries and museums reveals much about the city's art, but also about its architecture and performance culture. Here's a small selection for the design-interested art enthusiast.

Art Gallery of NSW

Offering regular courses, lectures, workshops, films, performances, concerts and a never-ending round of exhibitions from Australia, overseas and the Gallery's own archives, there is always something to inspire in this extensive turn-of-the-19th-century building. The annual exhibition of children's art from around the state each November is a don't-miss, and you can build your own exhibition on the myVirtualGallery page. The Gallery even has a publishing arm, recently releasing the celebration of Indigenous art *One Sun, One Moon*, accompanied by a comprehensive exhibition in the Yiribana gallery. In The Domain on Art Gallery Road, you can walk from the Opera House through the Botanic Gardens to get there.
Art Gallery Road, The Domain
9225 1700
artgallery.nsw.gov.au

CarriageWorks

Sitting on the ridge between Newtown and Redfern, an old railway workshop has been transformed into one of the most interesting art venues in town, both from a programmatic as well as an architectural perspective. Providing an environment that pulses with creativity and innovation, CarriageWorks presents theatre, spoken word, music, dance and visual and hybrid arts. CarriageWorks' vast brick shell invites guests to explore a series of pockets inside this heritage-listed building, recently regenerated by architects Tonkin Zulaikha Greer. Containing two large, flexible theatre spaces, a

smaller gallery space, a scenery construction workshop, exhibition spaces, offices, a bar and a cafe, CarriageWorks has hosted a range of events including launches, exhibitions, gala dinners, cocktail functions, film and photo shoots and fashion shows by local celebrity designers such as Josh Goot. So make sure your, ahem, carriage works, then go for a ride to this place.
245 Wilson Street, Eveleigh
8571 9099
carriageworks.com.au

Museum of Contemporary Art

While the focus is on art rather than design, the Museum of Contemporary Art features an ongoing schedule of exhibitions and events that will inspire and educate, including international exhibitors and speakers. They hold workshops for adults, tours for babies (who are encouraged to bring their grown-ups along), and collections of modern photography, sculpture, video and installation that will complement your design leanings. The calendar on the website is a handy little tool for checking out what's on and when, the MCA building itself is worth a look and – hello – there's a store that emphasises Australian design.
140 George Street, The Rocks
9245 2400
mca.com.au

Museum of Sydney at the site of the first Government House

The byline is a nod to the heritage of the place, as the Museum is built on the original footings of the first-ever Australian Government House, now a feature exhibition. The permanent exhibitions are a play through the history of Sydney from Dreamtime up to the present day, using 1788 as a turning point. A good resource for learning about Sydney history and its architecture, they hold architecture-related exhibitions and the building itself is a heritage feature. Also, the MOS shop has a great range of books on Australian architecture, and is renowned for its Sydney souvenirs.
Cnr Phillip and Bridge Streets, Sydney
9251 5988
hht.net.au

Things to see

If you like to combine outdoor fun with an artistic experience, check the following destinations. Not all of them are permanent, so find out what's happening first.

Biennale of Sydney

Australia's largest celebration of contemporary visual art is held every second year from June to September in spots all over the city, and most events are free. Get a packed program from the website.
biennaleofsydney.com.au

Cockatoo Island

The largest island in Sydney Harbour, Cockatoo Island was once a convict prison, later developed as a naval shipyard and a school and reformatory for naughty girls. Since 2001, it has become a favourite art and cultural destination, featuring music and arts festivals. While still an industrial site, with work in progress, the Sydney Harbour Trust is now offering individual, business, community groups and institutions the opportunity to make their own history by using facilities on the island. There are lots of art-related and cultural events on all the time. Access to Cockatoo Island is via ferry from Circular Quay.
harbourtrust.gov.au

Sculpture by the Sea

Each year in November this spectacular show takes over Sydney's beaches. Australia's largest annual, outdoor, free-to-the-public sculpture exhibition displays a wide selection of work by hundreds of artists from different countries. Founded by David Handley from his lounge room 11 years ago, Sculpture by the Sea is now a huge event for locals and tourists alike, loved for both for its location and the atmosphere it generates. Past exhibitors include Tim MacFarlane Reid, Jon Denaro and Jennifer Cochrane. Take the coastal walk

240 ART_THINGS TO SEE

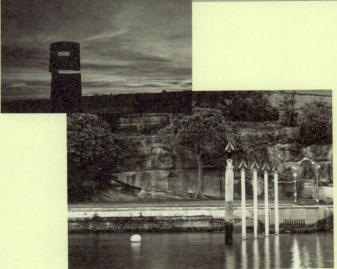

left, top and centre
Australian icons the beach and Ned Kelly – pop up in Sculpture by the Sea.

left, bottom
The Archeology of Bathing was one of the artworks commissioned prior to the Sydney 2000 Olympics. Both the Public: Art Place & Landscape walk and the Sydney Sculpture Walk visit its site.

photography
Courtesy Simeon King

from Bondi to Tamarama to take it all in. Although it's a true Sydney staple, there's now also a Sculpture by the Sea event in Perth.
sculpturebythesea.com

Public: Art, Place & Landscape walk

If you've got a couple of hours to spare, we highly recommend you take this fantastic guided tour led by the lads from Sydney Architecture Walks. It examines the city through its evolving attitude to the design of its public domain and the elements it contains: art, architecture and landscape. They map a living history on contemporary architectural, sculptural and urban projects and consider the role of art, architecture and design in the creation of some of Sydney's best-loved and most-used public spaces. The walk leads from the city towards Woolloomooloo Bay. Check the website for details (and have a look at the other tours while you're at it).
sydneyarchitecture.org

Sydney Sculpture Walk

The Games may be long over, but remaining is a legacy for all to enjoy. In and around the Botanic Gardens, you'll find ten specially commissioned contemporary artworks by some of Australia's (and the world's) finest artists. You can explore these artworks and at the same time enjoy the city and the harbour foreshore with the help of the Sydney Sculpture Walk map, which also provides information about the work and a walking route. Pick up the map at a tourist information stand or on the City of Sydney website.
cityofsydney.nsw.gov.au

Terminus Projects

For many people, public art is a cringe-worthy term conjuring up bronze statues of dead white men or incomprehensible blobs on street corners. Sarah Rawling and Clare Lewis, curators of Terminus Projects, set out to change that perception at the beginning of 2004. Since then, the two have co-directed and curated numerous site-specific projects including an inflatable cloud of recycled umbrellas that drifted across the city, live performances with politically charged recordings and an interactive video installation in Pitt Street Mall. Terminus' latest raft of projects was shown in mid-2007. Check out the website for details of upcoming events.
terminusprojects.org

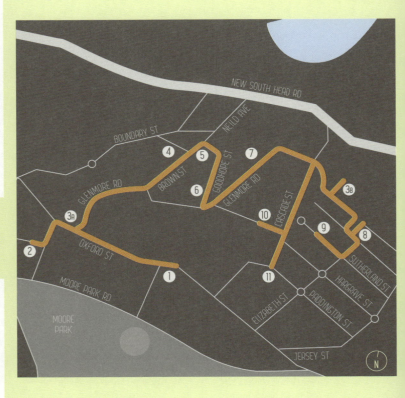

Take a walk: galleries

Katrina Schwarz, Editor of leading art mag *Art & Australia*, introduces ten not-to-be missed art destinations on her stomping ground, the suburb of Paddington.

More than just an affluent inner-city suburb where shopgirls are disdainful and coffees are $3.50, Paddington is a hub of contemporary art. The 2021 postcode embraces the smallest gallery (Three Foot Square) as well as the most influential (Roslyn Oxley9) and the most cluttered (Josef Lebovic). Contemporary art institutions (Sherman Contemporary Art Foundation, ACP) and commercial galleries, an art school and arthouse cinema all make Paddo a must-visit for Sydney's cultural tourist.

ACP – Australian Centre for Photography

As the name implies, ACP focuses on exhibiting photo-based art, and is supported by an expansive education program. Founded in 1973, it's Australia's longest-running contemporary art space, and also publishes *Photofile*, a journal esteemed for rigorous critical writing and high production values. ACP has two exhibition spaces: a foyer display area and a project wall for emerging artists. The exhibition program is diverse; both Australian and international artists are well-represented and there is a notable willingness to tackle confronting and controversial subjects. ACP's extensive workshop has facilities including b&w and colour darkrooms, a digital suite, a lighting studio and library.
257 Oxford Street, Paddington
9332 1455
acp.org.au

Ivan Dougherty Gallery

The University of NSW College of Fine Arts (COFA) has four galleries, including the alternative exhibition space Three Foot Square, which is little more than an illuminated hole in the wall. Ivan Dougherty Gallery is COFA's major space. Host to some ten exhibitions each year, IDG's focus is on 20th century and contemporary art across all disciplines. With a strong curatorial ethos, IDG has a deserved reputation for rigorous and innovative thematic exhibitions.
Selwyn Street, Paddington
9385 0726

Australian Galleries

Celebrating its 50th anniversary in 2006, Australian Galleries is a true national institution. Originating in the Melbourne suburb of Collingwood, where Tam and Anne Purves converted their pattern-manufacturing business into a gallery showcasing post-war Australian art, the business has expanded to include four gallery spaces in both Melbourne and Sydney. Now under the sole direction of Stuart Purves, a rare second-generation art dealer, there are two Paddington outposts. Painting and sculpture are shown in Roylston Street and the Glenmore Road space specialises in prints, drawings and watercolours. While Australian Galleries represents

above
Exterior view of Sherman Galleries.

photography
John Gollings
(Courtesy the artist and Sherman Galleries, Sydney)

a roster of established artists, look out too for the charcoal-on-paper works of Mika Utzon Popov, and for the diverse practice of Louis Pratt.
24 Glenmore Road, Paddington
9380 8744
15 Roylston Street, Paddington
9360 5177
australiangalleries.com.au

Stills Gallery

A commercial gallery entirely devoted to contemporary photography and multimedia art, Stills Gallery occupies an expansive warehouse conversion in residential Paddington. Since its inception in 1991, Stills has nurtured both emerging and established artists, and their roster of female photographers – including Pat Brassington, Petrina Hicks and Anne Noble – is particularly strong. The Gallery's program is accompanied by a series of artist talks and don't miss the extensive collection of prints in the Gallery stockroom.
36 Gosbell Street, Paddington
9331 7775
stillsgallery.com.au

left
Installation view of Michael Parekowhai *Eerst me fiets* (First my bicycle), 2006 at Roslyn Oxley9 Gallery showing *The Horn of Africa*, 2006 and *Parliament of Fools*, 2006.

photography
Courtesy of the artist and Roslyn Oxley9 Gallery, Sydney.

Sarah Cottier Gallery

A gallery with many lives and a long history, Sarah Cottier arrived in Paddington after a three-year hiatus and previous incarnations in Newtown and Redfern. Minimalist and abstract works dominate, bringing together established players – John Nixon, Andreas Reiter Raabe, Stephen Bram – and new lights – Gemma Smith, Koji Ryui, Huseyin Sami. Since re-opening late in 2006, the gallery has also staged a number of thoughtfully curated group shows.
3 Neild Avenue, Paddington
93563305
sarahcottiergallery.com

Sherman Galleries Contemporary Art Foundation

Gene Sherman, gallerist, French literature specialist and influential member of Sydney's cultural community, announced in early 2007 that the commercially-focused gallery she ran for 21 years would become a scholarship-led, not-for-profit foundation. Sherman Contemporary Art Foundation (SCAF), launched with a specially commissioned project by Chinese artist Ai Weiwei, engages specifically with contemporary art from the Asia-Pacific rim and emphasises education and creative partnerships. It's a natural and exciting expansion for a space that has always served as a cultural complex, encompassing an art gallery, sculpture garden, study and artist residence.
16–20 Goodhope Street, Paddington
9331 1112
shermangalleries.com.au

Harrison Galleries

Occupying the former site of Brian Moore Gallery, Harrison Galleries represents a promising stable of young artists. Their light-filled space hosts monthly exhibitions of artists working with a range of media. Group shows are a strength as is the gallery's clutch of super-talented painters – Dane Lovett and Anthony Lister chief among them.
294 Glenmore Road, Paddington
9380 7161
harrisongalleries.com.au

Roslyn Oxley9 Gallery

This is a gallery with a deserved international profile and a star-strewn line-up of artists. In a quiet pocket of Paddington, sharing a back lane with the *Art & Australia* office, the volume is turned up a notch at the much-anticipated exhibition openings where the crowd, A-list and art student alike, swells. Established in 1982 with a group of largely unknown artists, the Gallery now represents many of Australia's most visible, renowned and globe-straddling practitioners, including Patricia Piccinini, Tracey Moffatt, David Noonan, Bill Henson and 2007 Venice Biennale representative Callum Morton. When a new artist is added to the Roslyn Oxley9 roster, such as recently signed Newell Harry, you know they are one to watch.
8 Soudan Lane
(off Hampden Street),
Paddington
9331 1919
roslynoxley9.com.au

Kaliman Gallery

First established in 2001, owner Vasili Kaliman shifted this dynamic gallery to its current, high-ceilinged premises in 2006, formerly the site of iconic Sydney galleries Gitte Weise and Chandler Coventry. Kaliman has forged some interesting international connections, exhibiting the work of Louise Bourgeois, for example, and the Swiss-based Australian Glenn Sorensen. But it's the hot names and the rising stars – The Kingpins, Del Kathryn Barton, David Griggs, Ms & Mr, to name a few – that ensure every Kaliman opening is an unmissable event.
56 Sutherland Street,
Paddington
9357 2273
kalimangallery.com

Sullivan + Strumpf Fine Art

Joanna Strumpf and Ursula Sullivan are the wonder duo behind this warm and accessible Sydney gallery. Friendly and fierce talentspotters, they nurture an exciting and vibrant stable of artists, ranging from master abstractionist Syd Ball to emerging photographers

below
The large spaces of Stills Gallery were designed by Jackson Teece Architecture.

photography
Ridwan Hadi

Emily Portmann and Elana Vlassova. If you think Sydney galleries are foreboding or unfriendly, this is the art space that will change your mind.
44 Gurner Street, Paddington
9331 8344
ssfa.com.au

Josef Lebovic

An iconic and eccentric gallery space celebrating its 30th birthday in 2007, Josef Lebovic specialises in Australian and international photography and vintage works on paper dating from the 15th century. A happy antithesis to the white cube gallery norm, at Josef Lebovic a Lautrec lithograph jostles against a Kandinsky woodcut and is surrounded by Australian theatrical posters, printed paraphernalia, books and sculptures. A new exhibition opens every two months and considering art critic Sebastian Smee's description of the space as 'a sort of brothel for the history-starved, the picture-hungry, the detail-deprived', it's clearly a must-see.
34 Paddington Street, Paddington
9332 1840
joseflebovicgallery.com

250 VISUAL CULTURE_CONTENTS

VISUAL

Visual Culture

- 253 Introduction
- 255 The talent_designers
- 268 Publish or perish_publishing
- 274 Chest magic_T-shirts
- 279 Paper tigers
- 282 Florence in the city: Broadhurst's legacy_feature
- 287 Go shopping_stores & galleries
- 289 Bookish behaviour_bookstores

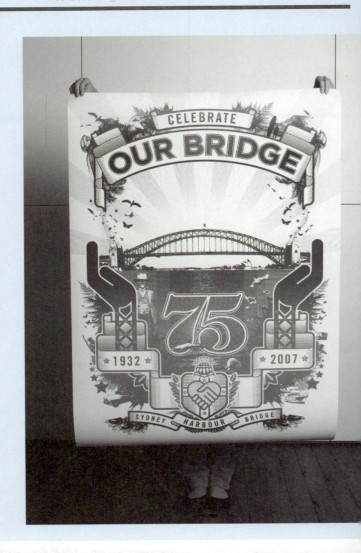

Introduction

left
Congrats, everyone! Deuce Design's Harbour Bridge 75th anniversary campaign. Shame we couldn't run this one in colour.

Some might say Sydney is all about looks, but in the case of its visual design industry, this ain't such a bad thing. If this city is the media heart of the land down under, imagery is its lifeblood, pulsing through the streets in an array of forms including animation, brand identities, broadcast design, publishing, art, advertising and of course the ubiquitous printed T-shirt.

While the nation's huge media players have settled in Sydney, some of the country's most exciting talent thrives alongside them. In a city obsessed with film, television and performance art, it's not surprising that much of the most innovative designers develop within it. Check out their work (we've listed some of the most interesting talent), peruse their product (we've include a stores and galleries section) take home some stationery (from the paper-obsessives around town), or just go on a wallpaper sightsee (that's our Flo). And did we mention the T-shirts?

above
Three-dimensional lettering for the Canvas Group's new identity.

right
Still from Sixty40's remake of *The Eguanda Panda Show* on Channel 9.

The talent

From worthy art projects to corporate commercials, 2D and 3D, emerging and established, one-man shows and international networks, Sydney visual design studios cross a lot of boundaries. Here's a cross-section of talent from B to W.

Billy Blue Creative

Back in 1977, Billy Blue began life as magazine, publishing colloqual Australian writing. As time passed and various companies began using the studio space, a consultancy was formed, namely Bill Blue Creative. They also opened a tiny design school to train people who would eventually work in the studio. It started with four places but six enrolled, and immediately there was a waiting list. Fast-forward to 2007, and there are now three campuses. Meanwhile, Billy Blue Creative produces brand identities, corporate and marketing communications, multimedia and web-based projects, signage and exhibition graphics, advertising and publishing. Their portfolio includes clients such as the City of Sydney, Kappa Clothing, Luna Park and Tourism NSW.
billybluecreative.com.au
billyblue.com.au

Canvas Group

Here's a truly international studio that manages the difficult symbiosis of corporate and creative, acting global but staying small. Born in early 2003 with the launch of the global press kit for the Mazda 3, Canvas' partnership of three has since tripled in size, moved studios twice and designed for clients in Australia, Germany, Japan and Canada. Canvas consists of nine computers, nine chairs, two fitballs, one badge machine, one very long custom-made desk

... continued p. 262

Animal Logic

above
You'd be jumping around like that too if you'd just pocketed the nation's first ever Oscar for best animated feature film.

The first Aussies to gong an Oscar for best animated feature film (*Happy Feet* in 2006), these digital production experts focus on storytelling through movies, TV and commercials, using sympatico artists from around the world, and recently signed a deal with Warner Bros. to produce a 'slate' of animated feature films. On the rise and rise since 1991, the Animal Logic team began as a visual-effects developer for TV programs and commercials, and they also develop animation software to feed this thriving industry. The 20+ crew has created material for a pile of films including *The Matrix*, *Moulin Rouge* and *The Quiet American*, and produced one of the most-loved ads on TV in 2006, the 'Big Ad' for Carlton Draught, in which huge crowds of extras were replicated to create a joyous, human, beer-guzzling mosaic that made Aussies all over the country sit up and smile (check it out on the website).
animallogic.com

Collider

above
Rock my world!
Still from a
Digitalism
video clip.

With such a cool name, you'd expect design and film company Collider to turn out top-notch work, and yes, they don't disappoint. Having hooked up with clients such as Ministry of Sound, Dior, Air France and BMW, the trio behind Collider act as both a design and production company for a multitude of different creative projects in various mediums. In doing so, Collider even managed to make Target look cool. They have produced music videos with bands such as Placebo, Phoenix, Digitalism and the mighty Pet Shop Boys. Apparently they're also holding the record for the longest amount of track ever laid for a single motion control shot. That was for a television commercial for Cadillac – and the track was laid for 2km along a single stretch of desert road outside LA. Their moniker reflects the different backgrounds of the three directors, who came together in 2001, driven by similar ideas and desires for their business. In the true sense of the word, smashing!
collider.com.au

de Luxe

above
Just the right type. De Luxe applies their eye for editorial layout and typography to the *Monash Business Review* and a catalogue for lighting firm Globe.

They are the guys newspapers call when it's time to – pardon the pun – turn a page. Established in 1993 by James and Nicola de Vries, de Luxe, as the name suggests, supply a pretty fancy standard of corporate print communications and magazine art direction. Their specialty, however, is the design of newspapers and other highly organised, text-heavy publications. As such, they've worked on titles including *The Australian Financial Review Weekend*, the *Hong Kong Standard* and the *South China Morning Post*. They also helped out in August 2000, when *The Sydney Morning Herald* readers complained the type size was too small, and beat Melbourne design studios to the task when it came to redesigning that city's beloved *The Age* newspaper in 2002. They do book design, including *John Howard's Little Book of Truth* – a satirical tome with the crazy, zealous look, but full of facts of course. When they get the time, they create cards, posters, rubber stamps, T-shirts, bags and stickers (email them if you want one).
de-luxe.com.au

Deuce Design

below
Railway Monument by Deuce Design.

They tend to attribute it to the Melbourne heritage or the art school background; whichever it is, Deuce Design's principal aim is to transcend the boundaries of traditional graphic design in a time when fast turnaround, tight budgets, strategy and InDesign reign supreme. Headed by directors Bruce Slorach and Sophie Tatlow, the studio follows the principles of 'more is more', 'considered disorder' and 'break the cookie-cutter mould'. Their outcomes aren't always two-dimensional. Examples include the design for the *Great Wall of China* exhibition at the Powerhouse and Melbourne Museums, and identity and collateral for the 2008 RAIA conference. They've applied their quirky style to various interpretive park projects and environmental signage jobs. Always keen to connect with the community, the Deuce crew loves to get involved with lots of non-client-based work when they find the time. You always know someone's good when other creatives are on the client list, and Deuce has that seal of approval from many, currently designing three architecture books for well-known Sydney architecture practices. As this book was readying itself for the printing press, they were about to don their smocks to paint murals in two Surry Hills bars.
deucedesign.com.au

Eskimo Design

above
The imagemakers: impression from the Westfield campaign.

VISUAL

This group of designers has been working away in their lofty rooftop studio since 1998. Often named in the same breath as prominent boutique studios like Frost Design and Moon, Eskimo are particularly chummy with the fashion crowd. The list of clients is long and impressive, including local fashion celebs Collette Dinnigan and Belinda. On the other hand, they produce particularly stunning art direction and design work for lots of corporate and lifestyle clients (think luxury, darling). In 2007, Eskimo got the coveted task of designing for all their peers, producing the annual calendar and invitations for the Australian Graphic Design Association (AGDA). As the collateral is meticulously studied by every graphic designer in the biz, they say that 'it pays to know your audience'. The guys proved their point by having their work double as a drink coaster.
eskimodesign.com.au

Frost Design

above
Bill for the Sydney Dance Company's hugely successful production *Underland*; design to the tune of Nick Cave.

Ever since British-born Vince Frost arrived in Sydney in 2004, leaving behind a successful business in London, the local design community has looked to what is now probably the most renowned among the boutique studios with a mixture of awe, admiration, jealousy and territorialism. Fact is, the studio's work is highly individual, interesting, creative and memorable. The 30+ designers chipping away in the Surry Hills office work on projects as diverse as designing exhibitions (the seminal *Freestyle: New Australian Design for Living* exhibition by Object Gallery in 2006 was one) and even stage sets (standing ovations for their stunning work with the Sydney Dance Company). Not one to shy away from self-promotion, Frost recently held a major retrospective exhibition of his work, titled *Frost*bite*, at the Sydney Opera House. It was accompanied by a large, beautiful book, *Frost*(sorry trees)*. The studio also plays an active role in the design community, chiefly through pro bono work for art and design related projects.
frostdesign.com.au

above
Ink Project sets SBS in motion with a series of clips known as 'Figures in Motion' – footage of dancers was treated graphically with animating ink.

… from p. 255

and of course nine highly creative people, making business look its best.
canvasgroup.com.au

Gentil Eckersley

Founded in 1998 by Franck Gentil, the diverse client base of Gentil Eckersley includes the Australian Chamber Orchestra and Virgin Mobile. With their main office in Sydney and a smaller one in Melbourne, Gentil Eckersley are particularly keen to support and nurture the design community. Their 2003 pro bono effort of designing the 'rulebook' for the Sydney Esquisse Art and Design Festival was rewarded with Victoria's Premier's Design Award a year later.
gentileckersley.com

Ink Project

Now producing work for clients from New York to New Zealand, Ink Project began in 2001. A large amount of their ventures is for international television channels including The Movie Channel, Nickelodeon, SBS and UKTV. Ink Project have also been involved in producing five five-second bumpers for the Sci Fi Channel in the US. These hands-on projects include digital doubles, fat explosions, growing beanstalks and making cats and dogs fall from the heavens, using animals, Sumos, stunt rigs, princesses and imported cane toads.
inkproject.com

Mandarin Creative

Now that's a name. Founder Annie Schwebel and team explain their choice by stating that their clients are 'like the seeds of a mandarin. They are the root of our momentum, source of our strength, catalysts for our imagination and partners in inspiration.' Not hard to guess that their services include all kinds of print communication, including copy writing. Founded in 2000, the studio is popular with arts and entertainment based clients, as well as government community sectors. They've produced branding, seasonal programs and ongoing collateral for The Studio, a Sydney Opera House venue. They have also worked for the Australia Council for the Arts, promoting Australian arts in the UK, the Sydney Symphony, The City Night Markets, MCA and the Actors Centre, to name but a few. They say there are 'no Chinese whispers, no egos, no dramas'.
mandarin.net.au

Mark Gowing Design

We need to say no more than 'Hopscotch films', and avid movie-goers will instantly know what Mark Gowing does. One of his most recognisable works is the Hopscotch promo featuring a neon light in a suburban park. From his big old warehouse studio in Redfern, Gowing chips away on an impressive portfolio, much of it culture or arts based. His work ranges from corporate identities to film campaigns, record covers and photography. Gowing has also designed artwork for a number of music releases in the last few years, as well as compilations for his own label, Preservation, which he runs with friend Andrew Khedoori. Books and typefaces are other Gowing favourites.
markgowing.com

Mathematics

The guys at Mathematics may claim that they were established in 512 by the Benedictine Monk Terry the Unlikeable, but that, of course, is entirely untrue. Firstly because the two young guys weren't around then (that didn't happen until well into the 1970s), but secondly because no one who's unlikeable could be behind such a cool, creative and, well, likeable ensemble. They do a lot of work with the music industry, whether animation or print, and their friends (i.e. clients) include Aussie music talents such as Eskimo Joe and

right
The August pin-up for Spring in Alaska's 2005 *Private Pink* lesbian calendar.

Missy Higgins. The list of all the cool stuff they've done is too lengthy to reproduce here, but luckily they have a website where you can check it all out. xy-1.com

Moon Design

Moon's graphic dynamic has helped shape Sydney's design culture for over a decade. One of their earliest jobs was to deploy a new Opera House logo throughout the building's entire promotional range, and although they were more recently gobbled up by Sydney's largest communications group, the quality of their work hasn't suffered in the slightest. They mainly develop identities and branding. On their client list are some of Australia's biggest (Qantas, BIT Financial, Jetstar) but they also service the arts community (Sydney Theatre Company, Sydney Symphony Orchestra). Creative Directors Carby Tuckwell and Mark Moffitt have their fingers in a few design pies around town. Tuckwell is also part of the unique motorcycle emporium Deus Ex Machina, while Moffit is one half of music magazine *DEMO*. moondesign.com.au

Naughty Fish

These fish are rapidly bubbling to the surface of the graphic design sector in Sydney. Working with clients in art, entertainment, education, retail and corporate, their capabilities include identity design,

packaging, websites, literature, publishing, environmental design, production and implementation. They have designed posters for Swedish scientists, against AIDS in Africa and have won AGDA awards. Say no more.
naughtyfish.com.au

Precinct

This brand developer and communications consultancy is a union of graphic design studio Precinct Design and financial services project managers Ideassociates. They help corporate types project new images and identities. For example, when the Diversity Council Australia needed a makeover, Precinct redesigned their marketing tools using strips of fabric – reflecting the different textures of Australian society. If you're looking for a brand new visual strategy to pull those elusive investors, Precinct might just be the guys for you.
precinct.com.au

PictureDRIFT

Established in 2002 by Brendan Cook, PictureDRIFT is a team of designers, directors and animators specialising in broadcast design and visual effects for TV and film. At the same time, Cook has continued his work on film, producing short films and music video projects for artists including Gotye, The Cops, Paul Mac and Smog. Recently, PictureDRIFT teamed up with Sydney visual effects studio Fuel to create an animated televison commercial for Samsung's new BlackJack mobile phone that references the ornate world of playing cards. PictureDRIFT has also worked with Nickelodeon on their campaigns and promotions.
picturedrift.com.au

Sixty40

Known for their varied motion design work, innovative approaches to design problems and their furiously fresh ideas, Sixty40 specialise in motion graphics and animation for promos, show titles and TVCs for a range of clients. Much of their work combines animation and other forms of broadcast design. Established over six years ago by duo Mark Simpson and Matt Taylor, their client base includes MTV, Jägermeister and the Comedy Festival. They also have their own cartoon. *The Eduganda Panda Show*, a revival of a kids' show of the 1950s, on Channel 9. Other projects include sock

above
Bold statements courtesy of Naughtyfish.

right
Bold type courtesy of Toko.

puppet video confessionals, In Situ (projected animation as public artwork), Ringtone Death Match and question / answer feedback from Dr Prawn. They also organise events like Rocket Car Day. Brilliant! sixty40.com

Spring in Alaska

It was formed in spring (2002), but not in Alaska. Founders Keren Moran and Noa Peer simply loved the visuals the icy place brings to mind. They're all about visuals, after all. Their clients are a mixed crowd hailing from diverse industries including architects, publishers, media companies, community organisations and corporates. They are also the folks behind T-shirt festival Shirty07. springinalaska.com.au

Toko

Eva Dijkstra and Michael Lugmayr only moved to Surry Hills from the Netherlands in 2006, but their venture, Toko, has already earned an excellent reputation around town for their well-executed and original print design. Their typographic work is especially sensational with its crisp appearance backed up by their religious use of the typographic grid. Check out their T-shirt label High Tee, especially if you're a type nerd. They say they were inspired by Sydney being the capital of T-shirt culture. Toldyouso. toko.nu

Wishart Design

Known as a 'designer's design practice' of sorts, Wishart Design was formed in the mid-1990s by Zoe Wishart and Martin Stone. The studio began with a strong connection to the interior design and architecture world, as Wishart was the inaugural designer for interior design trade magazine *InDesign*. They've designed for productions of the Sydney Dance Company and have gone beyond two dimensions when producing the environmental signage for the Sydney University of Technology. When they get a chance, they work on their own promotional pieces, such as a Wishart newspaper that can be folded, ripped and, like wine, gets better with age. wishartdesign.com

Publish or perish

Move over Rupert, it's time for big ideas. Sydney's independent magazine publishers aren't media moguls, but what they lack in cash they make up for in creativity. We've pulled together this city's finest …

Curvy

As an extension to the Semi-Permanent Conference in 2004, *YEN* magazine put together a book to document the event, inviting 100 leading artists from 20 countries to participate. Since then, two more books have been published (one a year), including work from almost all creative disciplines but within one context: it focuses exclusively on female designers, celebrating the achievements of inspiring women who make their mark. They are offered in limited edition, so get your hands on 'em while you can! The best places to look are art-based bookshops.

Cyclic Defrost

This electronic magazine is a testament to the fusion of music and design that's so unique to Sydney. The two people who've shaped its development from a photocopied zine to its current form as Australia's only electronic music mag are web-wizzes Sebastian Chan and Dale Harrison. For each issue, a guest designer is invited to produce the cover, most invitees being local artists whose design work is music-focused. The quarterly editions are available from record stores and can also be viewed on their website.
cyclicdefrost.com

Demo

Just over a year old at the time this book is going to press, *Demo* Magazine has made a big splash both with music and design fans. This not-for-profit (i.e. made with love and financed by its passionate makers) publication is out to uncover and expose some of Australia's most talented and

VISUAL CULTURE_PUBLISHING

above
Looks very little here, but *Demo* is huge. You can pull it all apart, plaster your walls with it and bathe in great graphic deisgn while keeping in tune with the music world.

fascinating musicians working today. That's what the makers say about it. We say it also uncovers and exposes some pretty fancy graphic design and editorial vision, namely that of twin brothers Andrew and Mark Moffitt, whose day jobs are at two well-known Sydney agencies, Precinct and Moon Design respectively. The oversized magazine can be pulled apart and pasted up on your bedroom wall. Available at the usual art-related haunts including Published Art, Red Eye Records and Deus Ex Machina.
demomagazine.com.au

Monster Children

It's not as scary as it sounds. Starting life as a magazine documenting street culture, skateboarding, surfing, snowboarding and art nearly five years ago, *Monster Children* is now a multi-layered project that encompasses a gallery, an online shop and the production of other publications including magazines, zines and books. Founded by Chris Searl (Editor) and Campbell Milligan (Art Director), these guys issue quarterlies with creative contributors and sometimes guest editors from all over the globe.
monsterchildren.com

01 Editions

above and below
It's huge and costs more than this editor's car, but the Murcut folio is destined to be the most beautiful publication you ever got your hot little hands on.

Designers Liisa Naar and Michael Tommasi set up their independent publishing company in 2001, after having had enough of the ephemeral 'stuff' they had been creating within their previous guise as a design consultancy. Aiming to create objects with lasting value, they decided that books were the way to go – no surprises there, but it's the 01 Editions approach that's special. Focusing on their shared passions of contemporary architecture, design and art, they embarked on one of the most expensive publications in Australian history – *Glenn Murcutt, Architect*. Since most of the Murcutt's buildings are private and not open to the general public, this folio is now the best way to view Murcutt's inspired architecture, his original hand-drawn designs and remnants of the thought process involved in the creations, in one gorgeous, hand-crafted volume guaranteed to last for 300 years. If you're feeling crushed by all that insidious mass-market pulp, make an appointment to visit the studio for an immersion in pure scripture that will save your soul. 01editions.com.au

VISUAL CULTURE_PUBLISHING

Dumbo feather, pass it on

above
Dumbo feather features mini-biographies and glimpses into the lives of many creatives. Great read, great to look at. Great.

This little magazine has made lots of friends, found lots of admirers and made some people famous, and it's all done on the one laptop. *Dumbo feather, pass it on*, is the work of Kiwi expat Kate Bezar, who had enough of high-flying management and instead focused on creating a 'mook', a cross between a magazine and a book, which she launched in 2004. Although it appears periodically, the publication is timeless, each issue featuring five individuals, their stories, lives and passions, on many, many beautifully laid out pages.

As to the name, we suggest you don't pass your copy on, but collect it. Everyone should buy their own, so that the Dumbo feathers keep flying.
dumbofeather.com

Empty

below
Empty has explored international illustration in ten issues over three years.

It really doesn't keep its promise, this well-established independent magazine that emanates from the same stable as Design is Kinky and the hugely popular Semi-Permanent event. *Empty* is not at all empty but choc-full of the finest (and at times controversial) international illustration, art and graphic design you could imagine. Founded three years ago by Andrew Johnstone (the designer who's also behind the above initiatives), *Empty* was in its tenth issue at the time this guide went to print and is going from strength to strength, gaining more and more cred in the illustration and art community. Entirely self-funded and put together in the precious spare time of its publisher, the mag is, however, empty in one regard: there's hardly any advertising. Just pages and pages full of rip-me-out-and-pin-me-on-the-wall pictures.
emptymag.com

Open manifesto

below
About to launch onto the global stage, *Open Manifesto* is attracting the attention of the international design intelligentsia.

After seven years climbing the career ladder Kevin Finn, then-Director of Saatchi Design in Sydney, found himself standing in a boardroom wondering 'if this is all we'll ever do'. The endless cycles of advertising – receiving briefs, creating strategies, coming up with solutions, implementing them – seemed to pass the native Irishman by. Finn's thoughts turned to the great masters and movements of the avant-garde, who discussed and debated their work through publications and manifestos. After carrying around his hunger for just this kind of debate for some time, Finn responded with *Open manifesto*, an A5-sized publication inviting authors to respond to a prescribed theme. Primarily text-based, *Open manifesto* is edited, designed, published, distributed and financed solely by Finn, who is careful to mix Australian contributions with those from international luminaries to help integrate Australian design into the international discourse. The responses are positive all round. After just three issues, Finn has secured the collaboration of design supremos such as New York design historian Steven Heller and Dutch typography rebel Stefan Sagmeister. *Open manifesto* is ready to take on the world. Be part of it: buy it at art and design bookstores.
openmanifesto.net

VISUAL CULTURE_T-SHIRTS

Chest magic

above
100% happy buying from the Love Jungle.

T-shirts, what can't they do? Dress them up or dress them down, make a statement or blend in with the crowd. T-shirts are synonymous with Sydney design culture.

Whether they stake out new ground at a weekend market or line boutique shelves, Sydneysiders love a good tee and have even given the T-shirt it's very own festival, aptly named Shirty. Many labels are the side projects of graphic designers – a creative outlet not governed by a client brief. Ranging from handmade one-off creations to screen-printed or, increasingly, digital prints, the diversity of tees available is an expression of Sydney's street culture and confidently casual fashion sense. Where other cities spray walls and hang banners, Sydney flaunts her design culture on her chest.

VISUAL CULTURE_T-SHIRTS

Not that we could cover them all, but we've aimed to put together a cross-section of the offerings of Sydney T-shirt culture. No more excuses for those who still relentlessly parade the logos of international chain stores. Here's some outstanding T-shirt talent …

Akina

Fashion designer and illustrator Lang Leav has attracted some serious attention with her collection of sweetly sinister girls who could obliterate Emily the Strange with a single creepy scowl. The stories of these 'villains with button fetishes' are played out over a range of postcards, pins and shirts, featuring appliqué prints with delicate lace finishes. Check online for stockists all over town.
akina.com.au.

Brown Paper Tiger

Like all good things, Brown Paper Tiger was imagined over a few beers by small-business owner Ollie Pennington and graphic designer Zoë Sadokierski at their local pub. Each series of tees is loosely linked by a narrative, featuring a peculiar cast of creatures including the Peafowl of Haughtiness, dancing yetis and a showdown between a cowboy and a petrol pump. The original designs are digitally printed in limited editions on politically correct shirts from American Apparel. Available sporadically at markets and always online.
brownpapertiger.com

emshop

Focusing on distinct, handmade, sweatshop-free clothing for individuals, emshop's Jess Macdonald creates original screens from scanned drawings and hand-paints deliberately old-school shirts in her lounge room overlooking the ocean. Each garment is unique, with much time and love injected into its creation. Beachwear or club gear, pastels or fluoro, emshop's got you covered for unique graphic tees. Stop by for a chat at Bondi Market, pick up a shirt at Local Derby on King Street, Newtown, or order online.
emshoponline.com

Enfant Terrible

Graphic designer and art director Mike Lind started his playful kids' label Enfant Terrible when his nieces were born. Lind declares his graphics are designed for future rodeo clowns

left, clockwise from top
Emshop = no sweatshop / the workings of People Like Us / Young Lovers walk all over you / monkey business by Brown Paper Tiger.

and stuntpeople and are not about fairytales. Urban hipsters can choose from a unisex range including a spray-stencilled bespectacled monkey, happy monsters and the Mouse-y Skull for apprentice metal heads. Shirts are stocked at Shorties on King Street, Newtown, and online.
enfant-terrible.com.au

Kitten

Partners Damien Fuller (ex-Mambo and Royal Elastics) and Fern Levack (ex-Collette Dinnigan) teamed up to create the internationally acclaimed label Kitten, winning an Australian Fashion Award for streetwear in 2004. Their distinctive, handdrawn graphic tees are perfectly suited to throw over one of their original swimsuits or jeans.
2 Glenmore Road, Paddington
9361 0651

Love Jungle

Dissatisfied with local fashion options, graphic designer Michael and business / law student Aaron formed the label Love Jungle, with the aim of creating a tee they would be 100% happy buying – soft, well-made, low neckline with minimal, simple designs. Strong geometric patterns, skulls and scribbly robots adorn the first range. Check them out at Somedays or online.
pitbullmansion.com
lovejungle.com.au

People Like Us

This is as much a philosophy as a design collective. Dynamic duo Jeremy and Jonathan realised people like them wanted limited-edition, hand-numbered shirts on quality fabric, and most importantly an experience, not just a product. For a little extra dosh, your tee arrives in a reusable cotton library bag with treats like stickers, toys and a profile of the designer. Their new range exploits a digital printer capable of printing millions of colours – these shirts are literally wearable art, created by an array of local and international designers.
peoplelikeuscollective.com

The End

Independent label The End began as a side project for Mark Drew, Manager and Co-Director of successful Surry Hills institution China Heights Gallery. Drew describes his tees as concept-driven: themes for the current and future ranges will always be based on aspects

above
Enfant Terrible: what will it do to your children?

of pop culture that are close to his heart – be they music, film or skateboarding.
Dobry Den, 326 Crown Street, Surry Hills

Young Lovers

Luke Nuto's indie street label is a full-time affair, run adjacent to his work for Surry Hills creative collective The Glue Society. He uses a special dyeing process to achieve a vintage fade and softness that ensures these shirts become immediate 'old favourites'. Limited to 100 shirts per edition and drawing inspiration from early 1990s daytime TV, and music ranging from the Lemonheads to Ratatat and the Grates, Nuto's big, punchy, graphic and text-based tees are sure to get you noticed on the street. Buy in-store at Beautiful on the Inside or online.
younglovers.com.au

Paper tigers

Did you start stealing stationery before you reached puberty? You're a lost cause. Don't fight it. Instead, make sure you invest in some quality local product.

Corban & Blair

A true Sydney stationery institution, this brand was created by cousins Gillian Corban and Amanda Blair in 1988. Producing journals, photo albums, cards and other stationery, the duo is still hands-on 20 years after throwing their doors open. Their range is now huge, with picture frames and other stationery-related paraphernalia produced in Australia and overseas, while simultaneously striving for utility and durability and considering the environment. Launching two retail collections a year, as well as designing unique products for the business sector, Corban & Blair also held the licence for the Sydney 2000 Olympics, making products for retail as well as designing items for the lineup of corporate sponsors. They now have dedicated space allocated in almost all David Jones stores, and their range is also stocked in lots of other stationery-related haunts.
corbanblair.com.au

kikki.K

Swedish by name, Swedish by nature, but an essentially Australian success story. After opening the first of her stores in Melbourne, Swede Kristina Karlsson has found a lot of support in Sydney, where she's now up to nine stores. Everybody loves the little empire that consists of streamlined, colour-matched boxes, cards, envelopes and knick-knacks. All of it is designed to bring some Scandinavian order to your home. While that's up to you, we can definitely guarantee you'll be delighted by the product. Kikki.K also supports the work of local designers,

VISUAL CULTURE_PAPER

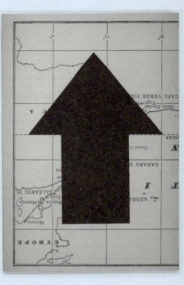

above
Me and Amber handprinted greeting cards.

stocking related products such as the stylish laptop bags of Melbourne-based All The King's Men. Kikki.K stores are at Westfield, Bondi Junction and the ground floor of the Queen Victoria Building. For more stockists, their online store or to subscribe to the new online mag, check the website.
Westfield Bondi Junction,
500 Oxford Street
9386 0804
QVB, 455 George Street
Sydney
8264 0123
kikki-k.com.au

Me and Amber

Who's Me, you might ask. We can help out: the duo behind the beautiful greeting cards and stationery comprises Karen Enis and Amber Molnar. Both are communications design graduates from the Sydney University of Technology. The best-bud duo makes a range of different objects, including books, graphic print T-shirts, artwork, cards and badges, which are sold at markets and stores around Sydney including Orson & Blake, Planet Furniture,

Published Art and the MCA store. The two also work on bespoke projects for a handful of clients; among them were fashion hotshots ksubi when they needed a set of business cards to take to London Fashion Week. Me and Amber came up with a design where no two cards were the same. The handmade asthetic indeed reflects a process of individually making each object, so rest assured that a lot of love comes with each Me and Amber birthday card, even if it's not the presenter's own.
meandamber.com

Modernmurri

From a small workshop in north-west NSW, in the Gamilaroi country, three Moree women supply Sydney's art galleries and design stores (among them is the Collect store at Object Gallery) with a range of exquisite handprinted cards and silk-screened textile accessories. Designs are inspired by the makers' surrounds, relying on traditional printmaking techniques such as linocuts, using locally sourced materials.
modernmurri.com

Paper Couture

This little store on South Dowling Street is certainly one you want to stumble across while snooping around the shops in Paddington. Filled with pretty paper goods and selected specialty books, it also stocks bespoke handmade creations by store owner Jo Neville, including writing paper, cards, invitations, tags, albums and decorative paper-based objects. Paper Couture doesn't have a website as yet, making for a really good reason to drop in.
284 South Dowling Street, Paddington
9357 6855

Florence in the city: Broadhurst's legacy

right
Florence Broadhurst in Shanghai, 1926.

photography unknown, collection of Powerhouse Museum, Sydney.

For a woman born in rural Queensland in the last year of the 19th century, it's surprising how much Florence Broadhurst radically changed attitudes to design in Australia, writes <u>Anne-Marie Van de Ven</u>, Curator of Graphic Design at Sydney's Powerhouse Museum.

The indefatigable and colourful Sydney-based wallpaper designer and businesswoman was particularly popular during the 1960s and 70s among the city's social elite, who rushed to hang her bold papers on the walls of their recently refurbished and modernised interiors.

Broadhurst had toured Asia as a troubadour at a young age, then travelled to London to start new careers as a dress designer and passenger boat operator. On returning to Australia in 1949, she became an artist and charity worker while helping her husband with his trucking business, and ten years later embarked on her final, and best known, venture – the successful Australian Hand Printed Wallpapers screen-printing business that became Florence Broadhurst Wallpapers when she moved to Paddington in 1969. Broadhurst created hundreds of unique and luxurious patterns, combining flamboyant colours with sumptuous oriental floral, gardenesque, naturalistic or geometric designs. After her mysterious death in 1977, it took 12 years for her designs to be recovered by David and Helen Lennie of Signature Prints (see p. 285), who hold the sole rights to reproduce Broadhurst designs worldwide and thereby keep this remarkable woman's legacy alive.

left
Handprinting the 'Horse Stampede' at Signature Prints.

right
Broadhurst's 1970s Japanese Bamboo wallpaper design, collection of the Powerhouse Museum.

photography
Marinco Kojdanovski

far right
'Geometric G' at Mr Goodbar.

Florence in the city: admire comptemporary applications of Broadhurst's work in the following places …

Leona Edmiston boutiques (see also p. 206) all over the country use Broadhurst's signature Cranes in cream and burgundy on matt brushed gold mylar.
The Strand Arcade, 412–414 George Street, Sydney

The Bayswater Brasserie (see also p. 300) features an homage to Australian design – including the Broadhurst Cockatoos.
32 Bayswater Road, Kings Cross

The Florence Broadhurst display in the Powerhouse Museum's *Inspired! Design across time* exhibition is another important Broadhurst destination, featuring many original designs and photographs.
500 Harris Street, Ultimo

The Greg Natale-designed Mister Goodbar nightclub chose Broadhurst's Geometric G design as a word play on 'G'ood Bar, and because the bold, ageless paper is based around patterns in G, in white on black gloss mylar.
11 Oxford Street, Paddington

 5

Renowned fashion designer Akira Isogawa is a big fan of Florence, borrowing from the Signature Prints library and using Broadhurst's designs on fabric for his collections. See if you can pick them in the Akira showroom.
12a Queen Street, Woollahra

 6

Pressed-metal ceilings and full-height columns set off a range of Broadhurst wallpapers at the restored Establishment Hotel. Dress nice-like.
252 George Street, Sydney
9240 3000
merivale.com.au

 7

Nestled against the snakeskin padded walls of the dark little Lotus bar (see also p. 326) is a great example of Broadhurst's iconic Japanese Bamboo paper. Have a cocktail and toast her ageless style.
22 Challis Avenue, Potts Point

 8

Last but not least, the Signature Prints showroom; featuring hundreds of designs and samples, it's a treasure trove and a most popular destination for interior designers and the frenzied design media.
3 Hayes Road, Rosebery
8338 8400
signatureprints.com.au

VISUAL

Go shopping

left
Horsepower meets manpower: Deus Ex Machina is a unique destination for visual culture fans with a penchant for mean machines.

While traipsing the steets is the only way to grasp what visual culture really means in this city, there's also nothing like taking a bit of that vision home to light up your life. Here's our pick of where to find picturesque products … or just pictures.

Deus ex Machina

Translated from Latin 'god out of a machine' is a combined shop, gallery and cafe celebrating the motorcycle. It's the brainchild of a group of passionate bike enthusiasts, united in the belief that 'motorcycling has been hijacked by corporate marketing forces'. Their desire is to create a new motorcycle culture, one that relies on custom design. The team behind the store features some prominent Sydney characters: Dare Jennings, the founder of famous surf brand Mambo; Rod Hunwick, a revving rider and bike collector; and Carby Tuckwell, a bike-obsessed graphic artist, also founder and Creative Director of Moon Design. The supremely grand showroom is certainly worth the trip to Camperdown to see the boys' collection of bikes and other paraphernalia. Great feature murals are complemented by a range of Tuckwell-designed work-shirts, hoodies, caps and tees sporting the Deus logos and handdrawn graphics guaranteed to make you go faster. The three are avid supporters of local design culture and many an interesting project has been launched here.
98–102 Parramatta Road, Camperdown
9557 6866
deus.com.au

Egan

Visual artist David Egan manoeuvres between art and design. After losing his job as an art director in the advertising industry in 1990, the native Irishman took his chances as

VISUAL CULTURE_STORES & GALLERIES

below
Following from the successful publication *Vinyl Will Kill!*, Jeremyville and Sydney-based publishers IdN joined forces again to create *Jeremyville Sessions*.

an artist. Fifteen years later, he opened his own gallery. Having come a long way since selling his first works at Glebe Market, celebrity collectors of his work include U2 and Elton John, who asked for a painting to commemorate his Australasian tour. The managements of Apple, Qantas, Amnesty International and Greenpeace have all commissioned work from him. He was also appointed to complete public works and murals throughout the city during the Sydney Olympics, as well as designing the official T-shirt for the Museum of Contemporary Art's blockbuster Andy Warhol exhibition.
It's a far cry from being a wage slave. Check out his gallery.
3a Glenmore Road, Paddington
9361 0066
egangallery.com

Jeremyville

This wacky projects-based concept is the vision of one self-described artist, product designer, animator and 100-year-old human swinger, Jeremy (no surname, no pack drill). He is the ideas man known for writing and producing the first-ever book on designer toys, *Vinyl Will Kill!*, and for working with an incredibly diverse range of collaborators, from Converse to Murakami. Focusing on comic-style character animation, the Jeremyville crew work with artists (like singer Beck), designers and toymakers to create an over-the-top range of noisy sneakers, T-shirts, mags, prints, skate decks and Darth Vader masks, among other things. Take a ride at the online store.
jeremyville.com

Bookish behaviour

If you're after design and architecture books, there are a few places you don't want to go past. Here's a handful in the city's design hotspots.

Architext

Housed in the fantastic Tusculum Building, the headquarters of the Royal Australian Institute of Architects (and worth a look for that significant building alone), this is a specialist architect's bookstore and is run by real architecture freaks. They have lots of international publications you won't find elsewhere.
3 Manning Street, Potts Point
9356 2022
architext.com.au

Ariel Booksellers

Opening in 1985, Ariel's convivial atmosphere quickly attracted a loyal clientele of artists, actors, writers, students and other book-loving regulars who it continues to cater for today. Specialising in art, architecture, design and film, Ariel offers complimentary coffee to sip on while you leaf through the books.
42 Oxford Street, Paddington
9332 4581
103 George Street, The Rocks
9241 5622
arielbooks.com.au

Berkelouw Books

One of the largest and earliest established bookshops in the country, Berkelouw sells new, second-hand and antiquarian titles. The original Oxford Street premises has a little cafe on its first floor, and downstairs behind the counter you'll see lots of illustrations by Emma Magenta, who's managed the store for many years.
19 Oxford Street, Paddington
9360 3200
berkelouw.com.au

Better Read Than Dead

'More than just a bookstore', BRTD prides itself on individual customer service and the specialised knowledge of its staff. Owned by President of the Australian Booksellers Association Derek Dryden, it has a great range of diverse literature.
265 King Street, Newtown
9557 8700
betterread.com.au

Borders

They're not Australian, we know, but especially when it comes to independent international magazines on art and design, Borders has a great selection. Also, they let you peruse the mags for hours on end, until you're completely drunk with inspiration. There are six stores in greater Sydney, with one in the city centre.
Skygarden, 77 Castlereagh Street, Sydney
92352433
bordersstores.com

Gleebooks

The definition of independent bookseller, this place is a true Glebe institution and is filled to the brim with great reads. The entire upstairs section is devoted to art and architecture, and they have regular readings and bookish events.
49 Glebe Point Road, Glebe
9660 2333
gleebooks.com.au

Kinokuniya Bookshop

Kinokuniya's selection of art and design related books – including manga graphic novels – is mind-boggling. An in-store feature displays work by national and international artists, including specially conceived installations by local talent who sell their wares in the store, such as Me and Amber.
500 George Street, Sydney
9262 7996
kinokuniya.com.au

Museum of Sydney Bookstore

With a good range of architecture titles, including history of architecture, this store focuses on work coming out of Sydney. A favourite lunchtime hangout for many city workers, it's got great designer knick-knacks too.
37 Phillip Street, Sydney
9251 4678

Published Art Bookshop

Specialising in contemporary art, architecture and design, as well as personal service, Published Art stock the most interesting art and design publications available internationally. Drop in at lunchtime and you'll see the Surry Hills creative crew purchasing towering stacks of books – looking away as they sign the credit card receipt.
23–33 Mary Street, Surry Hills
9280 2839
publishedart.com.au

UNSW Bookshop

This great uni bookstore sources its books through small distributors of avant-garde publishing, and will order in titles from pretty much anywhere in the world. The shop is independently owned by UNSW Press and NIDA, and as such also caters for subjects such as fashion design, staging and theatre.
Quadrangle Building, UNSW Campus, Kensington
bookshop.unsw.edu.au

EAT/DRINK/SLEEP_CONTENTS

Eat/Drink/Sleep

- 295 Introduction
- 296 Water & views
- 300 The classics
- 303 Dress to impress
- 307 Breakfast
- 309 Small, dark & handsome
- 312 Lunch
- 315 La vera pizza
- 317 Orient express
- 320 RSL's
- 322 Something fishy
- 324 Late at night
- 327 Hotels

EAT/DRINK/SLEEP_INTRODUCTION

above
Ventuno at Miller's Point, designed by Fitt de Felice architects and catered by specially imported Calabrian chefs (we're told).

Introduction

Let's get one thing straight – this ain't no *Good Food Guide*. But we know you need sustenance from sources other than inspired design, and it's always interesting to note where the people behind the product hang out, where they think the best exteriors, interiors and ingestibles are, where you might 'accidentally' bump into one or two of the sly little creatures … So in the course of putting this guide together we asked dozens of designers to list their favourite eating, drinking and sleeping spots. Then even when we had struck off the back yards, boudoirs and, in some cases, bathrooms(!) of the designers themselves, we were still left with a huge and diverse list. That's when we called in the big guns, Lisa Dabscheck and Joel Meares, to find the common ground, sort through the best of the best and give us their expert opinions on what they unearthed. So here are the Sydney spots chosen not for their fame, not for their chi-chi-ness, not because you 'should' go there, but because this is where Sydney designer types actually do hang out.

Water & views

Oh, Sydney and its sweet sea scenery. If you're a local and you don't often consume by the coast, or you're a visitor who hasn't yet supped by the seaside, you just don't get it. Here's a few Sydney versions of surf + turf to get you started – and they're not all followed by that other standard, a crazy bill.

The Bathers' Pavilion

Built in 1921, and as the name suggests, the old Bathers' Pavilion was a shed where swimmers swapped their civvies for their cozzies and ran the ten steps down to the sea. Now, this whitewashed Spanish Mission-style building houses a busy cafe at one end and a swanky restaurant at the other. The cafe is a refuge for milkshake- and spaghetti-seeking kids who hoe in while their parents hide behind newspapers and make like they've still got time to read them. The restaurant is a dining affair of the finest kind, where they want to know if you take foie gras with your boned duck, both of which will be suitably superb.
4 The Esplanade,
Balmoral Beach
9969 5050
batherspavilion.com.au

Icebergs Dining Room and Bar

If only wicker furniture could talk. The pages of *NW* would pale in the face of the stories the candy-coloured cushions could convey. What did Our Nicole discuss with her 30 closest friends on her 40th birthday? Who did Paris fancy when she turned up in a bikini to launch Bondi Blonde beer? What did the first ladies of the world have to say during a quiet APEC lunch, when a Greens MP flashed his surfboard at them, sporting a message that suggested they follow the example of Greek heroine Lysistrata, who recommended withholding physical pleasures

above
The view from North Bondi Italian Food / Moorish architecture paired with moreish food and views at the Bather's Pavilion.

from spouses at war? We will never know. Why don't you go write your own celebrity history in the Mario Terzini-designed restaurant and bar? The location couldn't be more glamorous.
1 Notts Avenue, Bondi
9365 9000
idrb.com

The Kiosk, Rose Bay

Maybe the staff have had military training (move that table an inch and they'll call in the troops) but who's to argue when you're sitting on the end of a sun-soaked pier from which you can actually dangle your toes in the water. The food is good, but don't ask for breakfast after 12 (they discipline latecomers). Still, it's pretty cheap and you get free entertainment: watching the rich play with their superyachts. And the location can't be beat.
594 New South Head Road, Rose Bay
9362 3555

Opera Bar

What more can we say than this: the views and location are unbeatable, and the food exceptionable. Make your way down to the Opera Bar after a show and you might just bump into those dainty ballerinas you admired on stage, and you could learn how to do the splits – perhaps with a bit of help from the extensive and unusual cocktail list.
Lower Concourse Level,
Sydney Opera House
9247 1666
operabar.com.au

North Bondi Italian

It's hard to remember where all the fabulous Bondi people hung out before this beachside diner opened in 2005 – if an anthropologist wanted to study the natives, this'd be the place. In between decorating the bar and populating the terrace, they do sometimes eat, and the food is blessedly free of the overwrought flourishes weighing down so many Sydney dishes. Here, order the crumbed veal cutlet and that's exactly what you'll get. Dreamt up by Thomas Jacobsen, the design is unashamedly patriotic – red, white and green Perspex panels run the length of the restaurant. The waiters wear ksubi T-shirts in the same colour scheme. Well, this isn't a wallflower kind of place.
118–120 Ramsgate Avenue,
Bondi
9300 4400
idrb.com

The Orbit Bar at Summit Restaurant

Back in the day when hairspray was a staple in every woman's bathroom cabinet, a restaurant on a revolving platform on the top floor of the city's highest building had residents gaping with awe – more than they did at the mini-skirt that was making a scandalous entry into the Sydney scene at the time. While (almost) everyone got used to the latter, the former still gets an occasional gobsmacked reaction.
The Orbit Bar – part of the Summit Restaurant – has been rediscovered by the city's cool cats and creative crowd, who enjoy a Singapore sling at sunset while spinning around within the wonderfully kitsch decor.
264 George Street,
Sydney
9247 9777
summitrestaurant.com.au

EAT/DRINK/SLEEP_WATER & VIEWS

Otto Ristorante

Only a Melburnian could have thought of opening a darkened Italian ristorante on one of the most watery wharves in Sydney. A local would have stuck with bright white, blonde and chrome, as they almost all did until Maurice Terzini came along and changed the rules. Now there are lots of other dark Italians, from Surry Hills to Glebe, but Otto was the template. Terzini's since sold out to shock jock John Laws, who keeps the best table on the terrace permanently earmarked for him and his wife Princess. It's that kinda place, but James Kidman's food (strozzapreti ai gamberi – artisan pasta with Yamba prawns) more than makes up for it.
6 Cowper Wharf Road,
Woolloomooloo
9368 7488
ottoristorante.com.au

Redleaf Pool Cafe

We'd prefer not to tell you about this place, ok? Right now, we really like the fact that you can drop in, pull up a plastic chair at one of the four tables, order one of the best no-frills egg-and-bacon breakfasts in town (with a view straight down to sailboats bobbing up and down in the harbour) and not be disturbed by any Sunday morning rabble – just a few kids lining up for Paddle Pops. Then you can dive off a pontoon with the handful of others who know about this (mostly) secret spot. So we're not telling you, ok?
536 New South Head Road,
Double Bay
9327 8813

Sean's Panaroma

Ok, so it's not exactly waterfront. The views are what real estate agents might describe as 'glimpses', but does anyone care when the food's this good? The interior owes something to the classroom, with its straight-backed chairs, sensible tables and blackboard menus strung from the ceiling. Maybe there's something in that: owner and chef Sean Moran could give Sydney restaurants some lessons about how to make honest food served with humility, warmth and not one drop of att-i-tude.
270 Campbell Parade,
Bondi
9365 4924
seanspanaroma.com.au

The classics

above
The Hollywood Hotel; it couldn't be more of a classic.

Whether your definition of classic involves fine dining, notoriety, individuality or just being open late, this selection covers some true Sydney institutions.

Bar Italia

We're not pretending that Bar Italia offers great service or that its pastas and mains are more than adequate, but this Sydney staple in the heart of Italian Leichhardt churns out solid heart-quickening coffee and authentic gelato every time. The customers are loyal – some are older Italians sipping on a taste of home (or shadily playing *Sopranos* in a corner), others are bookish students venturing a little further from Sydney Uni for a pastry and espresso. The definition of cheap and cheerful local.
169–171 Norton Street,
Leichhardt
9560 9981

Bayswater Brasserie

In a city that thinks endless reinvention is the way to satisfy its infamously fickle population, you can count the stalwarts on one or two hands. The 'Bayz' has managed to convincingly

approximate a Left Bank bistro for the last 25 years. Nestled between a row of thumping clubs and a former pole-dancing joint, it's a little slice of je ne sais quoi on one of Sydney's seediest strips. As well as a nostalgic menu (gruyere soufflé and steak frites anyone?) the kitchen always knows where to get the best oysters, which are shucked to order. And the back bar has a ruby-red banquette made for getting smoochy.
32 Bayswater Road, Kings Cross
9357 2177
bayswaterbrasserie.com.au

Bill and Toni's

If you think fast food means a spongy hamburger and fries in a cardboard box, you obviously haven't been to Bill and Toni's. Climb the narrow staircase to this reliably dingy dining room and be rewarded with a $6.50 mound of spag bol, with vinegary iceberg salad, bread and orange cordial thrown in for free, all delivered within 90 seconds. Now that's what you call a happy meal. Downstairs, old school baristas churn out industrial-strength espresso while you munch pellets on the original Pac-Man console.
72–74 Stanley Street,
East Sydney / Darlinghurst
9360 4702

Golden Century

Take a number, sit down and shut up. We'll tell you when your table is ready. This place seats 600 and if you think the waiters are offensive, get used to it. This is one of those Chinese seafood restaurants where you choose your fish while it's still swimming, then the chefs knife it in the guts. Speaking of chefs, it's open till about 3am, so if you've ever wondered what big Sydney cooks eat, wander down to Chinatown in the wee hours and watch them demolish mountains of pipis with XO sauce.
393 Sussex Street, Sydney
9212 3901

Hollywood Hotel

One of the last original art deco hotels in Sydney, the Hollywood is much more than a pretty facade – it's a magnet for interesting people with fantastic hairstyles and lots of good stories. The usual Australian tradition calls for naming establishments after a neighbouring landmark, but neither a cricket ground nor a railway line was within the vicinity when this hotel opened in the late 1940s. So the country's fledgling film industry, at the time at home in Surry Hills, played godfather. Just as well, since Doris Goddard,

the publican who took over the premises in 1977 (when it was a watering hole for local police journos and private detectives), is a genuine film star who acted alongside Bob Hope and Katherine Hepburn in her day. Now over 70, she still gives impromptu singing performances for her hip punters, who love the place even more for them.
2 Foster Street, Surry Hills
9281 2765
hotelhollywood.com.au

Kinselas

Sydney lacks 24-hour venues, so Kinselas gets a tick by default (9am–6am). It's hard to ignore the seedier side of its Taylor Square location, full as it is of frenzied teenagers and passed-out beggars, but there's something to be said for a decent 4am drink at Kinselas' long marble bar. The venue itself is better than most late-night dives, with bright red chairs contrasting nicely against industrially dark brick walls, and a spot on the middle bar balcony gives you a vantage of always frenetic Bourke Street below.
383 Bourke Street, Darlinghurst
9331 3100

Tropicana Caffe

The birthplace of John Polson's Tropfest is a casual diner in popular Darlinghurst, just on the cusp of the Cross. Grab a number and sit on a pavement table for some of the city's best people-watching, or take a table inside for a salad or pasta fix before a big night out. The vibe is bright and buzzy and attracts Kings Cross eccentrics, tourists after a bit of affordable nosh and the occasional celeb playing incognito (it's too well-lit for that, Hugh).
277 Victoria Street, Darlinghurst
9360 9809
tropicanacaffe.com.au

Dress to impress

Er, you might not believe this but there are some nosebags in Sydney where you have to dress nice to get in. We know, astonishing. But worth it. You won't get any more cream-of-the-crop than this lot.

Becasse

Chef Justin North moved his former Surry Hills eatery to the city's Clarence Street in 2005 and with the new locale came a new food philosophy. It's still a divinely French affair, with slow-cooked fish and offal cuts du jour, but North has moved away from the old thick and heavy butter sauces and embraced a cleaner approach to continental cooking. The result is one of the city's finest diners that doesn't weigh too heavily on the wallet or thighs. North's emphasis is on fresh and tasty produce and the room is warmly elegant with crystal ceiling lights and plush carpet. Even the French would approve.
204 Clarence Street, Sydney
9283 3440
becasse.com.au

Bistro Moncur

The first thing you notice is the gigantic black-and-white Michael Fitzjames illustration on the wall. The second thing you notice is that the people in the picture bear rather a resemblance to the people in the restaurant. You've got a good feel for this place already. And if you're still paying attention, you might notice that owner and head chef Damien Pignolet (wearing his trademark circular specs) is still cooking in the kitchen, after 14 years. He's got the talent, bloodline and chutzpah to have weaned Sydneysiders onto boudin noir long before anyone knew what they were really eating.
116 Queen Street, Woollahra
9327 9703
woollahrahotel.com.au

Buon Ricordo

Any restaurateur who knocks back a request to cater for Tom Cruise's long-haul flight home with the words 'we don't do take away' is the stuff of legend. Armando Percuoco, who's been running this Italian institution for 20 years, has a reputation for other good stuff too, like throwing out customers who don't get it. He can afford to do that for two good reasons: one, he's just spent half a million bucks kitting out the joint, and two: he invented the signature dish: fettuccine al tartuvo (truffled egg fettucine), a plate of pasta so good somebody should write an opera about it.
108 Boundary Street, Paddington
9360 6729
buonricordo.com.au

est. at Establishment

If you're happy to trade harbour views for one the of plushest interiors by masters of chic Hecker Phelan Guthrie from Melbourne, est. is the place to go. The opulent surroundings, where the young and beautiful mingle, will have you yearning for a glass of expensive French boujoulais and a cigar the minute you walk in the door. But with the 18/20 nod from the foodie's bible *Good Food Guide*, you'd better have a look at the menu first.
252 George Street, Sydney
9240 3010
merivale.com

Guillaume at Bennelong

When it comes to gastronomic triumphs in world-class architectural spaces, Sydney has usually got the plans stuck at council. Guillaume's is an exception. A bureaucratic error must have given the green light for some of the city's finest fare to be served in its most remarkable building. A pair of Jørn Utzon's sails provide the shelter and Guillaume Brahimi does his bit with five-star sustenance, like his legendary basil-infused tuna. And if you've worked up a bit of an appetite during *La Traviata*, the mezzanine bar does a smashing late-night supper.
Sydney Opera House,
Bennelong Point
9241 1999
guillaumeatbennelong.com.au

La Sala

Sydney people are always banging on about how this place is 'so New York' (it's a bit warehouse-y) or 'so Melbourne' (the lighting's dim). But actually, the sunken dining room is

below left
Regal dining at est.

below right
Dress nice for dinner at Becasse.

photography
Steve Brown

designed so that patrons can study new arrivals as they descend the staircase. And that's about as 'Sydney' an entrance as you can make. Really, everybody should be focusing on the food: Italian-inspired primi piatti like Carpaccio Cipriani is a good copy of the Harry's Bar original and, for dessert, Chocolate Nemesis does the originators – Rose Gray and Ruth Rogers of London's River Cafe – proud.
23 Foster Street, Surry Hills
9281 3352
lasala.com.au

Tetsuya's

What do you know about the Franco-Japanese relationship? Not much? You'll find out it's a genuine love affair when you indulge in the world-famous (people have crossed the earth to come here) degustation menu of chef Tetsuya (Tets) Wakuda. Having scored pretty much every epicurean accolade there is, the waiting list for a coveted spot in the old Suntory restaurant site stretches over months. Once you've been wined and dined in the private, interconnecting rooms with adjoining Japanese garden, you'll know why.
529 Kent Street, Sydney
9267 2900
tetsuyas.com

EAT/DRINK

above
So very Surry Hills: the Wall Cafe.

photography
John Gollings

Breakfast

From the famous to the infamous, here's a sextet of canteens representing the range of early morning (or afternoon) nosh-ups available in this big brekky town.

bills

If only Bill Granger had taken out some patents, he'd be a very rich man. Actually, scratch that – with his three 'bills' cafes, his cookbook empire and his television career, he is a very rich man. But next time you tuck into some ricotta hotcakes with honeycomb butter at some other gaff, remember they were invented by Bill. And next time you pull up a pew at a communal bench, think of him. Granger pioneered the shared table concept to adhere to arcane trading laws that stipulated he was allowed only a certain number of tables. Now that everybody else is doing it, he's ditched it. But his breakfast institution is still going strong with the blonde-on-blonde aesthetic – that applies to the wood finishes as well as most of the customers.
433 Liverpool Street,
Darlinghurst
9360 9631
bills.com.au

Green's Cafe

Didn't make the 10.30am cut-off at McDonald's? Thank God. Still, if the glare of early morning Sydney has you reaching for your blinds, Green's has an all-day breakfast you can visit right into the afternoon. The feel is rustic, with blackboards, pale green walls, offbeat art, tea cosies and racks of jam, and the food is homely with gentle twists – a touch of parmesan in your scrambled eggs, perhaps? A solid brekky and an almost singularly unpretentious vibe for Bondi.
140 Glenayr Avenue, Bondi
9130 6181

Three Eggs

If the open kitchen looks like it might turn out some grease with your brekky, don't be dissuaded, it'll only enhance the flavour. As well as a damn good Eggs Benny and the obligatory bacon,

tomatoes and snags, this cafe does a mean scrambled tofu – designed to please the palates of the yoga bunnies next door. Housed in two unconnected shopfronts, the waiters walk out one door, onto the footpath and back inside another to deliver the food, but it all adds to the atmosphere of improvised theatre. After all, virtually everyone in here is an actor / director / filmmaker 'between projects'.
100 Brighton Boulevard, Bondi
9365 6262

Una's Coffee Lounge

For Sydney the 90s meant sharp bobs, skateboards and schnitzels, schnitzels, schnitzels. The Eastern suburbs were schnitzel central – you could barely move for flat-crumbed fillets – but most Wiener-pushers died out in the new millennium migration to paninis and pork bellies. Una's keeps the dream alive in a divey Darlo den serving plate-sized slabs of crumbed meat in seven varieties, including the very naughty Cordon Bleu (ham and blue cheese). The beer, sides (including a great sauerkraut) and decor are suitably Bavarian.
340 Victoria Street, Darlinghurst
9360 6885

Yellow Bistro and Food Store

An institution among the tight-knit community of Potts Point, The Yellow Bistro and Food Store ain't yellow at all, but has an interesting dining room decked out in pink and red where you can have breakfast, lunch, or dinner from a modern Australian menu. Or you can sit out on the footpath if you need a bit of greenery. Or just stay the whole day if you want to feel like a true-blue local.
57–59 Macleay Street, Potts Point
9357 3400

The Wall Cafe

This favourite with the local creative crowd has an older sibling and role model in Melbourne that dramatically changed that city's cafe culture. The Wall boasts idiosyncratic seating configurations that are a trademark move of its designers, Six Degrees Architects, the darlings of Melbourne hospitality design. They serve exceptionally good coffee over their little counter, which caters both to the street and the interior of the cafe. You've really got to go there to see what it's all about.
80 Campbell Street, Surry Hills
9280 1980

Small, dark & handsome

A fiery Spaniard? An existential Gaul? An amorous Italian perhaps? Sydneysiders are flocking to these haunts. Check them out and then do the latest thing: make one of these continent-inspired bistros your second home.

Bambini Trust Cafe Restaurant & Bambini Wine Room

A horizontal strip of mirrors pitched precisely at eye-level runs the gamut of the bistro, with an interesting result – everyone can see everyone else's face. That makes for an intimate atmosphere in this L-shaped dining room with its wood-panelling, black banquettes and white linen. Things get even more interesting when you look up. A bernabeifreeman-designed chandelier hangs from the ceiling like an upside-down crinoline, Indigenous dot paintings line the walls and the waiters have personality as well as ability. Next door, the wine room is invariably packed, with good reason – it's a little piece of Paris; the smartest bar in town.
185–187 Elizabeth Street, Sydney
9283 7098
bambinitrust.com.au

Bodega

With its polished concrete floors, exposed brickwork and crowd of impatient people hovering outside, Bodega looks like it could be too cool for school. Uh-uh. The place is more love-in than la-di-da. Co-owners and chefs Ben Milgate and Elvis Abrahanowicz are good friends, Elvis's girlfriend is on front-of-house and her sister waits tables. First-timers and regulars are treated with equal quantities of affable charm, which is just as well coz after you've consumed the best tapas in

EAT/DRINK/SLEEP_SMALL, DARK AND HANDSOME

above
The epitome of Sydney's next big thing, the bistro, is Vini.

photography
Anthony Gill

town (white anchovies, heavenly jamon and morcilla – black pudding) your body content will be 51% water, 49% garlic.
216 Commonwealth Street, Surry Hills
9212 7766

Buzo

When Buzo moved from one end of Jersey Road to the other, the residents must have had a street party to celebrate their good fortune. The rest of us could only wish for a local like this in our 'hood. Now housed in a Victorian corner terrace, it somewhat improbably pulls off Italian-inspired food with French-style furniture in a very British building. It's one of those where the staircase is vertiginous, the wood is dark and the spaces between the tables are so narrow you have to sidle sideways to get to yours. Best to do your walking around before dinner then, because after a generous slice of the Vincisgrassi (porcini mushroom, prosciutto and truffle lasagne) you probably won't fit.
3 Jersey Road, Woollahra
9328 1600
buzorestaurant.com.au

Cafe Sel et Poivre

A guy riding a bicycle wearing a beret, a stripy T-shirt and a row of garlic strung around his neck wouldn't be half as French as this place. In all probability Daniel Perchey, the maitre d' and proprietor, will greet you on the street with a chipper bon soir, and you'll find yourself mumbling poorly-recalled high school Francais while he raises an eyebrow in mirth. Bonne chance if you fancy one of the tables on the front terrace, but it really doesn't matter where you sit; the garlic snails, steak tartare and profiteroles taste just as delicieux at any table, n'est-ce pas?
263 Victoria Street, Darlinghurst
9361 6530

Gertrude & Alice Bookshop Cafe

Order a latte or a Moroccan mint tea, take a number and prop yourself up under Biographies L–S. Pull a title off the shelf and settle in for as many hours as you like. If Laurence Olivier or Joseph Stalin isn't as interesting as you'd hoped, you can always eavesdrop on the conversations of your neighbours, who are probably sitting just a few inches away. Perhaps they'll provide some material for your own bestseller, or maybe you'll make a new friend. Either way this little hidey-hole will warm you up on the darkest of days.
40 Hall Street, Bondi
9130 5155

Fratelli Paradiso

Potts Point residents really do think they live in paradise when digging into the beautiful yet unpretentious fare at this minimalist, chalkboard-menued abode in the little restaurant area on Challis Avenue. It's dimly lit and the frenzied waiters negotiate between tables like Roman Vespas at peak hour. The Lasagnetta is beautiful both for breakfast or lunch, and the goods of the adjoining bakery can't be beat. Just don't turn up on Saturday night, that's when the Fratellis take time out.
12–16 Challis Avenue,
Potts Point
9357 1744

Vini

Sydney didn't know what an enoteca was until Vini came along and showed 'em. The education doesn't stop there – the wall of wine covering one quarter of this small, dark box is all from Italy, so slow learners can catch up quickly. Those who have really done their homework will know you can't book, so you need to be here by 6.30 if you've got any chance of snaring a seat. Try your luck later at your peril – nobody's in a hurry to leave. Not that they're poring over the menu – it's so brief it can be scribbled on a sliver of paper. Crostini, pasta and meat options change daily but whatever you get will be very good. Did we mention get here early?
3/118 Devonshire Street,
Surry Hills (shopfront is actually on Holt Street)
9698 5131

Lunch

Ok, so there's no such thing as a free one, but there's plenty of freedom of choice in the home of ladies – and gentlemen – who lunch.

Bourke Street Bakery

For this section of the guide we asked dozens of designers to list their hotspots for breakfast, lunch and dinner. The suggestions were wide and varied, but this place popped up on almost all the hit lists. Why? Go there and find out for yourself. Perhaps it's the staff (they look like they've been cast, rather than recruited), the fellow breakfasters or lunchers (ten bucks if the person next to you isn't an architect or designer) or simply the wonderful croissants, sandwiches and rolls this little place turns out.
633 Bourke Street, Surry Hills
9699 1011

Cafe Sopra

Hidden up a level at one of Sydney's premier provedores, Fratelli Fresh, Sopra has the advantage of an in-house veggie garden and uses it well. Chef Andy Bunn's paninis and salads, that might include globe artichokes, kipfler potatoes and oyster mushrooms, are fresh and more sophisticated than the pared-down, white-walled, casual room suggests. A Jerusalem artichoke and crab soup is superb – enough to warrant the sometimes 40-minute wait it can take to secure a table. And who doesn't love a man-high blackboard?
7 Danks Street, Waterloo
9699 3174

Single Origin Roasters

A cafe that roasts its own sustainable coffee beans has got to be serious about coffee. When that cafe has a coffee-roasting machine named Boris, you know it's got a sense of humour too. If you arrive and find a man in

above
A favourite game at Il Baretto is 'What pedigree is that pooch?'

photography
Eoghan Lewis

the corner playing with Boris' controls, don't worry, that's just (co-owner) Gavin Folden fine-tuning his toy. Everything will be perfectly clear when you taste his ristretto: a short, dark, strong reminder that few things in life taste this good. At lunchtime, the district's designers and architects drop in for a pit-stop salad and a shot of the black stuff.
60–64 Reservoir Street,
Surry Hills
9211 9055

Danks Street Depot

The most striking feature of Danks Street Depot might be the pig and lamb carcasses hanging in the cool room, visible from certain points on the floor. Chef Jarred Ingersoll doesn't see the point of hiding them. He wants people to know what they're eating. His earthy approach to food means he butchers the carcasses himself and combines cuts with seasonal produce for some of the city's freshest and tastiest cafe dishes.

The decor – concrete floors, timber tables, breathtakingly high-peaked ceilings – is subtle and won't distract from the eating.
2 Danks Street, Waterloo
9698 2201

Il Baretto

Leafy Bourke Street is a catwalk for weird and wonderful canines and their quirky owners. If the comfy cafe seats in this bustling Bourke Street joint are all taken, try sitting on one of the stools, stooping your head out the window and playing 'What pedigree is that pooch?' Back inside, perfectly al dente pasta is the order of the day and duck ravioli – a dish copied all over town – is the star. No bookings, no cards, definitely no frills but a fabulous place to while away the arvo.
496 Bourke Street, Surry Hills
9361 6163

Paddington Alimentari

Originally opened to provide the Italian immigrant neighbourhood with staples of prosciutto, mozzarella and parmigiano back in the days when Aussies ate meat and three veg, half of this lovely relic is still a deli. The other half squeezes in a few stools and a counter, where a lucky few are treated to plates of the AlimentARIs own antipasto and coffee with a crema just like they make it in the old country.
2 Hopetoun Street, Paddington
9358 2142

Via Abercrombie

It's hard to believe someone had the temerity to put something other than a skip bin in a Sydney laneway, but here you have it. And if you thought the queue was as long as your arm, you should see the sandwiches. Anyone interested in examining dental work should pay attention as the city suits arch their jaws over four-inch-deep paddles of bread filled, if they're early enough, with chilli chicken and about 17 salads. Once upon a time the staff bore a distinct resemblance to Seinfeld's soup nazi (in spirit at least) but now the long wait to the counter is rewarded with big smiles – and those bloody big sandwiches.
1 Abercrombie Lane, Sydney
9251 0000

EAT/DRINK/SLEEP_LA VERA PIZZA

La vera pizza

right
Pizza e Birra: simple, but beautiful Italian fun.

When it comes to skill, expertise and centuries-old technique, you've gotta hand it to the pizza-makers. After all, if you really had some talent you'd be designing them too, wouldn't you?

Love Supreme

This brand-new pizza joint on Oxford Street is part of Sydney restaurant folklore. Along with charismatic proprietor Bosko Vujovic, Love Supreme is the continuation of a legend that began a little further down the road, at Arthur's Pizza, the epic honky-tonk Bosko used to run. It was famous for its quirky service, trendy punters and upside-down sign. Then, a soap-opera-style dispute over the name of the place saw Vujovic move to Customs House. Since 2007, however, he's back home in Paddington. The residents couldn't be happier.
180a Oxford Street, Paddington
9331 1779

Pizza e Birra

It hasn't been around for all that long but Pizza e Birra is already an essential destination for pizza fans and Surry Hills foodies. Designed by Melbourne-based interior designer Chris Connell, the restaurant's insides, like its name, are simple and understated. The wood-fired pizzas couldn't be more authentic, and for that matter neither could the dining crowd – the former is la vera Napoli and the latter fair-dinkum Surry Hills, mate. With all that talk about pizza and people, we almost forgot about the pale. It's made by the Hopping Mad boutique brewery in Orange.
500 Crown Street, Surry Hills
9332 2510

Pizza Mario

David Cowdrill knows how to make a crust so good it could be divine. After breaking our hearts when he sold his beloved Mario's, he made a pilgrimage to the birthplace of pizza.

In Naples, he earned his Vera Pizza Napoletana certification (Accreditation No. 153), then returned to Sydney to open this temple to pizza, where hearts are mended as we sink our teeth into gorgonzola with parmesan and radicchio. And now that it's traded its piccolo digs for a sizeable slice of the St Margaret's design precinct, we don't even have to queue to worship.
St Margarets, 417–421 Bourke Street, Surry Hills
9332 3633
pizzamario.com.au

Pompei's

George Pompei has nothing to do with Mount Vesuvius, unless you count the blasting temperatures inside his pizza furnace. This is an oven so hot, the discs of dough need only a minute or two inside before they're crispy. On a Bondi corner quite unlike any other, Pompei's belies its modest size by cramming twice its bodyweight into tightly-packed tables inside and out. Friends munch, families feast and toddlers do endless runs to the legendary gelato counter.
126–130 Roscoe Street, Bondi
9365 1233

Rosso Pomodoro

They say you shouldn't talk religion or politics. In Sydney, that should read coffee or pizza. However, should the latter topic arise, you're guaranteed to hear the name of this pizzeria championed with ravenous passion. Rightly so. The pizzas are thin and delicate but hold firm, and the toppings are minimalist and bitey. Within its art-smattered tomato-red walls you'll find the best capricciosa in town. Retort?
24 Buchanan Street, Balmain
9555 5924

Ventuno

Designed by Melburnians Kylie Fitt and Elida de Felice of Fitt De Felice architects, Ventuno is as much a design destination as it is a spot for some good Italian pizza and coffee. Set by the water on Hickson Road Ventuno has become a haunt of theatre goers and urban aesthetes. With a cast concrete bar, a diverse and relaxed atmosphere, and about as much Flos lighting as you can get in one place. Ventuno offers traditional Italian faire - prepared by specially imported Calabrian chefs.
21 Hickson Road, Millers Point
9247 4444

Orient express

Sydney must be the city with the most Thai take-aways after Bangkok, but there's much more to Asian fare here than Tom Yum. From upmarket and refined to downtown and no frills, these places are really all about the food and the atmos. Let all roads lead East.

BBQ King

This well-lit step in from Chinatown's Goulburn Street is a favourite of the pre- and post-theatre set, most of whom flood in straight after curtain call at the nearby Entertainment Centre. The interior leaves a bit to be desired and many have called for an overhaul. But renovations be damned, there's something very cool about being here at 2am. Diners share massive plates of slippery noodles and hoe in with impolite abandon. When in Rome …
18–20 Goulburn Street, Sydney
9267 2586

Billy Kwong

Whereas Londoners flock to Jamie Oliver's Fifteen to get their own slice of TV chefery, the Sydney equivalent is Billy Kwong, the restaurant of ubiquitous celebrity chef Kylie Kwong. Like Fifteen, Billy Kwong also sticks up for a worthy cause – the surprisingly small restaurant fills its windows with posters and advertisements for international campaigns against poverty. Once past the literature, the food in the canteen-like interior is spectacularly fresh and largely organic, and a strict no-bookings policy means that everyone will get a seat, provided you're happy to wait, and you will be.
355 Crown Street, Surry Hills
9332 3300

Longrain

Located in an expansive converted warehouse, Longrain was all the rage when it opened just before the turn of the millennium and transformed

the eating-out culture of the Emerald city. Its wood-panelled interior with communal tables is still at the top of the visit-list of many visitors to this city, and the Thai-fusion dishes are as popular and mouthwatering as ever. A couple of years ago, the popular eatery expanded to Melbourne, and while that city's denizens are still celebrating their own Longrain as the hot newcomer, the Sydney original has long-since entered the all-time-favourites list and that's where it'll no doubt stay for many years to come.
83–85 Commonwealth Street, Surry Hills
9280 2888
longrain.com.au

Matsuri

Some people stand outside Matsuri scratching their heads. 'Will I get take-away, eat in at the take-away, or dine in at the restaurant?' Watch their faces contort as they agonise over the decision. But the ohitashi spinach and teriyaki tuna will taste just as good at home or in-house, and the sashimi is so fresh it's hard to believe it's stopped swimming.
614–618 Crown Street, Surry Hills
9690 1366

Phamish

Could this be the busiest Vietnamese restaurant in Sydney? There might be times when it's empty, but nobody's ever witnessed them, except when this place is shut (and even then people are probably still queuing). When it's open, it's a noisy hive of heads bent over bowls of rice paper rolls, duck pancakes and sesame lamb, most of which are sold out before the last sitting has been sat. Bright red chopsticks match the cylindrical stools and retractable windows blur the lines to the street – where hungry hordes wait to take your place.
354 Liverpool Street, Darlinghurst
9357 2688

Red Lantern

Define incongruity and you may come up with this: a Vietnamese restaurant in a Surry Hills terrace. That's Red Lantern, which pulls off incongruous so well you might never get in. Or maybe the crowds are here just for that food. If you manage an entry, go for a spot on the verandah and order a plate of rice paper rolls stuffed with duck, enoki mushrooms and Vietnamese herbs. An inside table is a suitable second,

with red menus, napkins and furnishings contrasting nicely with dark timber floors. Praise the Red Lantern.
545 Crown Street, Surry Hills
9698 4355

Sailor's Thai Canteen

Not so long ago, a 1980s thinking-girls crumpet on tour went out for one of the best Thai meals he ever had (or so he said to this very writer). The crumpet was Lloyd Cole, the venue was Sailor's Thai Canteen in The Rocks. And it's not only the food that causes a commotion about the place, it's also the one long, communal stainless-steel table that makes talking to strangers easy pieces and – if you're new to this town – helps you feel part of the mainstream.
106 George Street, The Rocks
9251 2466

Sea Bay

It's just been refurbished, but this place ain't ever gonna win any design awards. That's no impediment for the gaggles of arty young things and Chinese locals who congregate to slurp noodles made here by hand every day.
372 Pitt Street, Sydney
9267 4855

Spice I Am

No one can keep a secret in Sydney. There was a time, not so many moons ago, when this Thai local was known only to a select few and one could chance upon it's low-key shopfront, grab a table and enjoy arguably Sydney's best Thai. Those days are over, and like most Surry Hills dives given decent newspaper reviews, the place is always heaving. The tom yum's more famous around town than most red carpet tragics, and the quaint decor, with tiny white tables, little potted plants and an open front, is daggy Austral-Asian genius.
90 Wentworth Avenue,
Surry Hills
9280 0928

Uchi Lounge

Something keeps Sydneysiders coming back to this popular Japanese diner. It could be that it's set back from the frenzy of Oxford Street, or that the bar downstairs is a bonafide star. Sake cocktails go down a tad too easy in this hip room, murmuring one minute, boisterous the next.
15 Brisbane Street, Surry Hills
9261 3524

RSL's

above
The RSL's, the last bastions of war veterans, have been discovered by the cool crowd.

photography
Olivia Martin-McGuire

Thanks to the tough licensing laws, the spot that is elsewhere reserved for bingo and bowls can in Sydney become a hangout of the coolcats. Several of them have been colonised by a much younger generation – veterans of style wars, if you like. And yes, there are even some with views.

Commercial Travellers Association

Originally 'an oasis in the city of Sydney' for workers employed to travel the country preaching the corporate gospel, this club in banked-out Martin Place is now a nice reprieve from all the travelling going on outside. Escape the flow of suits, awful grey fountains and piercing horns in the meat-and-three-veg bistro or settle down for what passes as fine dining in these parts (i.e. mains at $19.50 across the board).
MLC Centre, Martin Place, Sydney
9232 7344

North Bondi RSL

Where most RSL's offer views of octogenarians rolling little black balls across short green lawns, North Bondi spoils its drinkers with panoramas of Sydney's most famous beach and the sun-kissed bodies who call it home. Cocktails are not big here but you didn't come for muddled limes. Savour the view, tune out the pokies and head to the bistro for some reliable pub fare with a VB chaser.
120 Ramsgate Avenue, Bondi
9130 8770

Paddington RSL

Among the boutique fashion dens pocketing Oxford Street, Paddington RSL stands out as a beige-grey glass paean to suburbia. But the perfect opener to a night out in ultra-trendy Paddo hosts a surprisingly eclectic crowd. For many of the trendy things inside it's a throwback to home – good for cheap beer and maybe a flutter. The bistro is better than most of its kind, the taps reach beyond the Carlton / Tooheys set, but the carpet is very RSL and sporadic pot plants can be irksome. For better or worse, Saturday's comedy night.
226 Oxford Street, Paddington
9311 1203

Palm Beach RSL

Just a few breaths from another fabulous Sydney beachside icon, Palm Beach Wharf, this dramatically planted gem has views of the Pacific and a great summery vibe. It looks like a surf club and acts like an RSL, with beer gardens, pokies, meat raffles, bingo and trivia. The locale and the breezy feel means Palm Beach RSL is kid-friendly and the bistro is a lovely homage to old-school Aussie tucker – the homemade gourmet pies are worth the $20 membership alone. Pass the dead horse.
1087 Barrenjoey Road,
Palm Beach
9974 5566

Something fishy

above
The finest sushi you'll ever have is at sushi-e.

right
Have some atmosphere with your snapper at Flying Fish.

One, two, three four five, once I caught a fish alive; six, seven, eight nine ten, then I threw it back again – not bloody likely in this town, mate. Just a few are caught and cooked up a storm in this surf-obsessed city. Here's a selection of the best seafood shanties.

Fish Face

Some of the best Sydney beach fare can be found in this urban Darlinghurst crack-in-the-wall. The tiny room stretches the length of the high sushi bar and holds about five dark wooden tables. There are a few spots outside and you can always haggle for a stool somewhere. You should, because former fine-dining chefs Stephen Hodges and Zachary Sykes have packed their small place with some of the town's tastiest and freshest seafood creations. The perfectly balanced flavours of seared tuna with coddled egg and anchovy will flap around your mouth like a live mullet for hours.
132 Darlinghurst Road, Darlinghurst
9332 4803

Fishmongers

It hasn't taken Mongers (as it's known in the local dialect) long to become a Bondi Beach institution. Upon opening in 2005, a wave of newspapers and magazines declared it the source of some of Sydney's best chips. Crowds flocked like seagulls. The famous frites are creamy on the inside of a faint but crisp coating. A handful go perfectly with a thick steak of swordfish or dory. Squash into a sand-smattered timber bench or take lunch to the beach and enjoy Mongers' modern twists on beachside classics.
42 Hall Street, Bondi
9365 2205

Flying Fish

Set in a converted wharf, this restaurant got off to a flying start when it opened in 2003, scoring top reviews and a coveted IDEA award for its interior design. As if the killer views and inspired menu of fish dishes in all varieties and fusions weren't enough, the restaurant's bartender was also crowned the best of his ilk in Australia.
Jones Bay Wharf, Lower Deck,
19–21 Pirrama Road, Pyrmont
9518 6677
flyingfish.com.au

Mohr Fish

Every Sydneysider has a different opinion about where to get the best fish & chips in town, so we won't even get into that debate. But we can tell you the cutest – it's the tile-clad interior of Mohr fish, which is the tiny add-on to the Mohr and Mohr restaurant next door. Clamber onto one of the high chairs and order from a simple menu. Eating in is a lot pricier than taking out, but it'll be worth the experience. And yes, they might just be the best fish & chips in coathanger city.
202 Devonshire Street,
Surry Hills
9318 1326
mohrandmohr.com

sushi-e

It's a little bit of work to find Sydney's swishest sushi bar in the Establishment Hotel. Hint: it's behind the wooden slats by the fourth level Hemmesphere bar. Make the effort and you'll be delighted by bitsy dishes including a Balmain Bug Roll or Spider Roll (soft-shell crab with jalapeno mayonnaise) prepared by chefs behind the impressive white-marble counter. The chop and roll production is theatrical, but the attractive floor staff move about like a stunned audience.
Establishment,
252 George Street, Sydney
9240 3041

Late at night

right, top
The den-like atmosphere of Hemmesphere.

right, bottom
Lotus Bar is a favourite late-night haunt.

Can't stop the party? On a date you can't bear to end? Just want to see what happens in shindig central after hours? You'll fit right in with the locals at any of these establishments.

Barons

Beer goggles were probably invented in this late-night dive. The ceiling is as patched and worn as the carpet, making the mind boggle when you think about how, but therein lies the charm of this Shakespearean upstairs den, filled as it is with late-night lovers, misfits, drunks and persons of questionable profession. But no matter, this is a no-questions-asked kinda place, except when Sydney's absurd licensing laws come into play and you're asked to throw down a plate of lasagne before you can get your hands on a drink. (Editor's note: At the time of going to press, the building was due to be demolished, but the developers have pledged to re-let a space to the club's owners, who will 'distil the essence of the old Barons'.)
5 Roslyn Street, Kings Cross
9267 7160

The Gaslight Inn

If you're 23 and your wardrobe consists of Converse sneakers, stripy T-shirts and skinny jeans, then this is where you come to drink cheap beer, listen to Van She and feign boredom at 2am. If you're, ahem, slightly older than 23, you can just about get away with doing the same. Maybe just throw on a pair of (original) RayBans first.
278 Crown Street, Surry Hills / Darlinghurst
9360 6746

Hemmesphere

This ultra-swish nightclub in the Establishment hotel and restaurant complex is not for the faint-hearted. If you really want to let your hair down, kick your heels up and get your cleavage

out, do like Snoop Dogg did when in he was in town – turn the place into your crib for the night and hang a few ladies off each arm like cufflinks.
252 George Street, Sydney
9240 3040
merivale.com

The Judgment Bar

There is not much to recommend the Judgment Bar beyond its opening hours (all 24 of them) and yet ask any self-respecting hard partying Sydneysider and the sheer mention of this classic closer will bring a glint to their eye. Don't roll out of Sydney without having staggered out of here.
Cnr Oxford and Bourke Street, Darlinghurst
9360 4831

Lotus Bar

Many a designer will tell you that this is one of the best bars in Sydney. Tucked behind the restaurant of the same name, the cave-like, SJB-designed, Florence Broadhurst-clad interior will have you forgetting about time, space and all that jazz as you work your way through the extensive cocktail list.
22 Challis Avenue, Potts Point
9326 9000
merivale.com

The Lounge

Truly down-to-earth, this open space with its motley furniture, bar staples and pizzas is a favourite of many a Surry Hills local and is open late. Not a pub, not a cafe but the right kind of place to hang out in when you're not interested in starlet-spotting or fancy cocktails – this is what Sydney needs more of. And if licensing laws ever change, she'll get it. Let's not forget that The Lounge was there first.
277 Goulbourn Street, Surry Hills
9356 8888
9360 4702

Will and Toby's

Don't try talking to the big black beast in the middle of this bar. He's the silent type. And besides, he's wearing a lampshade on his head (Front Design's life-size Horse Lamp). But he does set the tone for the room. Although it's less than a year old, brothers Will and Toby Osmond have kitted out their latest baby like a gentlemen's club on hunting vacation. (Imagine Ralph Lauren in a dark, dark mood and you'll get the picture.) On the floor below is a supper club where local crooners sing away their sorrows.
134 Oxford Street, Darlinghurst
9331 7073
willandtobys.com.au

Hotels

above
The beautifully tranquil roof garden and hallway of the Regent's Court Hotel in Potts Point.

Whether it's a one-night stand, a long-term affair, a romance rekindler or just a flopbox between flights, this city's got lodgings that'll fix your fancy. The following are just a few.

The Blacket

Sharing the corner with landmark architectural site 363 George Street (see p. 49), the Blacket has a lot to live up to in terms of its design heritage. Named for the Edmund Blacket who designed the ANZ building next door, it too is a classic Sydney example of old-meets-new. An understated, no-fuss but fashionable place aimed at corporate and holiday travellers keen to lodge in the heart of the CBD, it's a great spot to grab a cocktail, mingle with other over-nighters and contemplate the great architectural minds that contributed to the site.
70 King Street
(Cnr George Street), Sydney
9279 3030
theblacket.com

The Blue

Shmancy but a rather nice place to be. Russell Crowe lives next door to this 5-star spot formerly known simply as the W, right on

the Finger Wharf. It's designer but it's warm, too, with an attention to detail you'd expect from a 5-star place. After dinner at Otto with Russ go down and lie in your spa and contemplate how to pay your hotel bill, or sit on the dock of the bay and watch the superyachts roll away in the harbour. The quintessential Sydney experience.
6 Cowper Wharf Road, Woolloomooloo
9331 9000
tajhotels.com/sydney

The Hilton

Woah, down boy. This OTT scratch crib is like an all-over Berocca, from the minute you're swallowed up at the door. It's a huge extravaganza, with 577 rooms, thousands of square metres of party space and a pile of marble they might have had to quarry half a continent for. The Hilton's got some amazing art pieces, services that aim for 'the absolute zenith of indulgence' and a regular run of swanky jetsetters you'll have to remember not to gape over. Are we having fun yet?
488 George Street, Sydney
9266 2000
hiltonsydney.com.au

left
Soak up history at The Blacket Hotel (top) or indulge in local art and sculptures at the Hilton (bottom).

The Kirketon

Smack-bang in the middle of dear old Darlinghurst, this inexpensive but not cheap boutique hotel has a European industrial feel – block colours, shiny surfaces, clean straight lines – designed by Burley Katon Halliday (they do lots of the stuff). It's filled with designer pieces, including Geoffrey Mance lights, and houses the newly opened Kell's Kitchen restaurant.
229 Darlinghurst Road, Darlinghurst
1800 332 920
kirketon.com.au

Medusa

Even though it's pink it's still one of the best hotels in Sydney. With 18 rooms in an old Darlinghurst mansion nurtured back to life by architect Scott Weston, the Medusa is a little bit theatre dahling but with all the mod cons. Encapsulating the locale's old-world charm, it's a favourite during Mardi Gras when patrons (and their dogs) can make full use of the snug and secluded courtyard.
267 Darlinghurst Road, Darlinghurst
9331 1000
medusa.com.au

Regents Court Hotel

We've shown you the fancy, the low-budget and the inner-city. Now we're bringing out the big guns. Regents Court Hotel is Sydney's answer to the Chelsea – where you stay to meet any artists, performers, photographers, curators, writers and general creative folk in town, all in a dear and convenient little spot on the border of Kings Cross and Potts Point. The family-owned 30-room hotel in a quiet side street is lovingly run by Paula and Tom MacMahon, who cultivate the creative atmosphere through their collection of iconic furniture and art, their beautiful roof garden – surely the best in inner-city Sydney – and their very warm reception. Many of their artistic guests show their appreciation by leaving their artworks and books behind. Others don't leave at all; the MacMahons practise what they preach by offering a residency program for artists and writers to help make projects happen. Find out more on the website.
18 Springfield Avenue, Potts Point
9358 1533
regentscourt.com.au

REGIONAL_RIVERSDALE

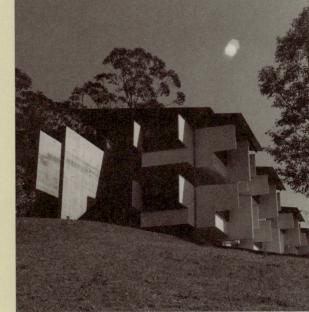

above and right
The only publicly accessible Glenn Murcutt Building; Riversdale is certainly worth the trip.

Out of town

There's a raft of design destinations just out of Sydney. Whether it's the only public building by Glenn Murcutt, or the arts and crafts haven that is Canberra, get yourself into the car or on the train and enjoy the great outdoors. We have a few suggestions.

Canberra

A compromise between Melbourne and Sydney as the nation's capital, this town is nothing like either of them but has its own distinct personality. Walter Burley Griffin enthusiasts shouldn't miss this place, but there's a few other national treasures besides.

The National Portrait Gallery

It's a bit obvious to say, but this place is about portraits – painted, drawn, photographed and busted in both permanent and changing exhibitions. Besides the interesting array of faces, it will soon be housed in a rather interesting building, designed by architects Johson Pilton Walker, who recently won the competition for the new building. Just a quick walk away is the second site at Old Parliament House, which has another history all its own.
Old Parliament House
King George Terrace, Parkes
6270 8236
Commonwealth Place
Parkes Place, Parkes
6270 8236
portrait.gov.au

National Museum of Australia

It took over a hundred years of gestation for this mighty creature to finally be born in 2001, and what a birth it was. There were lots who didn't appreciate the design of architects ARM in conjunction with Robert Peck von Hartel Trethowan, but it won a raft of architectural

accolades anyway. With its 6600 square metres of unexpected landscapes, bold angles and look-twice use of colour and texture, it's a visual feast.
Lawson Crescent,
Acton Peninsula, Canberra
6208 5000
nma.gov.au

Workshop Bilk

It's a little out of the way, but we didn't want to keep it from you. Another name that repeatedly emerged from our research as a focal point of jewellery and glass, Workshop Bilk opened in its present location in a factory space on the edge of Canberra, in the creative hub of Queanbeyan, in 2002. As a partnership formed by pioneering artists Helen Aitken-Kuhnen and Johannes Kuhnen, the name is homage to the Düsseldorf suburb where the two opened their first workshop in 1978. Their Aussie abode now functions simultaneously as a gallery space and a jewellery school, and has become a hub for collaboration. Their teachings focus on gold and silversmithing, as well as enamelling and kiln-formed glass. The gallery is devoted primarily to exhibiting contemporary jewellery and silversmithing, but occasionally shows furniture and glass. What's not on display is kept in drawers for visitors to admire. By showcasing the work of both established and emerging artists, Workshop Bilk encourages the creation of individual collections and fortifies the relationship between jewellery design in Sydney and Canberra.
53 Kendall Avenue, Queanbeyan
6232 9411
workshopbilk.com

The Glass Workshop

Founded in 1983 by internationally acclaimed artist Klaus Moje, The Canberra Glassworks, now headed by Ann Jakle, has set a standard of quality and diversity that is now the benchmark of graduates of the workshop. (Poor things!) Earlier this year, it moved into the supremely impressive old Canberra Powerhouse at Kingston. Yet to be fully occupied by artisans, the workshop is certainly worth a visit if only to see the demonstrations of glassblowing in the 'hotshop'. Visitors sit above, looking down on the workshop floor while glass-smiths extract the molten substance from the furnace and shape it into art as the audience watches. Built and funded by the ACT Government, it's the only centre of its kind in Australia

REGIONAL

below
The pool at Tonic in the Hunter Valley.

left
Test drive Koskela furniture by staying in their beautiful holiday house near Palm Beach.

and the largest of its kind in the Southern Hemisphere. Truly a defining space in the art glass industry in NSW, this is a focal resource where artists can utilise state-of-the-art equipment and access space and time to create their masterpieces.
11 Wentworth Avenue, Kingston ACT
6260 7005
canberraglassworks.com

Palm Beach

Just over half an hour's drive from the city is the hammerhead peninsula of Palm Beach, a Sydney playground where the rich enjoy their luxury shacks and the rest of us enjoy watching them (and the sand, sun and surf as well). It really is a tourist paradise, but don't let that stop you from enjoying one of the most spectacular, island-like spots in the state.

Patonga

How groovy is this: in a sleepy little fishing village bordered by national parks a million miles away from Sydney (but only an hour and a half drive) lives an old weatherboard house renovated and furnished by the folk from Koskela with their own and some restored pieces. Rent it, live the Koskela experience, then pick up something to take home from their Surry Hills showroom on your way back through town.
9280 0999

Hunter Valley

Hop in the convertible, drive through a rolling valley, pick up some vino, savour the local produce, cast an eye over some quaint old cottages – just don't miss this incredible area only a couple of hours out of the CBD.

Tonic Hotel

The design is based on a typical outback shed, but it's kitted out with designer furniture and homewares, and has all the mod cons like heated floors. Great views, an emphasis on privacy and non-invasive service, no one under 15 (this ain't a place for the littlies), the thing that really sets this hotel apart is that everything in your room is for sale – you really do have to pay for the stuff you take home with you, but considering Tonic's focus on high-quality goods, it might just be worth it.
tonichotel.com.au

Riversdale

An art pilgrimage, architecture journey and road trip down the coast rolled into one – visiting the Arthur and Yvonne Boyd Education Centre on the Shoalhaven River is a chance to explore the life of one of Australia's most celebrated artists (Boyd) and a chance to visit the only public building of Australia's most renowned contemporary architect Glenn Murcutt, designed in association with Reg Lark and Wendy Lewin. Known as Riversdale, the centre is set on Bundanon Trust's magnificent property overlooking the Shoalhaven River. The Centre provides arts education programs, hosts special events for visitors and is available for corporate functions, seminars and conferences. Up to 32 visitors at a time can learn from residential programs, which are based on the cultural and natural heritage of the property, or you can take advantage of the tranquil setting as a place to pause and think.
bundanon.com.au

Blue Mountains

Not quite contemporary – but at least it's perched on the edge of a cliff called Echo Point – Lilianfels in the Blue Mountains offers a modern spa retreat experience in a grand olde worlde setting, with a lap pool and some big hearth fires.
lilianfels.com.au

Newcastle

Take a drive to the 'steel city' of Newcastle only two scenic hours north from Sydney. Newcastle's claim to fame, aside from having steel mills and recently, an oil tanker parked on its main beach, is a growing array of award-winning architecture and cultural events. Two notable festivals are Electrofringe, a festival of experimental electronic arts, and the This Is Not Art festival, an independent, emerging arts soirée. Both make Newcastle worth the drive along a freeway that winds through bush and over rivers, especially in the September–October period.

After a stroll on one of the many city beaches you might fancy some architecture spotting, so grab a copy of *Architecture Newcastle: A Guide* (edited by David Stafford and former Newcastle Uni Dean of Architecture Professor Barry Maitland, who is now writing crime fiction novels). Many of the gems they reveal are located on the University of Newcastle Callaghan Campus, which had a permaculture landscape makeover in the early 1990s. Check out these major awards collectors: the BSC Building at the Faculty of Architecture (aka Red Square) by Michael Wilford of James Stirling Michael Wilford, the Design Building by Peter Stutchbury and EJE Architecture, the Architecture Design Studio by James Grose of Grose Bradley, the Life Sciences Building by Peter Stutchbury and Suters Architects, and Birabahn, the Aboriginal Cultural Centre by Leplastrier, Harper and Stutchbury.

Back in the city, have a look at the Art Pavilion at the Newcastle Regional Art Gallery (1 Laman Street, Cooks Hill), designed by Herd Architects, then head up Darby Street for some frock shopping at High Tea with Mrs Woo (see p. 185) and a coffee at Goldberg's.
electrofringe.net
thisisnotart.org

Events

above
Everyone loves Semi-Permanent. Not least because of its cool merchandise.

Animania Festival

This very independent Asian and Japanese animation party features a games room, karaoke, competitions, sword demonstrations and a food fair. All within the confines of the nice-and-central Sydney Town Hall over three days in September.
animania.net.au

Australian International Animation Festival

Late May. Three days. Wagga Wagga. The best of Australian and international animation from over 2000 entries. Need we say more?
aiaf.com.au

Australian International Furniture Fair

A three-day trade-only event, this fair is on every February at the Sydney Exhibition Centre in Darling Harbour. It's co-located with soft-furnishing fair Decoration + Design.
aiff.net.au
decorationdesign.com.au

Biennale of Sydney

Australia's largest celebration of contemporary visual art is held every second year from June to September in spots all over the city, and most events are free. Get a packed program from the website.
biennaleofsydney.com.au

Cut&Paste

Originating in New York and held in Sydney for the first time in November 2007, eight designers each have 15 minutes to produce a theme-based presentation while an eager audience looks on. A winning criterion includes 'overall dopeness', and the audience can participate too.
cutandpaste.com

DesignEx

Every second year in April Sydney plays host to this design trade fair. Interior Design Awards are held at the same time.
designex.info

DESIGN RESOURCES_DESIGN EVENTS

Form & Function

This trade event for the building, construction, architecture and design industries is held every April in either Sydney or Melbourne and showcases new products, services and technologies for residential, commercial and industrial projects.
formandfunctionexpo.com.au

Glenn Murcutt International Architecture Masterclass

Australia's most renowned living architect oversees this 'life-changing experience', a 14-day intensive workshop with alumni from all over the world. Only 30 lucky professionals can attend each year and the waiting list is huge.
ozetecture.org

Launch Pad

An initiative of *Indesign* magazine, Launch Pad is an awards event run in conjunction with their Saturday Indesign program, and is aimed at providing career development opportunities for emerging Australian product designers. Launch Pad includes an exhibition of the finalists' prototypes (which are then promoted to media and manufacturers here and overseas), mentoring and networking events and critique from Launch Pad judges as well as an international review panel.
launch-pad.com.au

New Design

Just another initiative of the inexorable Object, *New Design* is the annual high point of the design education arena where Object's curators and aficionados select the most promising work of design graduates. To final-out in *New Design* is one of the holy grails of final-year design students across Australia. The popular exhibition introduces the outstanding up-and-comers working across product design, textiles, fashion, ceramics, glass and furniture.
object.com.au

Newtown Flicks

Established to meet the demands of the underground Sydney short film industry, the festival is screened across a three-day weekend in April. There is action-packed footage, animation and documentaries, and everything else in between, as well as a program of short films for kids of all ages called Treehouse Flicks.
newtownflicks.com.au

Pecha Kucha Night

Started in Tokyo some years back, the Sydney edition of this worldwide slidenight bonanza is organised by a bunch of keen young architects and is a major social event. Twenty designers and artists have exactly six minutes forty seconds to get on their soapbox. Keep an eye on the website for details.
pecha-kucha.org

Rosemount Australian Fashion Week

Circular Quay lights up for three days every October to present trans-seasonal collections to the industry elite. With exhibits around town, designers from Australia and the Asia-Pacific presenting individual collections, as well as women's, men's and new generation group shows, and the new Australian Fashion Laureate award, it's a must-attend event for key players and newcomers alike.
afw.com.au

Saturday InDesign

An annual event for design professionals and interested laypeople, this late-July day out includes around 100 exhibits at around 60 locations, lots of them with free drinks and other fun things. The main event is held on a Saturday (with other smaller openings and events on the Friday) – pack your runners.
saturdayindesign.com.au

Semi-Permanent

This is a major feature on the Sydney design calendar. The event, with its huge guest-only after party (Semi-Intoxicated) is hosted by Design is Kinky every April, and has Perth and Auckland counterparts and others in the pipeline. Cream-of-the-crop designers speak over two days and anyone can go get themselves inspired.
semipermanent.com

Shirty

September in Sydney sees a shirt shindig where independent designers offer limited edition and one-off tees capped at a measly $69. At the Newtown Neighbourhood Centre, from midday to midnight.
shirty07.com

Sydney Architecture Festival

Inaugurated in October 2007 to coincide with World Architecture Day, this new fiesta takes over Sydney streets with walking tours, a Kids Design Challenge and an Iron Architect competition. Lots of fun.
architecture.org.au

Sydney Design

Presented by the Powerhouse Museum with their various industry partners, Sydney Design is one of the grand events that grace the streets, galleries and minds of Sydney once a year. It's a two-to-three-week festival packed with exhibitions, seminars, film screenings, design markets, tours, awards and exhibitions. Held every August, Sydney Design offers something for everyone – from the curious onlooker to the industry professional. Keep an eye on the website for details.
sydneydesign.com.au

Sydney Esquisse

Launched in 2003, Sydney Esquisse is the city's own art and design festival that hits the streets of Surry Hills, Darlinghurst, Redfern and Chippendale every couple of years with some of Australia's most talented creative individuals, exhibiting works in unpredictable public ventures for ten days of fresh, edgy and unexpected art and design. Sydney Esquisse was initiated by local design group Play, a trio (two Austrians and a German) who came together to form a business that runs huge design-focused events, whipping up a damn good time for the design hub in Sydney with talks, seminars, film screenings and parties.
sydneyesquisse.org

Sydney Film Festival

A winter wonderland of the hottest films from Australia and overseas, as well as talks, forums, debates, exhibitions and awards. Two weeks, hundreds of films. Get yourself a schedule and start planning well ahead of the June timeslot.
sydneyfilmfestival.org

Sydney Writers' Festival

A world-class cultural event and a most dynamic celebration of the written word. Showcasing around 250 of the world's leading writers from home and abroad, the festival, which runs over a week throughout Sydney, includes a diverse range of writing styles, including literary and popular fiction, journalism and poetry, screenwriting and drama.
swf.org.au

Tropfest

Although it goes to every capital city in Australia, Sydney is and always will be the home of the nation's most popular short film festival, and it's

impossible for any creatively minded Sydneysider to not have written, acted in, directed or otherwise been part of a Tropfest submission. It all began in the early 1990s as a modest screening at Tropicana Caffe in Darlinghurst. Held in the Botanic Gardens in February each year, picnic baskets are packed early, with viewers arriving in the early afternoon to see a piece of the action when night falls and the films aired are also broadcast via satellite across Australia. The competition is tough and guidelines are strict – each film must correspond to a stipulated theme to ensure it is specially created.
tropinc.com

Workshopped

Workshopped started as a series of successful design exhibitions at the Strand Arcade, traditionally held at the same time as Sydney Design. Independently curated, edgy and fun, the event has now evolved into an organisation that aims to promote Australian product designers by acting as agents for them both locally and internationally, facilitating production and locating suitable retail outlets.
workshopped.com.au

›
Institutions & Resources

Architecture Foundation Australia

Here's the (virtual) home of all things to do with Glenn Murcutt, Richard Leplastrier, Peter Stutchbury and Lindsay Johnston, including photos, articles, biographies and info about their master classes.
ozetecture.org

Ausglass

The Australian Association of Glass Artists is the principal body for glass workers across Australia and holds annual conferences at different locations every year. It works to represent members' interests both nationally and overseas, and aims to disseminate information about the glass-making industry to the general public.
ausglass.org.au

Australia Council Visual Arts Board

As a major facilitator of programs and grants for various design and craft practices, the Australia Council's Visual Arts Board supports the contemporary expression of art through the broadest range of visual media. They are advocates of craft, design, new media arts and visual arts through various initiatives directed at individual practitioners, groups and the industry as a whole. The Board aims to encourage the engagement of people in Australia and elsewhere in innovative visual art.
ozco.gov.au

Australian Architecture Association

The vision of the AAA is to 'enable the public to understand, enjoy and discuss architecture, locally and beyond.' With Glenn Murcutt as one of the founding fathers, the Association has a newsletter, holds tours and talks and runs the Sydney Architecture Festival.
architecture.org.au

DESIGN RESOURCES_INSTITUTIONS & RESOURCES

Australian Ceramics Association

The Association aims to support and promote Australian ceramic art and professional ceramic practice nationally and internationally. It lists special events, runs a discussion forum and publishes *The Journal of Australian Ceramics* as well as the *Australian Ceramics – In Touch* newsletter.
australianceramics.com

Australian Design Platform

Developed to provide mentorship and entrepreneurial training for small design businesses, Platform is run by Heidi Dokulil of Parcel (and our very own Ewan McEoin!) and connects small design businesses with leading mentors in branding, advertising, production, sustainability and other crucial skills for success.
designplatform.com.au

Australian Graphic Design Association

The representative body for graphic designers all over the country, AGDA is the home of awards, conferences, research, jobs, classes and so on and so forth. A one stop shop for visual culture information.
agda.com.au

Australian Institute of Landscape Architects

AILA is concerned with all aspects of landscape architecture, including land-use planning, urban design and landscape construction. They provide career advice and opportunities, an online magazine, publish *Landscape Australia* and offer membership for professionals.
aila.org.au

The Design Institute of Australia

Viewed as the voice of professional design in Australia, the DIA is the country's professional membership body for designers and design businesses. Membership in the DIA means you are a qualified, experienced, ethical, practising professional. It also provides you with support, networking, services and information to improve your professional practice.
dia.org.au

Dhub

Edited by Nicole Bearman and designed by Mark Gowing, Dhub (that's for Design Hub) is another project of the Powerhouse Museum drawing value from the content of the museum as well

as the broader design sector. It's an online resource that brings design treasures and curiosities out of the basement, connecting museum collections with news, interviews, opinions and ideas across the breadth of design. Search for yourself – it's grand.
dhub.org

National Association for the Visual Arts

For everyone interested in Australian visual arts and craft, NAVA runs the visualarts website that aims to connect people, answer questions and present latest news in the industry. The Association is also the peak body for professionals in the sector.
visualarts.net.au

Object

Behind the eponymous gallery is NSW's organisation for all things design and craft, Object: The Australian Centre for Craft and Design. It is one of Australia's most innovative design organisations. From Sydney to Singapore, Tokyo to London, Object's exhibitions, publications and *Object Magazine* take craft and design across Australia and to over 100 cities around the world. Aside from running the gallery, they support designers and craftspeople through mentorship programs and funding.
St Margarets, 417 Bourke Street, Surry Hills
object.com.au

Royal Australian Institute of Architects

The one-stop shop for everything you want to know about the industry in Australia. Check out the website for a suite of info and services.
architecture.com.au

The Society of Arts and Crafts of NSW

From their new address at The Rocks, this creatively entrepreneurial group exhibits and retails handicrafts to locals and tourists alike. Most of the work is the output of traditional craft practices and includes jewellery, ceramics, weaving, fabric collage and art glass, all made by members of the society.
104 George Street,
The Rocks
artsandcraftsnsw.com.au

Awards & Competitions

AGDA National Biennial Awards

The Australian Graphic Design Association provides biennial awards for creative excellence over 15 categories including Packaging / Label Design and Typography. Judged by professionals nominated by the Association's members, it's an Australia-wide award generally processed in Melbourne in July, but with a high percentage of NSW entries and winners.
agda.com.au

Australian Creative Hotshop Awards

Graphic design magazine *Creative* has its own awards in categories of advertising, animation & broadcast, design, interactive, photography, post & visual FX, production and sound & music. Always on the lookout for points of difference, the mag awards go to innovative creators and facilitators who are pioneers in their field.
australiancreative.com.au

Australian International Design Awards

Picking up the 'international' modifier in 2007, the AIDAs are Australia's most recognised industry awards and the organisation itself exists to promote Australian design culture and innovation across all product development sectors. The entry process runs from September through to December, but it's not until the presentation night in May that the winners are announced. Students can also apply.
designawards.com.au

Bombay Sapphire Design Discovery Award

Come October all eyes turn towards the Bombay Sapphire crew to see which bright spark picks up the $30,000 cash and Milan trip offered at the end of the two-month award process. Since its inception five years ago, the BSDDA has become a most coveted award, with many winners featured in this little book. Amazing what a bottle of gin can do for the creative process.
bombaysapphire.com

Caxton Awards

This newspaper advertising celebration is an awards ceremony, three-day seminar and weekend away in one, held in a different Australian or NZ location every year.
caxtonawards.org.au

IDEA Awards

This independent awards program applauding the best work in interior and product design across Australia is run by design mag *(inside) Australian Design Review*. The awards are presented each year in a different location for lucky attendees – the 2007 edition and gala party was on Cockatoo Island in Sydney Harbour. A great excuse for a knees-up, some prizes and a slap on the back for the country's makers and shakers.
idea-awards.com

Interior Design Awards

This awards night is described by some as the social highlight of a string of design functions in April (including Form & Function, the RAIA national conference and DesignEx). The submission process, for professional interior designers only, goes from November through to February.
interiordesignawards.com.au

RAIA National Architecture Awards

The Royal Australian Institute of Architects holds a national award that runs from September to June in NSW. The Institute also oversees the Peter Johnson Architectural Archive, a collection of entry folders for the award dating back to 1986.
architecture.com.au

The Team

Propped up by two degrees in journalism and design respectively, Viviane Stappmanns has spent years writing about stuff, places and people. Well-versed in and ever-curious about local design, Viviane explored, interviewed, wrote and edited while nervously keeping an eye on her ever-expanding waistline – the book and her first born share roughly the same due date.

Ewan McEoin likes a challenge, which might be why he likes to work on projects that aim to promote Australian design, like *The Sydney Design Guide*. Ewan dines on a mixed grill of experiences: editing, strategy development and networking as much as possible to ensure that he has his fingers firmly on Australia's design pulse.

Our Editorial Assistant needed two primary skills: flying fingers and dogged determination when it came to chasing information and images from all that elusive talent in coathanger city. Equipped for the task with a Diploma in Professional Writing & Editing and a motley history of freelance writing assignments, Caroline Clements was our woman for the job.

Our Sub-Editor, Josephene Duffy, has a Graduate Diploma in Editing & Publishing and is fully aware of both the essentials of English grammar and the nature of language as an evolving, fickle creature. For readers who take issue with a lack of agreement between collective nouns and their verbs – a style deliberately applied to company names throughout this guide – she says: prescriptivism be damned! It's the people behind the names who count.

Behind the design of this publication is the incomparable Studio Round, providers of superb graphic design work to many a cultural client across the country. Also behind the design of last year's *Melbourne Design Guide*, Round was once again up to the task; furiously creating, passionately debating and – when we were most desparate – whipping those mice till dawn.

THE SYDNEY DESIGN GUIDE TEAM

Sharing with us her insider knowledge of artist-run initiatives, Dominique Angeloro wears two occupational hats. Firstly, she's a freelance arts writer for publications including *The Sydney Morning Herald*; secondly, she's half of art duo Soda_Jerk who collaborate as remix artists, arts writers and curators.

A penchant for bright lipstick and an eclectic fashion taste have helped take Clare Buckley across the globe, styling fashion shoots for the big dailies in the UK and all sorts of fashion media in Australia. Naturally, she loves nothing more than a good shop. And that's precisely what she did for us; a fashion shopping spree.

Freelance curator and writer Grace Cochrane is a walking encyclopaedia of design, craft practice and creativity. A former Senior Curator of Australian Decorative Arts & Design at the Powerhouse Museum, Grace kindly allowed us access to her brain for info on craft, products and objects in and around Sydney.

Armed with her extensive experience as a writer and editor for heavyweight publications like *Australian Financial Review*, *The Sydney Morning Herald*, *Marie Claire* and most recently the *(sydney) magazine* – as well as her extensive appetite – we sent Lisa Dabscheck to the front line of Sydney's restaurant and bar scene. Whether it was selflessly tossing back champagne or chowing down on dumplings, she was on the ground, at the scene, in the line of fire … uncovering the truth.

One of this city's most celebrated new arrivals on the fashion scene, designer Kym Ellery has recently launched her own label and is also Market Editor for fashion bible *Rush*. Simultaneously working as a stylist, the former student of London's prestigious Central St Martin's College always knows what's cookin' in the city's fashion circles. So we asked her to show our readers …

Having developed numerous design websites and exhibitions as Curator of Product Design at the Powerhouse Museum, Angelique Hutchinson was just the right person when it came to revealing how product developments blend so well into our everyday lives that we barely recognise them (the vacuum cleaners, the asthma inhalers, the high-performance swimming goggles etc).

As Curator of Fashion at the Powerhouse Museum, Glynis Jones knows Sydney fashion history like the back of her hand. For the Museum, she collects contemporary and

THE SYDNEY DESIGN GUIDE TEAM

historical fashion and textiles ranging from colonial costumes to 1980s speedos and Mardi Gras costumes. Thankfully she managed to compress some of her encyclopaedic knowledge to fit into a spread in our little book.

Our architecture tour guide Vincent Lam is a young practising architect and one of the original volunteers and founding members of the Australian Architecture Association. He became a tour leader to promote an understanding of architecture's contribution to the city.

Eoghan Lewis reckons cities are society's greatest cultural expression, there to be talked (and walked!) about. To ensure he had company, he founded SAW (Sydney Architecture Walks) in 2000 alongside his practice Supple Design. Eoghan was an invaluable advisor on the project and contributed a few of his secrets to our architecture section (for the rest of them, you'll have to take his tours). He says he tries hard to cultivate a bohemian look and we've caught him staring out of windows, muttering to himself 'I wonder what Utzon would do …'

When tackling the fickle but fascinating world of fashion, we went straight to the top to ask for advice. Now Fashion Editor of *The Weekend Australian* Magazine, Edwina McCann has seen some sacred sites of Australia's fashion during her incarnations as Senior Fashion Editor for *Vogue*, Beauty Editor at *Harper's Bazaar* and Editor of *The Australian*'s *Fashion Extra*.

Your architecture tour leader David McCrae is one half of the first official romance in AAA history – he met his partner Luisa through the organisation's Tour Leaders Group. He's also been responsible for developing the AAA's highly successful series of bar architecture tours.

Joel Meares refines his palate for good food and wine as a writer for *The Sydney Morning Herald's (sydney) magazine*. His time on this monthly bible of the city's social set has seen him tackle the best and worst the city has to offer, and live to tell the tale. Thankfully, he shared some of that with us.

Our advisor for products and objects – curator, facilitator, author and new father Brian Parkes – is also Associate Director at Object: the Australian Centre for Craft and Design. He manages Object's artistic programs and curates exhibitions such as *Freestyle: New Australian design for living*. Brian can often be found at design events, feverishly spreading the gospel of creativity.

THE SYDNEY DESIGN GUIDE TEAM

Zoë Sadokierski is a book designer, illustrator, writer, T-shirt designer and self-publisher. She's also doing a PhD at UTS, where she tutors and lectures in design. Thankfully, she doesn't need much sleep, so she had time to introduce our readers to the bubbling, creative world of T-shirt design in Sydney.

Peter Salhani has been a writer and editor with leading design publications including *Vogue Living* and *Belle*, and a freelance contributor to *The Sydney Morning Herald* for over a decade. Recently appointed to Editor of design mag *Monument*, Peter takes our readers on an extensive reconnaissance of local product in the city's hotbed of design, Surry Hills.

Katrina Schwarz, Editor of *Art & Australia* is one of those great enthusiastic people who loves a collaborative project (there are too many to list here). In between all her tasks, she made time to take our readers on an enlightening art tour through Paddington. (Good on you, British Council, for recently awarding her the Realise Your Dream scholarship to move to London in 2008 – it's a prize well-deserved.)

Anne-Marie Van de Ven, a former teacher, is curator of Visual Communication Design and Photography at the Powerhouse Museum, Sydney. She has curated national and international exhibitions and of course she was the right person to introduce us to the legacy of one of Sydney's legendary figures in visual design: Florence Broadhurst.

The Australian Architecture Association's Executive and Publicist Stella de Vulder promoted architecture at the Royal Australian Institute of Architects before forming the not-for-profit entity AAA with Annette Dearing and Founding President Glenn Murcutt as well as several other leading architects. Their vision is to enable the public to understand, enjoy and discuss architecture.

Anne Watson has spent more time looking, thinking, talking and writing about furniture than she cares to remember! As Curator of Architecture and Design at the Powerhouse Museum she's contributed quite a bit to the development of the collection and curated various exhibitions on 19th and 20th century furniture and architecture. When it came to giving readers a brief overview of the museum's permanent design gallery Inspired!, Anne was naturally up for it.

PARTNER_BOMBAY SAPPHIRE

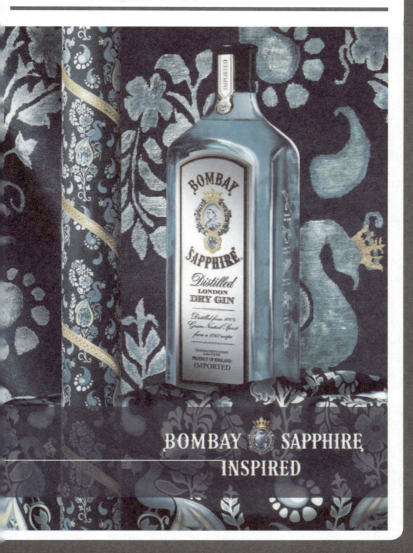

The book you are holding in your hands is a product of collaboration. To all those involved, thank you for your creativity, inspiration, support, advice, trust, energy and hard work.

Adam Haddow
Alaana Fitzpatrick
Amy Johnstone
Andrew Clarkson
Angelique Hutchison
Anne Marie Van de Ven
Anne Proudfoot
Anne Watson
Berto Pandolfo
Brian Parkes
Caitlin Beale
Cameron Stevens
Caroline Clements
Caroline Pidcock
Cecilia Heffer
Chad Willats
Charles Rice
Chris Bosse
Clare Buckley
Colin Rochester
Craig Allchin
David Clarke
Desley Luscombe
Dominique Angeloro
Edwina McCann
Eoghan Lewis
Eva Rodriguez Riestra
Fernando Navarro
Fiona Spence
Gabriel Clark
Glynis Jones
Grace Cochrane
Greg Blain
Heidi Dokulil
Helen Whitty
Ian Gwilt
Jacquiline Harvey
Jaqui Gothe
Javier Degen
Jennifer Kwok
Jenny Bonnin
Jim Griffiths
Joel Meares
John Parker
Josephene Duffy
Julie Donaldson
Kate Murray
Kate Scott
Katrina Schwarz
Kevin Finn
Kevin Jarrett
Kiersten Fishburn
Kym Ellery
Lana Alsamir-Diamond
Lily Katakouzinos
Lindie Ward
Lisa Dabscheck
Lisa Moore
Lisa Murray
Marcus Trimble
Maree Crosby-Browne
Mark Goggin
Michaela Webb
Michelle Mcewen
Neale Whitaker
Nicole Bearman
Olivia Martin-McGuire
Paul McGillick
Peter Faruggia
Peter Salhani
Phoebe Dawson
Prue Pascoe
Regents Court Hotel
Robert Nudds
Robyn Gower
Ross Longmuir
Simeon King
Simon Hörauf
Sophia Callaghan
Stella De Vulder
Steve Pozel
Tammy Wong
Tanya Wolkenberg
Tatjana Plitt
Terri Winter
Toby Willats
Vincent Aiello
Viviana Saccero
Zoe Sadokierski